W9-BNN-582

Understanding
O Pioneers!
and *My Ántonia*

The Greenwood Press "Literature in Context" Series
Student Casebooks to Issues, Sources, and Historical Documents

UNDERSTANDING
O Pioneers!
and *My Ántonia*

A Student Casebook to
Issues, Sources, and
Historical Documents

Sheryl L. Meyering

The Greenwood Press
"Literature in Context" Series
Claudia Durst Johnson, Series Editor

GREENWOOD PRESS
Westport, Connecticut • London

Library of Congress Cataloging-in-Publication Data

Meyering, Sheryl L., 1948–
    Understanding O pioneers! and My Antonia : a student casebook to issues, sources, and historical documents / Sheryl L. Meyering.
        p.   cm.—(The Greenwood Press "Literature in context" series, ISSN 1074–598X)
    Includes bibliographical references and index.
    ISBN 0–313–31390–3 (alk. paper)
    1. Cather, Willa, 1873–1947. My Antonia—Handbooks, manuals, etc. 2. Cather, Willa, 1873–1947. O pioneers!—Handbooks, manuals, etc. 3. Historical fiction, American—Handbooks, manuals, etc.   4. Frontier and pioneer life in literature. 5. Women pioneers in literature. 6. Nebraska—In literature. I. Title. II. Series.
PS3505.A87 M8944   2002
813'.52—dc21   2001050103

British Library Cataloguing in Publication Data is available.

Library of Congress Catalog Card Number: 2001050103
ISBN: 0–313–31390–3
ISSN: 1074–598X

First published in 2002

Greenwood Press, 88 Post Road West, Westport, CT 06881
An imprint of Greenwood Publishing Group, Inc.
www.greenwood.com

Printed in the United States of America

The paper used in this book complies with the Permanent Paper Standard issued by the National Information Standards Organization (Z39.48–1984).

10 9 8 7 6 5 4 3 2 1

To Brian Abel Ragen

Contents

Introduction

While Willa Cather is often thought of as a novelist of the Midwest, her works in fact have settings that range across America and beyond. The two novels discussed in this work, however, are those in which she captures the culture of the American prairies in the generation just after their first settlement. *O Pioneers!* and *My Ántonia* have been embraced by both the citizens of the prairie states and readers around the world because they give a glimpse into a world that has vanished, but to which many still turn when they seek to recall what is quintessentially American about the culture of the United States, with its blend of traditional Protestant British cultures and those of immigrant groups of many kinds. Cather looks back to the pioneers and the immigrants who joined them on the prairie with real affection and even admiration for the efforts they made to turn the wild land into the bountiful fields that now feed the world.

Cather's work, however, is not in truth that of a regional or even a national author, though she can certainly be read for insights into the Midwestern and American characters. She is, in fact, an author who deals with the unchanging themes that have occupied writers in the Western tradition for millennia. While her characters are often simple or unlettered, the authorial voice she presents is one steeped in the literary tradition, from the Bible and Virgil onward. She writes in a simple, thoroughly American style, one easily understood even by young readers, yet her work is enriched with allusions to classical authors, and she can even make the discovery of Latin literature a turning point in the life of one of her characters./

These two novels explore the same themes the classical authors explored. Cather's subjects are the bounty of the land and the labor required to bring it forth, the sweetness of youth and its poignant transience, and the power of love and the heartbreak that results from it. While her tales make every use of the American landscape—and her most moving symbols, such as a plow against the setting sun, are deeply evocative of the prairies—her central interest is in characters who deal with the joys and sorrows that are common to all humanity. In fact, part of her subject is how those joys and sorrows draw together men and woman of different creeds and nations.

Any reader who understands human hopes and disappointments can appreciate *O Pioneers!* and *My Ántonia*. Yet they are the product of a specific time and place, and readers who want to enter Cather's world more fully may want to know more about the places and eras she describes. They may also wonder how the issues she explored continue to shape American culture. The purpose of this book is to serve those readers.

Chapter 1 is a literary analysis of both novels. It describes the genres in which Cather placed her works and the literary traditions she evokes. It also explores the central themes of the novels, such as the healing power of memory, the influence of the land itself on human society, and the reciprocal feeling of devotion to the land that some of the pioneers feel.

Chapters 2–5 place the novels in their historical context. The subject of Chapter 2 is everyday life on the plains. It describes in detail the work the pioneers had to do and the hardships they had to face in order to survive in what was still a wilderness. Historical documents—including true narratives of personal experiences and articles from frontier town newspapers—explain how pioneers built houses from sod, dug wells, and endured grasshopper infestations and blizzards. Chapter 3 describes the arrival of the railroad, which made possible the settlement of the prairie. This chapter explores how the railroad brought the values of the cities, which some pioneers hoped to escape, into every town that had a depot. Articles from railroad propaganda publications and letters written to the editors of local newspapers by farmers who opposed the tactics of the railroad moguls are included here. Chapter 4 recounts the stories and challenges of immigrants to the prairie—Bohemian, Scandinavian, German-Russians, and others—who both formed ethnically homogeneous communities of their own and joined with Americans from the East to create a new culture on the plains. They overcame not only the hardships that the frontier presented to all pioneers, but also language and cultural barriers that native born Americans did not have to face. Chapter 5 focuses on the roles of women pioneers, whose experiences were often different from those of the men they accompanied to the West; it includes excerpts from the diaries and letters of some of those women.

Chapter 6 deals with the echoes of the world Cather evoked in the modern era and describes how the family farm, which is the goal to which Cather's characters devote their efforts and sacrifices, has disappeared in the years since she wrote, leaving behind a cultural legacy that is at once nostalgic and bitter as it gives way to corporate, impersonal forms of agriculture.

For those wishing to ponder aspects of Cather's work in more depth, topics are provided that may produce papers, oral reports, class discussions, or simply interesting reflections.

Page numbers refer to *Cather: Early Novels and Stories*, a volume in the Library of America's 1987 edition of Cather's works.

1

Fleeting Moments of Beauty: A Literary Analysis of *O Pioneers!* and *My Ántonia*

Willa Cather's novels are deceptively simple. Many readers perhaps do not look for complexity in her books, because they seem so much a part of the Midwestern American world that is often their subject. Some readers may feel that here, in a Nebraska writer, they have plain, old-fashioned storytelling, without any of the dazzling or frustrating innovations one finds in "Modernist" writers, such as James Joyce, or even in the American expatriate writers, such as Ernest Hemingway, who were Cather's contemporaries. While it is possible to read Cather naively—just as it is possible to read Hemingway as simply a craftsman of adventure stories—the truth is that Cather's novels are both highly complex and surprisingly innovative. A search for true models for *O Pioneers!* and *My Ántonia* will yield nothing. They are nowhere to be found. Cather took many elements from the traditions of European and American writing, drawing both on genres that predated realistic fiction and on the tradition of the novel itself, and she created something new with them, something as original as the culture that grew up on the plains of America when Czechs, Scandinavians, French Canadians, and the children of old East Coast American families sought a new life in the West.

These novels differ from the traditional novel in their very structure. A reader may not notice Cather's experiments in structure because of the clarity of each part of the narrative. It is only after the reader asks why the various parts are put together as they are that the innovative nature of Cather's work appears. The questions become, Why are these scenes juxtaposed? Why are these particular moments in a lifetime highlighted, when so much that might be considered more important is left out? Cather's novels are highly episodic, and the reader must make the effort to see how the episodes form a whole.

In contrast, the traditional novel often follows one generic pattern or another. We expect a story to turn out in one way or another because we know how stories of that kind are supposed to develop, just as we know the same about movies and television programs. Up until the twentieth century, most novels were essentially comedies in prose. That does not mean that they were funny at every moment, though they often were; rather, it means that they followed the traditional pattern of comedy, in which young people take their places in society after overcoming certain obstacles. Taking one's place in society, in this genre, means getting married and being recognized as an adult by the community. In stage comedy, we even have traditional names for the young people who, we know, will marry by the end of the play: the girl is the "ingenue," the boy the "juvenile." They often are not the characters in whom we are most interested, but without them we would not know what kind of play we were watching. The same is true of traditional comedic novels: whether their business is the center of attention or little more than a subplot necessary to make the novel fit the pattern, we know where we are—because we know who is the ingenue, who the juvenile, and what will happen to them in the end.

Cather knows what we expect. That is why she is able to frustrate our expectations. In both *O Pioneers!* and *My Ántonia*, there is a scene early on that introduces the shy, good-hearted boy and the lovely, innocent girl. The reader thinks he has met his ingenue and his juvenile, and that a predictable plot is under way. It will turn out, however, that the young people do not play out those roles entirely. Each novel ends with a marriage, but not for the couple we first see introduced. The comedic pattern is frustrated. It is not, on the other hand, so completely reversed that we have a prose tragedy. We do not end with the death of the central character, who has become completely isolated from society even before dying. Something more complex is happening, in which comedic and tragic elements intertwine.

O Pioneers! and *My Ántonia* fail to adhere to another important pattern for the novel as well. They do not follow the pattern of the *bildungsroman*, or novel of education, which has been an important part of the tradition of the novel since the late eighteenth century. Those works, among which we might include Charles Dickens's *David Copperfield*, for example, describe, often in the first person, the process whereby a character comes to intellectual and moral maturity. They tend to be detailed, continuous, and chronological, and they focus tightly on a single character's experience. Cather shows her characters growing and maturing, but she always keeps them in a larger social setting. *O Pioneers!* is no more Alexandra Bergson's *bildungsroman* than it is Emil's and Marie's comedy—or tragedy. Also, it differs from the Victorian novels that set out to describe a large social world, in that it focuses on a small society, literally at the margins of the civilized world, rather than on the great city at the culture's heart.

Cather's novels avoid yet another genre, one employed by many American novelists of the nineteenth century—the picaresque. In a picaresque novel, a hero, or more often, a rogue, goes through a series of adventures. (The genre takes its name from the Spanish word for "rogue," *picaro*.) These novels can be called "road novels," because the hero usually wanders from place to place—or runs from place to place to escape trouble of one sort or another. Mark Twain's *The Adventures of Huckleberry Finn* is firmly in this tradition, as are works by Herman Melville (*Moby Dick* and *The Confidence Man*) and James Fenimore Cooper (*The Last of the Mohicans* and *The Prairie*). Cather's novels share the episodic structure of those works. Her characters, however, are not wanderers. They remain part of a single social world, while the heroes of picaresque novels visit many societies and join none. When the *picaro* visits Cather's world, as he does in the form of Larry Donovan, Ántonia's seducer, we are invited not to follow in a series of dubious exploits, but to consider the disaster his exploits leave behind him.

Cather builds her novels from a series of vignettes—that is, of vividly described moments. These moments may be separated by years of time. In her work, plot is not as important as the impressions produced by the rare moment of intense feeling or perception. Indeed, the characters who are most central to the plot are often less important in one of Cather's novels than the observers. (To put it another way, Emil and Marie are the ingenue and the juvenile, but Alexandra is the protagonist of *O Pioneers!*) People who remember and treasure experience—including the experience of others—are Cather's central figures. Those who merely live out the plot—comic, tragic, or picaresque—are secondary.

Cather's experiments in structure are profoundly related to the themes she explores. That is, of course, true of all good fiction. Twain uses the picaresque in *Huck Finn* because it is best suited to his examination of how far a person can be part of a society that will not allow his dearest friend to be anything but "property." Cather's central interest is in the passage of time and the power of memory, and she structures her work in such a way as to explore those subjects.

Readers have, of course, read Cather's novels as many things, ranging from patriotic celebrations of American ideals to covert defenses of lesbianism. There are justifications for those readings—though not in their most extreme forms. Her works interweave a variety of themes and resist any pat political interpretation, conservative or radical. But it is not hard to say what her central interest is. She writes to remind the reader of those numinous moments of beauty that come into life unexpectedly and fleetingly—of the inevitability of failure and disappointment, and of the nobility of people who face the latter unflinchingly while holding as best they can to the former. Since those moments are transient and yet may echo through the rest of one's life, Cather's disjointed, episodic form is perfectly suited to her purpose. The passage of time, with its inevitable effects on men and women, is thus both Cather's central theme and the organizing principle that structures her work.

O PIONEERS!

Cather makes it clear from the beginning of *O Pioneers!* that her focus is not primarily on the development of an individual. The reader is given several clues that this work is not a *bildungsroman*, as is Cather's own *The Song of the Lark*, which literally traces the education, the musical education, of a single heroine. In *O Pioneers!* the focus is broader. Cather's central theme is the place of humankind in the natural world. The title—a quotation from Walt Whitman's "Pioneers! O Pioneers!"—calls to mind a poem that addresses the whole "race" of "western youths" who set out as an army to conquer the vast empty spaces of the continent. It is worth remembering that while Americans always think of the civilian settlers of the West when they hear "pioneer," that word originally referred to soldiers who went in advance of an army to prepare roads and defenses for it. In other words, it denoted an organized group, not solitary individuals. While we now may question the doctrines of "Manifest Destiny," which celebrated the movement of white settlers into the plains, Whitman and Cather did not. They saw each man and woman who went out to turn the West into farmland as part of a great—and good—movement in history.

Between the title page and the actual opening of the novel, Cather gives the reader two epigraphs and a dedication, all of which make clear what the novel will explore. The first epigraph—"Those fields, colored by various grain!"—is a quotation from the Polish poet Adam Mickiewicz. It, of course, names the other great player in Cather's drama, the land itself. The dedication, to Sarah Orne Jewett, also sets the theme, for Jewett is known for writing stories that deal with the ways human beings interact with the natural world. In her short story "A White Heron," for example, a young girl must decide whether or not to reveal the location of the heron's nest to a hunter. Finally, the second epigraph is Cather's own poem "Prairie Spring," which describes the flat prairie land and the weariness and bleakness of the labor required to wring crops from it. The poem goes on to describe how out of that same land, "youth" brings forth joy. The reader who has paid attention to the "front matter" of the novel knows that Cather will be tracing the meeting of two forces, each of them larger than any of the characters she will describe. One is clearly nature. The other is a bit harder to define, for it is not so much humankind as it is a life force that works through individual men and women, driving them, triumphantly or tragically, to seek fulfillment and fruition, in bringing forth their crops or in consummating their love.

The prairie is, therefore, much more than the setting for Cather's story. As she explores the theme of man's place in the natural world, she makes the landscape almost a character. It is important in every strand of the story, for both Alexandra's and Emil's confrontations with the forces of nature are connected with the nature around them.

It might be said that Alexandra's primary relationship is not with any of the characters in the story but with the land itself. For Alexandra, Carl Linstrum is secondary to the land. Cather regularly personifies the land, attributing to it human qualities, so that it comes to seem that Alexandra's feelings are requited. The land responds to her as it does not to others. Describing John Bergson's troubles with farming, Cather makes the land sound like an unruly child: "It was still a wild thing that had its ugly moods; and no one knew when they were likely to come, or why. . . . Its Genius was unfriendly to men" (147). ("Genius" here means, as it meant in Greek mythology, the god who presides over a place.) But it reacts differently to Bergson's daughter. She falls in love with the land, and her feelings are requited:

> For the first time, perhaps, since that land emerged from the waters of geologic ages, a human face was set toward it with love and yearning. It seemed beautiful to her, rich and strong and glorious. Her eyes drank in the breath of it, until her tears blinded her. Then the Genius of the Divide, the great, free spirit which breathes across it, must have bent lower than it ever bent to a human will before. The history of every country begins in the heart of a man or a woman. (170)

This relationship with the land is what allows Alexandra to see its potential. The other pioneers have come to see the land on the Divide as almost worthless and to covet the more expensive land of the river valleys. Cather is reversing the imagery often associated with the pioneers, which is heavily masculine. The male pioneer, associated always with phallic implements, such as the plow, ravishes the land. Or, like an invading army, he "conquers" it. Here, the female pioneer draws the Spirit of the land to her.

Alexandra's success is thus based not just on the "will," which is often associated with male pioneers, though Cather does explicitly mention her "will." It is also based on her, Alexandra's, wits. She has both the cleverness to adopt the ways of the shrewd businessmen rather than follow the example of her neighboring farmers, and the insight to think about farming intellectually, to "reflect on the great operations of nature" (173). But the real source of her success is her love for and affinity with the land, for both her will and her understanding grow out of those feelings. It is something her practical, unimaginative brothers have a difficult time accepting. When Lou asks her how she *knows* that the land she wants to buy is going to be worth enough not only to pay the mortgage but to make them rich in a few years, she answers, "I can't explain that, Lou. You'll have to take my word for it. I *know*, that's all. When you drive about over the country you can feel it coming" (171). She feels not like the conqueror of nature but like a part of it: "She had felt as if her heart were in hiding down there, somewhere, with the quail and the plover and the all the little wild things that crooned or buzzed in the sun. Under the long shaggy ridges, she felt the future stirring" (173).

While Cather's version of the settlement of the prairie lacks the imagery of domination found in the work of other authors, she does recognize that something was lost in the "winning of the West." The prairie in its pristine state, as Cather describes it, is beautiful. The vast expanses of red grass, stretching like an ocean in every direction, are glorious, and pioneers like Alexandra are profoundly moved by the sight of them. Then they destroy them. The oceans of grass give way to geometric fields, plotted on a section grid and bounded with fences. The earth itself is broken and turned and turned again, so that great squares of wheat arise, but the red grass is hardly to be seen. Cather represents this transformation as bittersweet. The tamed earth is lovely in its own way, but there is a real loss in the destruction of the wild.

While Cather shows the triumph of the pioneers who set out to domesticate the wild land, she also shows the power of nature, a power that often cannot be resisted. That power is present in the description of the struggles of John Bergson and his daughter to make their farm a success—and is seen still more in the descriptions of their neighbors' failures. In a larger sense, however, it is present throughout the book, for Cather structures her novel to correspond with the great cycles of nature, and she depicts nature as working through human beings to bring them both joy and tragedy.

O Pioneers! is full of imagery of the seasons. The novel opens in the bitter cold of a prairie winter. Its climax is on a perfect day in June. The extremes of the seasons, products of the great natural forces, are linked with the forces of nature within the characters.

Emil and Marie meet as children in the bitter cold of winter. They fall in love and die in high summer. Alexandra, on the other hand, is always associated with autumn. It is in that season that she falls in love, first with Nature, in the September when all the other farmers are selling out, and then with Carl Linstrum, when she is recovering from the loss of her brother. By the end of the novel, she is also in the autumn of her life, an autumn marked by what the Romantic poet John Keats called "mellow fruitfulness." She lives in a friendly, loving, balanced relationship with nature, one that corresponds symbolically to the temperate fall.

The summer story of Emil and Marie shows a different aspect of humans' place in the natural world. The power of sexuality is linked with the loveliness of the natural world. As Cather describes the day that ends with his death, Emil is at every point drawn by the natural world into the experience of the power of the life force that leads to his moment of union with Marie and then to both their deaths. The perfect warm weather, the liveliness of the horses and their young riders, the sight of Marie lying under the white mulberry tree, all seem to conspire to lead him to destruction. In fact, the very fruitfulness of the countryside that farmers like Alexandra have created also seems part of the natural force that impels him:

> Everywhere the grain stood ripe and the hot afternoon was full of the smell of the ripe wheat, like the smell of bread baking in an oven. The breath of the wheat and the sweet clover passed him like pleasant things in a dream. He could feel nothing but the sense of diminishing distance. It seemed to him that his mare was flying, or running on wheels, like a railway train. The sunlight, flashing on the window-glass of the big red barns, drove him wild with joy. He was like an arrow shot from the bow. His life poured itself out along the road before him as he rode to the Shabata farm. (265)

Emil is carried away by nature, the nature outside him serving as a reflection of the life force inside him—specifically, by the power of sexuality.

Interestingly, Alexandra, who represents a person in harmony with nature, even one in control of it, often dreams of being carried away by some force more powerful than herself:

[S]he used to have an illusion of being lifted up bodily and carried lightly by some one very strong. It was a man, certainly, who carried her, but he was like no man she knew; he was much larger and stronger and swifter, and he carried her as easily as if she were a sheaf of wheat. She never saw him, but, with eyes closed, she could feel that he was yellow like the sunlight, and there was the smell of ripe cornfields about him. (238)

This powerful but gentle male force, redolent of the fields and shining like the sun, invokes a desire to union with nature as much as any sexual longing. The forces of nature are always stronger than the individual, but some people, like Alexandra, are more able to live in harmony with them than others.

Another theme that Cather explores in *O Pioneers!* is time. It is hardly possible, of course, to create fiction that does not, in some way, address the inevitability of the passage of time. The novel always, to a greater or lesser extent, deals with the influence of time on characters, for good or ill. Lyric poetry can celebrate a single instant or treat an image or perception as if it were outside the inevitable processes of development and decay, but prose fiction cannot. The very necessity of a plot requires that time and its effects be dealt with. Some novels, however, foreground the issue of time. In *O Pioneers!*, Cather both shows the inevitable passage of time and points up the human yearning for the permanent or the changeless. To put it another way, she shows the flow of events as given meaning by fleeting moments that seem so perfect in their beauty that one can almost take them as eternal.

The structure of *O Pioneers!* calls attention to both time and change, and to the "timeless" moment. Widely varying amounts of time pass between the different parts of the novel. We meet Emil as a small boy. Then he is a youth in the full vigor of manhood. Then he is only a bittersweet memory for the sister left behind. Years pass between the early parts of the novel, months between the later ones. Events disrupt whatever smoothly developing plans the characters may have—or the reader may have for them. Yet in images like the white mulberry tree, something that is itself fleeting (few things are more subject to mutability than a flowering tree) remains, giving a hint of the timeless.

The two strands of the plot center on missed opportunities—in other words, on relationships that "time has passed by." One in-

volves the young people. The reader initially expects Emil and Marie to take their roles in a traditional comedic plot. That is no
longer a possibility after Marie marries Frank Shabata. Their attempt to recapture what is no longer a possibility leads to their
destruction. It is worth noting that among the many things that
seem to conspire to compel Emil toward his final, sweet, and fatal
evening with Marie is his own heightening knowledge of the transitory nature of life. He makes his visit to the Shabata farm—an
attempt capture a moment of happiness, though he knows it is
folly—only after he has seen his friend Amédée, who has put off
rest and pleasure to prepare for the future, die with shocking swift-
ness. It is almost as if he has decided that he will not, like his
friend, be robbed of his moment of joy, no matter what the risk.

The other strain involves Alexandra. The chance that she will be
part of a traditional comedic plot seems to disappear early in the
novel, when Carl Linstrum leaves the Divide. She seems, indeed,
to have chosen a path that does not include traditional domestic
happiness. She is, after all, portrayed more as a manager than as
a housekeeper; she is certainly not going to be a prairie "angel in
the house," like Amédée's wife Angélique. In the end, however,
the path of domestic happiness that seemed closed to her is re-
opened, and she is perhaps like her brother in what finally pre-
pares her to accept it. She is ready to seek love at the end because
loss—the loss of Emil himself—has led her to see how transitory
happiness can be. When Carl returns, Alexandra is ready to embrace what time seemed to have taken way forever.

Cather's treatment of the theme of time is related to her experiments in plot in *O Pioneers!* and to the novel's resonances with
several literary genres. *O Pioneers!* is not what might be called a
"plot-driven" novel. In works that can be appropriately given that
label, the reader's main interest is in what happens. (The most
extreme form is the sort of mystery story called a "whodunit," in
which there is little of interest beyond what happens.) Cather's
work implies a reader who is more interested in perceptions and
sensibilities than in mere plot. Nevertheless, Cather's plot is important, for its development underscores the themes of time,
missed opportunity, loss, and second chances that are central to
the novel.

The reader who expects a traditional comedic plot—and that is,
to some extent, almost all readers—assumes there will be a happy

union of Emil and Marie at the end. That expectation is frustrated by what time actually brings. The reader thus shares in one of the great patterns of the novel, for many of the characters Cather depicts have great hopes, visions of what time will bring them, hopes and visions that are mostly disappointed. Alexandra is to some extent an exception to this rule, since she is perceptive enough to see how some patterns of events will turn out. But even her sagacity is limited to farming and real estate. She can neither shape the fate of her brother, whom she has raised almost as a son, nor foresee her own, happier fate. Cather's disruption of traditional patterns of plot, therefore, reinforces her depictions of the effects of time and of its inevitable but never predictable impact on every human creature. Cather's novel thus seems to be a comedy for Emil and Marie but is not; it seems not to be a comedy for Alexandra but turns out to be one.

Comedy is not, however, the only genre Cather invokes. Just as powerfully, she invokes the long tradition of the pastoral in European literature. From the ancient Greeks onward, Western authors have often described an idyllic world, unlike the world of work and suffering and loss that we actually inhabit. We take the very word "idyllic" from some of those early poems, which were called "idylls." The ancient poems and romances (prose fictions that predate the rise of the modern novel in the eighteenth century) that describe this world are called "pastorals," because their central figures are "pastors," shepherds. These works are often set in an idealized version of the region of Greece called Arcadia; we still use "Arcadian" to mean bucolic, innocent, and unspoiled.

The pastoral as a genre has always celebrated innocence and uncomplicated happiness. It has, in other words, had little to do with the realities of farming. At the same time, however, it has always included a recognition that death and suffering intrude everywhere. The most famous pastoral works are, therefore, not the romances that describe the course of innocent young love but the pastoral elegies by ancient poets that lament the death of the very shepherds who embody youth, vigor, and innocence. The same is true in visual art: while there are many paintings of pastoral scenes, probably the most famous is one by the seventeenth-century French artist Nicolas Poussin in which he depicts shepherds discovering a tomb that bears the enigmatic legend *Et in Arcadia ego*—"I [death] am also in Arcadia."

At the heart of *O Pioneers!* is a pastoral chapter, "The White Mulberry Tree." For one day Emil seems to be living in Arcadia. The day is warm. All the youths are joyous and full of vigor. They are also touchingly innocent—the excuse for their gallop across country, after all, is to meet the bishop. The whole countryside seems alive. What is more, he is not, like the older farmers (or indeed most of mankind) struggling with nature. He is, for a moment, at one with it. Emil's day of pastoral joy, of course, ends in the mulberry grove—for death is on the prairie, as well as in Arcadia.

Cather's invocation of the pastoral is complex. It joins innocence and guilt, life and death. Emil and Marie seem very much like good, unspoiled children, driven together by innocent, animal spirits. Yet they are, in fact, adulterers—and Ivar, at least, doubts that they have left this world for Paradise. Cather uses the pastoral to represent the life force that both gives fleeting moments of happiness and, almost instantly, destroys them.

Alexandra, again, does not fit the usual generic pattern. As she is seemingly too old (and too wise and experienced) to be the ingenue of comedy, so she is as unlike an innocent shepherdess as can be imagined. Yet she too feels at one with the fruitful land around her. In fact, for her the prairie is Arcadia, not just for one glorious day but forever. She loves it and makes it fruitful—and Cather ends the novel by creating a positive image of her at one with it, even in death: "Fortunate country, that is one day to receive hearts like Alexandra's into its bosom, to give them out again in the yellow wheat, in the rustling corn, in the shining eyes of youth!" (290).

Not all Cather's themes are built on timeless archetypes, such as the comedic and the pastoral. She also deals with the specifics of the time and place she describes. One of her purposes was to describe the sorts of men and women who lived and struggled in the vanished world of the newly settled West. By the time she wrote, the pioneers were gone, and the immigrants who had brought foreign ways to the prairies had become almost indistinguishable from their Yankee neighbors. The final great theme of *O Pioneers!* is the memorializing of that gallant generation.

In handling this theme, too, Cather presents a complex picture. Her pioneers are a varied lot. Some, like Alexandra, face the struggles of prairie life joyfully. Others, like Frank Shabata, are soured by them. Still others, like the Linstrums, simply cannot make a go of it and move on. But the effort to tame the land and make it fruitful seems to ennoble all of them. They are, as the language used to describe Alexandra's relationship with the land shows, not simply exploiting an economic opportunity. They are, through their wooing of the spirit of the place, creating a new people, a new country.

O Pioneers! is essentially about how the individual human being lives in the natural world. Some are broken by their struggles to conquer nature. Some are led to folly by the natural drives within them, which are amplified by their reflection in the fertile earth. Some are lucky enough to be in harmony with nature. Unlike so many of the other characters, Alexandra is at peace with both the natural world and her own natural drives. Her farm flourishes and, as the closing sentence of the novel implies, her marriage will be fruitful. More than once she is associated with the image of one carried away by a benign force, which she does not resist. Her relationship with nature—like her relationship with Carl—is a happy union, not a struggle. Alexandra is indeed far too mature to play the role of ingenue in the novel, but that is the very point. While the youthful joy of Emil and Marie has its bittersweet intensity, the mature, balanced, temperate happiness that Alexandra draws to her is in fact the life worth struggling for.

MY ÁNTONIA

> They told me Heraclitus, they told me you were dead;
> They brought me bitter news to hear and bitter tears to shed.
> I wept as I remembered how often you and I
> Had tired the sun with talking and sent him down the sky.
>
> And now that thou art lying, my dear old Carian guest,
> A handful of grey ashes, long long ago at rest,
> Still are thy pleasant voices, thy nightingales, awake,
> For Death, he taketh all away, but them he cannot take.
> —William Johnson Cory (1823–92)

In *My Ántonia,* Cather's central focus is on the power of memory. Cather structures the novel so that the reader experiences not so much a succession of events as a succession of memories. She emphasizes that the memory of events, as much as events themselves, are her subject by the use of the literary device known as a "framing narrative." When this device is used, the first narrator of a work of fiction—usually someone quite like the author, even someone with the author's name—does not present the body of the story but rather recounts how the narrative came to be told or written by someone else, and then steps back while the reader experiences the story told by a second narrator. Many authors use frame narratives to tell stories with a good measure of the exotic or adventurous. Cather uses the device for quite another purpose. The events that Jim Burden recounts are not wild or particularly adventurous, and the prairie frontier he describes has none of the improbable elements of Kipling's Afghanistan or Conrad's Congo. What Cather seeks to underline is that memories of youth can continue to give meaning, hope, and some measure of happiness to later life, however dull and passionless that life may appear.

The Jim Burden we meet in the introduction seems in one sense to have missed his chance for happiness in life. His marriage seems cold and loveless. As the narrator describes the New York woman he has married, there is nothing genuine about her: "I am never able to believe that she has much feeling for the causes to which she lends her name and her fleeting interest" (712). Her reasons for marrying Burden in the first place seem to have had to do with her own self-dramatization. Marrying the unknown westerner allows her to seem daring and original, which is what she wants to be after playing the role of a girl jilted by another member of Old New York society. Why she wishes to remain married to Burden is something the narrator cannot explain. If domestic happiness is the criterion of success, Burden's life must seem a failure.

Yet he does not seem to be a broken man—or not entirely broken. He seems to be untouched by time or experience, and he projects an ever-boyish image. He is still capable of the greatest enthusiasm, and he is willing to share that quality with others. Young men are often attracted to him because of his eagerness to explore whatever is wild in America, and women still excite his "sympathetic, solicitous" interest (712). Furthermore, as the lawyer for one of the large western railways, he is a success in business. The root of all that is still young, active, and attractive about him seems to be the same: "He loves with a personal passion the great country through which his railway runs and branches" (712). In other words, the memories he has of his youthful home and the people he loved there are what keep his life from being deadened by his loveless existence in New York.

For both the narrator of this framing introduction and for Burden himself, Ántonia is more than just a friend of their youth. She is the embodiment of all the treasured memories that go on giving their lives meaning. The structure of the novel emphasizes the importance of recognizing the life-giving power of certain memories that, unlike the rest of one's possessions, can never be taken away.

The introduction falls into two parts: the first meeting of the narrator and Burden on the train, with their talk about Ántonia, and Burden's presentation to her months later of the manuscript that is the body of the novel. In between he writes the story of his and Ántonia's young lives and of the moments of transcendence they would learn to hold dear. Also, and still more importantly, he writes of his own return as an adult to see his old friends after twenty years of separation. That reunion seals his realization that his early joys and loves are never lost, no matter what disappointments have intervened. His closing act in the introduction—which in terms of strict chronology is the last thing that happens in the novel—makes that point. He adds "My" to "Ántonia" in the title of his manuscript, because the girl he knew on the prairie, and the feelings he experienced as a boy and a youth, are forever his.

If *My Ántonia* ended with Book IV, it would be close to tragic in its tone, but its real ending shows that it is part of a much less heart-wrenching genre. All the good and loving people, including the "ruined" girl, are at last joined together on a happy, fruitful farm.

In the final chapter, "Cuzak's Boys," we see that in the twenty years that have passed since Jim Burden last saw her—and heard the sad story of her seduction—Ántonia has become the mistress of a fine farm, blessed with a good husband and many strong children. It is in meeting the mature Ántonia that Jim Burden recaptures the friend of his youth—and with her all that has been most nourishing in his life. Ántonia is now presented in some sense as Ceres or Pomona—a goddess of fruitfulness.

During the night Jim spends bunking with Ántonia's boys in the barn, he realizes that in his memories of Ántonia he has a source of strength and happiness to draw on despite the disappointments of his New York life—which he never mentions, but which the frame narrator has ensured that the reader will imagine. Ántonia is his link to the sources of what is real and good and lasting:

> Ántonia had always been one to leave images in the mind that did not fade—that grew stronger with time. In my memory there was a succession of such pictures, fixed there like the old woodcuts of one's first primer: . . . Ántonia in her black shawl and fur cap, as she stood by her father's grave in the snowstorm; Ántonia coming in with her work-team along the evening sky-line. She lent herself to immemorial human attitudes which we recognize by instinct as universal and true. I had not been mistaken. She was a battered woman now, not a lovely girl; but she still had that something which fires the imagination, could still stop one's breath for a moment by a look or gesture that somehow revealed the meaning in common things. She had only to stand in the orchard, to put her hand on a little crab tree and look up at the apples, to make you feel the goodness of planting and tending and harvesting at last. All the strong things of her heart came out in her body, that had been so tireless in serving generous emotions. (926)

To have those pictures in the mind—and to know that they are there to be called up—is almost in itself to have a meaningful life, if not a happy one.

The body of the novel can be seen as a series of episodes leading up to iconic moments—that is, to moments that are given highly visual descriptions and seem to carry great weights of meaning. Those moments all seem at once transitory and, because of the power of memory, timeless. As in *O Pioneers!*, Cather frustrates any easy assignment of this novel to a traditional genre but gives it a strong flavor of the pastoral. It has that flavor not simply because its central figures are young people who often work the fields. It is also because memory makes possible the impossible fantasy that underlies the whole genre of the pastoral. In memory, youth is eternal and the Arcadian fields always ripe and inviting.

But Cather invokes another, and more complex, classical model besides the pastoral. Virgil began his career with his pastorals, the *Eclogues*. The work of his maturity, however, was the *Georgics*, and it is that poem that Jim Burden studies at the University of Nebraska. In the *Georgics*, Virgil describes not the pastoral world, with its eternal Spring, but something more like the real world of farming, where there is work appropriate for every season. Virgil is also well aware in the *Georgics* that peaceful, fruitful farms are very much the product of human effort: he describes them so lovingly in part because he hopes to see them take the place of the desolate landscape left by Rome's civil wars. The fruitful farms of Nebraska also come after desperate struggles, and just as Virgil recalls the weapons that are still to be found in the fields of Italy, Jim Burden recalls the images that mark the struggles—and defeats—of the pioneers. Some of the images that remain ever fresh can be read as the memorials to the first generation that broke the soil. The grave of Mr. Shimerda, where the red grass still grows undisturbed, is one such image. The sight of the plow against the setting sun is another, though it is several other things as well.

The world of the *Georgics* is also unlike the world of pastoral poetry in that it is not a world of endless youth. Cather quotes as the epigraph of *My Ántonia* a line in which Virgil makes that most clear: *Optima dies . . . prima fugit*, "the best days are the first to flee." But Cather is also careful to show that although those best days may have fled, they are not, thanks to memory, really lost. Even as a young man studying Virgil, Jim Burden finds himself as much among his old friends on the prairie as on Virgil's farm by the Mincio: "Whenever my consciousness was quickened, all those early friends were quickened with it, and in some strange way they accompanied me through all my new experiences" (875). As a mature man, he finds that they are, like the images supplied by literature itself, touchstones that can strengthen him.

Beyond the power of memory, the novel explores several themes. Each of them is associated with one or more visual images, which are sometimes elaborated into iconic moments.

A theme that constantly reappears throughout the novel is the interaction of the human beings with the natural world, on the one hand, and the world of human culture and artifice, on the other. Both seem necessary for human happiness. Cather's characters are often in danger of being cut off from one or the other of these two sources of integrated humanity, and when they are cut off, they are often deformed in one way or another.

The invocation of the pastoral world and of the *Georgics* shows the importance of contact with the natural world. Ántonia's world is a hard one for the pastoral genre, but it is still innocent in its way. It is when the mechanized world, associated with the railroad, intrudes that bad things happen: the rape planned by Wick Cutter turns on railroad schedules; the seducer, Larry Donovan, who accomplishes Ántonia's ruin is a railway employee; and it is the railroad itself that has taken her away from the world where she was loved and valued. She attains happiness again through her marriage with a man close to the land, who is both a husband and a husbandman.

When we first see Jim Burden, he is himself associated with the mechanical world. He is on a train, and he represents the railway company. He lives in the least bucolic of settings, New York City, where his life seems to be unhappy and artificial. By the end of the novel, it becomes clear that what keeps him alive and humane—and less unhappy than the reader of the introduction might have thought—is his continuing connection to the natural world. That connection exists mostly though memory, where, thanks to Ántonia and the other friends of his childhood and youth, he always has entry to the pastoral world. But we see him seeking that connection again in the present, both in the introduction and in the novel's final chapter. The excursions he takes to the wild lands with younger men—like the hunting trip he plans with Cuzak's boys—keep him always, in some sense, in Arcadia, though clearly he is wise and sad enough by then to know that he is not a citizen of the green world, only a visitor in it.

Cather does not, however, in any way suggest anything as simple as that the natural world represents salvation while the world of culture and refinement represents decay and perversion. In fact, she shows that being cut off from the world of culture deforms people still more profoundly than does separation from nature. The first book of *My Ántonia* describes the grinding poverty of the Bohemian immigrants, but their worst privations are not material. Mr. Shimerda is a truly cultured man. He is a musician, and he had loved the artistic life and rich culture of his homeland. In the prairies, all of that is gone. Cather underscores that lack in another iconic moment. When Mr. Shimerda visits the Burdens' home at Christmas, he is drawn to all the good things there—the peace, the order, the hospitality. But he is especially attracted to the religious images, sent from the old country, that Otto Fuchs has used to decorate the Christmas tree, making it—with images including a sacred heart as well as a Nativity scene—an oddly Catholic tree in a Protestant household. Mr. Shimerda prays before the icons, and Jim's grandfather, rather than bridling at what might have been seen by a Protestant as idolatry, declares that "the prayers of all good people are good" (770). Art, even in the form of brightly colored paper, has brought a moment of peace into the life of a man on the brink of despair, and it has allowed another man to teach his grandson the value of the yearnings of all his fellow humans.

Mr. Shimerda's final collapse and suicide are also clearly related to his exile in a land without culture (his sharp-tongued, grasping wife and selfish son bear some blame for it as well, of course). The foreshadowing of his death—which he accomplishes with a fine, beautiful gun, another relic of his cultured homeland—is his ceasing to play his violin. Once he gives up his last contact with art, he is truly in the grip of despair.

While the effects of deprivation from art and culture are most extreme in Mr. Shimerda, they are present in the other pioneers as well. These individuals are not broken by it largely because they are not sensitive enough to know what they lack; nevertheless, the lack is there. Cather shows the longing for art and culture in many ways. In another iconic moment, she shows the schoolchildren of Black Hawk, Jim Burden among them, clustered around the one example of color and form in their desolate town. Jim writes of his walks home in the dead of winter:

> I can remember how glad I was when there happened to be a light in the church, and the painted glass window shone out at us as we came along the frozen street. In the winter bleakness a hunger for color came over people, like the Laplander's craving for fats and sugar. Without knowing why, we used to linger on the sidewalk outside the church when the lamps were lighted early for choir practice or prayer-meeting, shivering and talking until our feet were like lumps of ice. The crude reds and greens and blues of that colored glass held us there. (823–24)

The longing for art will be satisfied, one way or another.

Book II of *My Ántonia,* "The Hired Girls," is also largely about a longing for art, but not for art in any of its high forms—Jim will encounter that in the following books of the novel, when he is awakened to the glories of Virgil and of the theater and the opera. Rather, it is a longing for anything that brings together form and emotion. Part of what brings the girls to town is the desire for art—in the form of music and dancing. What attracts Jim to the hired girls rather than to girls of his own class is that they are not too staid to be moved by art but abandon themselves to it gaily. They live in a world where most art is associated with danger. Ántonia risks rape to live in town and be allowed to dance; Jim displeases his beloved grandparents when he goes to dances. But the lure of art—whether a dance band or a blind African American piano player—is always alive in them and keeps them from becoming mere drudges. In the case of the hired girls, there is always the danger that the price of their separation from high culture will be their own coarsening. (Jim's grandmother fears what too long a time as a farm laborer will do to Ántonia, for example.) Their joy in what art they can have, no matter how tawdry it seems from the perspective of New York, seems to save them from that.

A related theme is that of exile and exposure. The first book of *My Ántonia,* "The Shimerdas," is named for the Czech immigrants, who are, of course, foreigners a world far away from their homeland. But it is important to remember that Jim Burden himself is an exile in a new world—almost a castaway adrift on an endless sea. That is his own feeling when he is first alone on the vast prairies, which have hardly yet begun to be broken into farms: "As I looked about me I felt that the grass was the country, as the water is the sea. The red of the grass made all the great prairie the color of wine-stains, or of certain seaweeds when they are first washed up. And there was so much motion in it; the whole country seemed, somehow, to be running" (722).

The Shimerdas, of course, have literally crossed the ocean before being thrown up on an island of broken ground in the sea of red grass. In another of the iconic moments of the novel, Mr. Shimerda rests in an island of unbroken prairie amid the cultivated fields that have grown up since he was buried at the crossing of section lines. The red grass amid the fields of wheat and corn fittingly marks the resting place of a man who died a lonely exile.

But as in *O Pioneers!,* the theme of the grandeur of the transformation of the prairie into farmland always recurs. Today's readers may find it harder to admire that achievement than Cather did, since it brought in its wake many of the tragedies—the extinctions, the pollution—of which the environmental movement has made us so aware. Nevertheless, it is still the achievement on which all Americans depend, quite literally, for their daily bread. When

Cather wrote, the generation that had worked and suffered to make the wild land fruitful was passing away, and her acknowledgment of their heroism is bound up with her knowledge that because of their very success, the world they knew, with all its hardships and all its virtues, was also passing away. Therefore the central iconic moment of the novel is a fleeting image of human labor against the most powerful force of nature, the source of all the others. When Jim picnics with the hired girls soon after his graduation from high school, they are aware their world is changing. They are also aware, as their discussion of the explorers they learned about in school shows, that the country they love was won at a price—and a high one. When the girls ask why Coronado had "never gone back to Spain," Jim cannot answer. He can only report what the schoolbooks say, that the explorer "died in the wilderness, of a broken heart." Clearly thinking of her father, Ántonia adds, "More than him has done that" (865). Then they are granted what seems a vision:

> There were no clouds, the sun was going down in a limpid, gold-washed sky. Just as the lower edge of the red disc rested on the high fields against the horizon, a great black figure suddenly appeared on the face of the sun. We sprang to our feet, straining our eyes toward it. In a moment we realized what it was. On some upland farm, a plough had been left standing in the field. The sun was sinking just behind it. Magnified across the distance by the horizontal light, it stood out against the sun, was exactly contained within the circle of the disc; the handles, the tongue, the share— black against the molten red. There it was, heroic in size, a picture writing on the sun. (865–66)

This image unites many of Cather's themes. For a moment, the effort to break the land has its heroic image, and then "that forgotten plough had sunk back to its own littleness somewhere on the prairie" (866). The very fact that the image exists for but a moment underscores the theme of the transitory nature of life and happiness, where the best days are the first to flee. Most importantly, it leaves a memory that can be treasured in future years and casts a ray of the joy of youth over the dark days to come.

Like *O Pioneers!*, *My Ántonia* suggests traditional patterns of plot and then either fails to fulfill them or fulfills them in unexpected ways. We have characters we can assign to the traditional comedic roles. Despite the years of age that divide them, Jim and Ántonia could conceivably play the roles of comedic hero and heroine—and Ántonia's early life mistake would not necessarily make that impossible. But what we get in *My Ántonia* is an ending with all the resonances of the ending of a true comedy without the event usually essential to the plot—the marriage of the hero and heroine.

That all the resonances of comedy are present in the novel is undeniable. We move from disorder to order. Those who loved at first are reunited in love again. All mysteries have been revealed. The happy ending has been brought about not just by a marriage but by a fruitful marriage. But Ántonia is not married to Jim. The question is, then, what role does Ántonia play in Jim's life?

Among the many readings the novel has attracted recently, many deal with sexuality. Critics who posit Cather's lesbianism (something for which there is some degree of evidence, if not proof), see Jim Burden as Cather's surrogate. Like Cather herself, he hopelessly loves a woman to whom he cannot be united. Nevertheless, the love, which can never result in the marriage that defines traditional comedies, makes his life seem still a happy one. Whatever one thinks of that interpretation—and Cather's students include many who think that lesbianism is irrelevant to her works as well as many who think it is the key to understanding them—it is clear that Cather is describing a sort of love that gives life meaning, even if it does not result in an exclusive or legally sanctioned union.

In the end, Cather is clearly most interested in the power of memory to alleviate the disappointments of life. The novel is full of iconic moments that Jim Burden can draw on when seeking solace for the disappointments of his later life. Still more importantly, it includes in Ántonia an iconic character, one who embodies all the themes discussed above, and more. Having the memory of the young Ántonia and the promise of enjoying the friendship of her progeny in the years to come, Jim Burden is left with more than enough to compensate for whatever is lacking in his domestic life in New York.

TOPICS FOR WRITTEN OR ORAL EXPLORATION

1. Write an essay comparing and contrasting Alexandra's personality with Ántonia's.

2. As part of a classroom debate, support or refute the following statement: In *O Pioneers!* and *My Ántonia*, Willa Cather tends to romanticize the land specifically and nature in general.

3. What role do you think the seasons play in the two novels?

4. Choose one of the novels and explain whether, in your opinion, it is primarily a story of hope or one of despair. Using evidence from the novel, defend your position as part of a class discussion.

5. In both *O Pioneers!* and *My Ántonia*, Cather often refers to Old World notions and ways. Find several of these references and write an essay explaining what they contribute to the novels.

6. Alexandra Bergson is sometimes thought of as not very maternal. Partly, perhaps, that is because she is not married and has no children. Write an essay in which you argue that Alexandra is, nevertheless, very maternal in many other ways.

7. Contrast Alexandra's relationship to the land with that of her father and her brothers, Oscar and Lou.

8. What do you presume to be the significance, if any, of the name "Burden"?

9. Write an essay on how Jim Burden has enriched Ántonia's life, or on how she has enriched his.

10. Some readers are dissatisfied with Alexandra's forgiving attitude toward Frank Shabata after the murders. Are you? If so, why? If not, why not?

11. In *My Ántonia*, memory is represented as a healing or redeeming force in later life. Write an essay in which you describe the way in which one or more of your own memories has had a positive effect on your life.

12. Cather does not describe Ántonia's mother very sympathetically. Is there a way, nevertheless, that we can feel compassion for Mrs. Shimerda? Discuss in class.

13. Pick one of the following characters and in an essay explain how he or she changes throughout the course of the novel: Jim Burden, Ántonia Shimerda, Alexandra Bergson, or Carl Linstrum.

SUGGESTIONS FOR FURTHER READING

Bennett, Mildred. *The World of Willa Cather*. Lincoln: University of Nebraska Press, 1961.

Curtin, William. "Willa Cather: Individualism and Style." *Colby Library Quarterly* 8 (June 1968): 36–58.

Harris, Richard C. "Renaissance Pastoral Conventions and the Ending of *My Ántonia*." *Markham Review* 8 (1978–79): 8–11.

Middleton, Jo Ann. *Willa Cather's Modernism: A Study of Style and Technique*. London: Associated University Presses, 1990.

Murphy, John J. *My Ántonia: The Road Home*. Boston: Twayne, 1989.

Rosowski, Susan J. "Willa Cather—A Pioneer in Art: *O Pioneers!* and *My Ántonia*." *Prairie Schooner* 55 (1981–82): 141–54.

———. "Willa Cather and the Fatality of Place: *O Pioneers!*, *My Ántonia*, and *A Lost Lady*." *Geography and Literature: A Meeting of the Disciplines*. Edited by William E. Mallory and Paul Simpson-Housley. Syracuse, N.Y.: Syracuse University Press, 1987. 81–94.

Slote, Bernice. "Willa Cather as a Regional Writer." *Kansas Quarterly* 2 (Spring 1970): 7–15.

2

Everyday Life on the Plains

Willa Cather was born in Back Creek, Virginia, on December 7, 1873, and spent the first nine years of her life in this lush Shenandoah Valley area. The landscape she knew as a child was one that most people would consider idyllic—hilly and green, covered with trees, creeks, and wildlife. She spent her days exploring the woods and a nearby mill, finding places to hide in her family's large sheep barn, visiting her grandparents, and listening to the stories they told about the Civil War and its aftermath. Her grandparents had done fairly well as Virginia farmers, despite the fact that the land was rocky and sloping and therefore not especially well suited to farming.

Cather's Virginia childhood, then, was characterized not by want and struggle but by plenty, stability, and endless diversion. Besides exploring the surrounding landscape, she particularly enjoyed watching the women of her family go about their work, and listening to the stories they told as they did so. Her memories of the domestic activities of her mother and grandmothers, for example, especially their gardening, cooking, canning, pickling, and preserving, find their way into both *O Pioneers!* and *My Ántonia*. The narrator in *O Pioneers!* tells us that one of the "pleasantest rooms in the house [was] the kitchen—where Alexandra's three young Swedish girls chatter and cook and pickle and preserve all summer long" (178). Likewise, in *My Ántonia*, when Jim Burden returns to see Ántonia after twenty years away, one of the first things she wants to show him is her new "fruit cave" (617). Her children take him to the outside cellar and proudly show him "three small barrels; one full of dill pickles, one full of chopped pickles, and one full of pickled watermelon rinds. . . . [They] kept shyly pointing out . . . the shelves of glass jars. They said nothing, but . . . traced on the glass with their fingertips the outline of the cherries and strawberries and crabapples within, trying by a blissful expression of countenance to give . . . some idea of their deliciousness" (918).

Despite the Cathers' peaceful, orderly existence in Virginia, however, they were not untouched by the westering mood that had overtaken so many other Virginians, and easterners in general. Cather's father, grandfather, and uncle managed to run successful farms, but because the soil was difficult and sometimes unyielding, the enticement of more fertile, flatter, and virtually free farmland farther west was strong. In addition, tuberculosis had reached epidemic proportions in the Shenandoah Valley, and the Cather family had been uncommonly affected by it. Four of Cather's great-uncles had died from the disease, and two of her aunts had contracted it before her grandfather, William Cather, left Virginia. The high elevations and dry air of the West were considered therapeutic for people with lung problems, and William wanted both to cure his two daughters and to prevent other family members from getting the disease. Unfortunately, in spite of all their efforts, both women died of the disease, one shortly after the family left Virginia and the other some time later, while they were living in Nebraska.

The first member of Cather's family to strike out for the West was her Uncle George Cather, her father's brother, and his wife Frances, who left Back Creek to claim a homestead in 1873, the year Cather herself was born. After finally settling on their land in Nebraska, they wrote to their Virginia relatives urging them to come west also. Cather's grandparents, William and Caroline Cather, joined George and Frances in 1877 and began urging Cather's father, Charles, to make the move as well. As much as William Cather wanted his whole family to be together, Charles was reluctant to leave Virginia, partly because his wife was opposed to the idea and partly because he himself was not especially discontented in Virginia. He did, however, agree to visit his father and brother in 1880, by which time they had built new farmhouses and were managing thriving, well-established farms. Shortly after Charles returned to Virginia, still uncertain about becoming a Nebraskan, the deciding event occurred: his sheep barn at Back Creek burned to the ground. Because William Cather's goal was to gather all his children and grandchildren around him in Nebraska, he refused to finance the building of a new barn for Charles, leaving his son no choice but to join him in the West.

The family left Virginia forever in 1883, when Willa was nine years old. The experience was emotionally wrenching for her, one she describes during a 1913 interview in terms of nearly unbearable loss and homesickness: "I would not know how much a child's life is bound up in the woods and hills and meadows around it, if I had not been jerked away from all these and thrown out into a country as bare as a piece of sheet iron. . . . For the first week or two on the homestead I had that kind of contraction of the stomach which comes from homesickness. I didn't like canned things anyhow, and I made an agreement with myself that I would not eat much until I got back to Virginia and could get some fresh mutton" (*The Kingdom of Art* 448).

All Cather's fiction is informed by her intense interest in the landscape and in the people who make their marks on it, whether those marks are in the form of a sheep barn or a bridge over a creek in Virginia, or of a prairie graveyard, a plowed furrow, a sod house, or a dugout in Nebraska. What gradually assuaged her grief over the loss of her childhood Virginia home was her growing awareness that in some ways the same things that had captured her imagination back home were also available in Nebraska. Although drastically different, the landscapes and the routines of daily life were equally interesting in both states. In both places she paid close attention to wildlife, vegetation, and the lay of the land. In both places she listened to the women talk as they went about their domestic chores.

Nevertheless, adjusting to the landscape and everyday life in Nebraska did require some effort. The flat, seemingly endless Nebraska plain looked and felt foreign to Cather; she reports that she "felt a good deal as if [she] had come to the end of everything— it was a kind of erasure of personality" (*The Kingdom of Art* 448). Jim Burden's memories of his introduction to the country in *My Ántonia* are similar. Jim reached Black Hawk depot and "stumbled down from the train to a wooden siding" (718). From there he was picked up by his grandfather's hired hand and put into a farm wagon, where he "rode on the straw in the bottom of the wagon-box, covered up with a buffalo hide. . . . Cautiously [he] slipped from under the buffalo hide, got up on [his] knees and peered over the side of the wagon. There seemed to be nothing to see: no fences, no creeks or trees, no hills or fields. If there was a road, [he] could not make it out in the faint starlight. There was nothing but land: not a country at all, but the material out of which countries are made. No, there was nothing but land—slightly undulating" (718). The character of Jim Burden is actually experiencing Cather's own sensations of arriving at the Red Cloud, Nebraska, train depot in 1883. She, like Jim, was driven in a farm wagon out to her grandfather's farm: "My grandfather's homestead was about eighteen miles from Red Cloud—a little town on the Burlington, named after the old Indian chief who used to come hunting in that country. . . . We drove out from Red Cloud to my grandfather's homestead one day in April. I was sitting on the hay in the bottom of a Studebaker wagon, holding on to the side of the wagon box to steady myself—the roads were mostly faint trails over the bunch grass in those days. The land was open range and there was almost no fencing" (*The Kingdom of Art* 448). The land that Cather was seeing for the first time was punctuated by strange-looking buildings and other objects—sod houses, dugouts, windmills, pig-yards, and sod-breaking plows pulled by oxen. Even the vegetation was alien to her: rough, shaggy grass grew everywhere, along with sorghum patches and cornfields. Perhaps strangest of all, she, like Jim Burden, could not see any mountain ridges, which she had grown up with.

Cather's fondness for this new land was some time in coming. In fact, despite her reputation as a writer who consistently celebrates the lives of frontier farmers, she never really came to love Nebraska until she was a mature woman and had moved far away from the plains. Time and distance gave her a new perspective that allowed her to believe that "life might not be so flat as it looked there" (*The Kingdom of Art* 448). Ironically, what made it less "flat" were Cather's memories of those very facts of the landscape that at first had seemed so foreign and impossible to appreciate: sod-breaking, dugouts, sod houses, booming crops, failing crops, stories of triumph, and stories of defeat.

TRANSPLANTING: LEAVING HOME FOR THE WEST

If Congress had not passed the Homestead Act in 1862, many of the people, including Cather's grandparents and uncle, who emigrated to the American West from Europe and the eastern United States, would never have left their native places. Although many of these people dreamed of owning and farming their own land, most of them simply could not afford to buy tracts of land large enough to support their families. During the first half of the nineteenth century, the federal government was pressured by westerners to provide financial incentives for people to settle in the West and cultivate the land (Foner and Garraty 878). The argument was that "land ownership would give people a strong economic stake in society and an interest in good government and political stability" (Foner and Garraty 878). This pressure finally resulted in the passage of the Homestead Act, which made land available to anyone who would agree to settle on it after paying a nominal fee—an offer so attractive that it lured thousands of people to the prairies and the plains. In fact, while the Homestead Act was in force, "homestead entries totalled 718,819" (Foner and Garraty 879).

Because the interest in obtaining a homestead was so strong, several western newspapers ran columns similar to the following unsigned one. It answers some of the most commonly asked questions about the homesteading process.

FROM "ALL ABOUT HOMESTEADS" (1871)

What is a homestead?

It is a farm given to any man or woman who lives on it and cultivates it for five years. I say "given," for the charges are only about ten cents an acre—that is the cost of surveying and recording, amounting in all to one-fourth of a square mile, to $18 at most, and $4 of this sum is not payable for five years.

How large a farm is a homestead?

It is a farm of 160 acres, except on tracts one-half of which has been granted in aid of railroads or other public improvements. On such tracts the homestead is of no more than half the usual size, unless the homesteader has served at least 90 days as a soldier. In that case his homestead is a quarter section anywhere.

Who may become a homesteader?

Any man or any woman—that is, any native of legal age, and any foreigner who has declared his intention of becoming a citizen, which any immigrant may do immediately after he arrives in America.

How does one become a homesteader?

He goes to the United States Land Office, and there has free access to maps showing all the vacant lands in the neighboring region. He then goes and picks out the one he likes best, returns to the land office, makes an application according to the legal forms furnished by the officers there, leaves those forms to record, pays at most $14, and is henceforth monarch of all he surveys on the farm of his choice. But a homesteader is not obliged to go in person to the land office. In most cases he can ascertain from local land agents or residents what lands are vacant and then make his application for the homestead he wishes to occupy, before the clerk of the court in the county where it lies, sending with it an affidavit with his reasons for not appearing in person.

How soon must a homesteader begin to occupy his land?

At any time within six months after his application is put on record, and he may journey away from his land at will, if not absent for more than six months at once, and provided that he fixes his residence nowhere else.

Can a homesteader become a full owner of his farm sooner than at the end of five years?

Yes; after six months residence, he can at any time purchase the land by paying the government price, the maximum of which is $2.50, and the minimum half that sum per acre.

What if a homesteader is in debt?

His homestead is exempt from liability for any debt contracted previous to his perfecting his claim to his land for any subsequent debt.

How is the full title finally received?

After the homesteader has resided on his land and tilled it for five years, if at any time within two years he proves that fact to the Register of the land office where his application was recorded, that officer will obtain for him from Washington a full title of his land, charging him a fee of only $4.

Is not one man as good as another?

. . . Our last Congress enacted that every soldier is equal to two other men. The act was approved by Gen. [Ulysses S.] Grant July 15th, 1870. It provides that every person who has served loyally in the National army or navy for 90 days is entitled on terms above explained, "to enter and receive a patent for one whole quarter section of land"—that is 160 acres—where other men can only enter 80, "of the alternate reserved sections along the lines of any of the railroads wherever public lands have been granted by acts of Congress." In order to gain these privileges, the soldier must pursue the same routine and pay the same fees as if he were a civilian. But he gets twice as much land.

Columbus, Nebraska, *Platte Journal*, June 28, 1871.

BUILDING A FRONTIER HOME

The first homesteaders came to Nebraska in covered wagons known as "prairie schooners," driving their wagons onto the land they had filed claim upon. Many of these settlers had little or no money left after paying their filing fees, and typically they lived in their wagons for as long as it took to build a home. Because timber was unavailable on most sections of land, log cabins and frame houses were rare in the early pioneer days. Much more common were dugouts—excavations in the sides of hills, roofed with sod—and small houses made entirely of sod but built above ground. When Cather's grandparents and her Uncle George and Aunt Frances first moved to Nebraska, both families lived for a time in sod-roofed dugouts of the kind Cather describes several times in *O Pioneers!* At the beginning of that novel, when Alexandra and her young brother Emil ride back to the farm from their excursion in town, they see "here and there a windmill gaunt against the sky, a sod house crouching in a hollow" (144). Crazy Ivar, from whom the Bergsons buy a hammock, lives in a dugout: all that was visible of it was "a door and a single window . . . set into the hillside. You would not have seen them at all but for the reflection of the sunlight upon the four panes of window-glass. . . . But for the piece of rusty stovepipe sticking up through the sod, you could have walked over the roof of Ivar's dwelling without dreaming that you were near a human habitation" (155). The Shimerdas in *My Ántonia* lived in a dugout, too, of course—perhaps the most famous one in all of Cather's work set in Nebraska.

Before a settler could build either a sod house or a dugout with a sod roof, however, he had to obtain his building material. Breaking the sod was a relatively slow and labor-intensive process that required a strong body, the right kind of plow, and usually three yoke of oxen (that is, six animals). W.G. Edmundson, an agricultural correspondent writing in a farm periodical called the *Cultivator,* explains the process and offers some advice.

FROM W.G. EDMUNDSON, "PRAIRIE FARMING—BREAKING THE
SOD" (1852)

Many false impressions have gone forth among the eastern farmers, in regard to the expense of breaking a prairie sod; and to those who many contemplate removing to a prairie country, a few facts exemplifying the method of executing this work . . . might be found interesting. The plow mostly used in breaking sod, turns a furrow two feet wide, and in some cases as high as thirty inches are turned, requiring three yoke of oxen to do the work with ease. . . . From two and a half to three inches is the usual depth that the soil is broken. . . . A prairie sod has no equal as a test, to put to trial the skill of a scientific plowman. . . . Some of the most improved steel mould board plows [are] so perfectly adapted to the character of the work, that any further attempt at improvement would be abortive. The best plows are suspended on two wheels, supported by an axle near the end of the beam. The wheels are twelve inches broad on the surface, the one following in the furrow guides the width of the furrow slice, and the one on the sod acts as a roller to break and smooth down the prairie grass. By the aid of a lever the wheels are hoisted up, so as to expedite the turning of the plow at the head lands, and the only thing the plowman has to do, is to set the plow at the turnings, as the wheels guide it quite as perfectly as could be done by the most experienced plowman.

Cultivator. Albany: New York State Agricultural Society, 67.

INSIDE FOUR SOD WALLS: "NEBRASKA MARBLE AND SOD HOMES"

The houses on the Divide were small and were usually tucked away in low places. Most of them were built of the sod itself, and were only the unescapable ground in another form.

O Pioneers!, 147

Our neighbors lived in sod houses and dugouts—comfortable, but not very roomy.

My Ántonia, 722

Mrs. Bergson, Alexandra's mother in *O Pioneers!*, refuses to live in a sod house, presumably because she wants her surroundings in a new country to be as much as possible as they were in the old one. Neither sod houses nor dugouts were as prestigious on the plains as was a log house. When Carl Linstrum returns to Nebraska after an absence of more than a decade, Alexandra's brother, Lou, assumes he'll want to see his old place. "You won't hardly know it," Lou says. "But there's a few chunks of your old sod house left. Alexandra wouldn't never let Frank Shabata plough over it" (191). In both *O Pioneers!* and *My Ántonia*, the sod houses that dotted the landscape are symbols of the endurance and industry of the first settlers.

In *Pioneers of the West: A True Narrative*, an early settler named John Turner describes his experience of building a sod house. Except that Turner built a larger-than-usual sod house, his account is representative of what most pioneers would have undergone, including Cather's own grandparents, aunt, and uncle when they first arrived in Nebraska.

FROM JOHN TURNER, "MARBLE AND SOD HOUSES" (1903)

First, then, of course, after plowing the sod, about three inches thick, say, which was done with an ordinary breaking plow, was to cut it into the required length. As the walls usually were built three feet in width, a twelve-inch sod, as we called it, had . . . to be cut two feet in length. In laying the sod, open spaces were left for doors and windows, the frames being built in as the walls went up. When the foundation had been laid, the order of laying the next course was reversed. This reversal process was repeated with every course till the walls had reached the desired height. At the proper height spaces were left for the windows, and the frames built in, as in the case of the door frames. When the walls were up to about the thickness of a couple of sod above the frames, lintels were then laid across, and the sod laid over them, continuing the wall right through. The vacant space over the frames was necessary on account of the walls settling so much, that process going on for years, perhaps. Old rags, or an old gunny bag, was usually stuffed into the open space, and a portion of it removed, as occasion required. When the walls were high enough, about six or seven feet usually, the gable-ends were then built up, a few inches or a foot higher, for, to prevent the dirt from washing off, as much as possible, by heavy rains, the roof was made almost flat. It was the general custom to trim down the surface of the walls with a sharp spade after they were up; but it was invariably the rule with me to trim each course as I laid it, thus giving a better chance to keep them up straight. We used to shave off the top surface of each course with a sharp hoe, filling in the cracks and openings between each sod.

The walls being completed, we are now ready for the ridge-pole, usually a tree from ten to fifteen inches through at the larger end, and as near the same size the whole length as was possible to find one. Sometimes the bark was stripped off; for the wood lasted much longer that way, as well as having a cleaner and neater appearance. Raising the pole into position was done by rolling it upon skids, and necessitated the help of several of the neighbors. Skids were placed with one end resting on the edge of the wall, and the lower end extending away out on the ground. Some stood on top of the walls, and pulled on the ropes, and others, on the ground, lifted and pushed on the pole from below. Of course, there were other ways in which many of these things were done, depending on circumstance. Next came the rafters, poles from four to six inches through, and placed about fifteen inches apart. Over these was laid willow brush, and this again covered with a good quantity of hay, and finally, dirt piled on to the depth of six or eight inches. The plaster for the inside of the walls was composed of about one-third part clay and two of sand. Two coats were put on usually. With the walls trimmed down tolerably smooth, and [with] a little care in putting on the plaster a smooth, hard surface could be made, and wallpaper could be put on about as neatly as on the plastered walls of a frame or brick building. Of course, it would not bear getting wet, and it was often washed off by the rain coming through the roof. Many of the houses, however, were never plastered, and few had floors in them in the early days. The ground usually was the floor, and the door and window frames were hewn out of the scrubby timber that could be found anywhere.

In making a dugout, all the difference in that and building a house was that an excavation was dug into a bank, and walls built up in front, and also on the sloping banks at the sides, and the roof put on. . . .

Every sod house consisted of only one room, but once in a while could be seen a curtain stretched across the room, thus affording some little privacy. So I laid my plans for putting up a house of three rooms, making the partition walls of sod, but not so thick as the outer walls—a thing that I have never seen in any other house. The house, being eighteen feet wide and twenty-two feet in length inside, required an enormous amount of sod; and, having no team nor wagon of any kind, and feeling the need of going to as little expense as possible, we carried all the sod in our arms. And, on that account, we had the sod plowed as near to the "building spot" as possible; but, being on the level prairie, it was exceedingly poor material. It will be seen, therefore, that we had no small job on our hands. We started in, however, our friend and I, nothing daunted. Day after day we toiled on. . . . I laid all the sod myself, and, when I would catch up and run out of sod, I would help carry in more. At the close of the first day, having worked like beavers, the progress that we had made was but little more than perceptible. After cooking and eating our supper, we spread our blankets on the floor of our six feet square cabin, and lay down to rest; not, however before bowing our heads in prayer in acknowledgment of blessings bestowed through the day, and asking for a continuance of God's protecting care throughout the night.

Day after day for more than three weeks we labored steadily on. . . .

Pioneers of the West: A True Narrative. Cincinnati: Jennings and Pye, 67–70.

JOHN TURNER'S "BIG BLIZZARD"

There had not been such snowstorms in twenty years, and the path across the fields was drifted deep from Christmas until March.

O Pioneers!, 235

The weather in Nebraska was often erratic; homesteaders became accustomed to searing heat and drought in the summer, and bone-chilling cold and killing blizzards in the winters. In *O Pioneers!* Alexandra is kept from seeing her dear friend Marie Shabata by heavy snow: "When the two neighbors went to see each other, they had to go round by the wagon-road, which was twice as far" (235–36). When Mr. Shimerda commits suicide in *My Ántonia*, the body has to stay where it fell for several days because a blizzard prevents the coroner from getting to the Shimerdas' homestead. Cather provides a vivid description of the storm through the eyes of her narrator, Jim Burden:

> The snow did not fall this time, it simply spilled out of heaven, like thousands of feather-beds being emptied. . . .
>
> Next day our men had to shovel until noon to reach the barn—and the snow was still falling! There had not been such a storm in the ten years my grandfather had lived in Nebraska. He said at dinner that we would not try to reach the cattle—they were fat enough to go without their corn for a day or two; but to-morrow we must feed them and thaw out their water-tap so that they could drink. We could not so much as see the corrals, but we knew the steers were over there, huddled together under the north bank. (773)

Cather's account is strikingly similar to the following one from John Turner's true narrative about a three-day storm he and his family survived in 1873.

FROM JOHN TURNER, "THE BIG BLIZZARD OF '73" (1903)

This was the 13th day of April, and was the ushering in of that never-to-be-forgotten blizzard of blizzards of 1873. The rain continued to pour down; but during the night it turned to snow, and the wind blew a perfect gale, and it turned freezing cold. The storm came directly from the north, and when we got up the next morning, the south window, which reached nearly to the roof, was completely blocked. Opening the door, this also we found blocked; in fact, the whole south side of the house, clear onto the roof, was covered with a big bank of snow, and extended away out several feet. Not being able to look out on this side to find out what was going on in the outer world, we went to the door on the east side—almost all the sod houses had only one door, and a dugout never more than one—and, on opening it, O, what a sight! If, indeed, it could be called a sight; for you couldn't see your hand held at arm's length, the air being so full of snow, almost as fine as flour, drifting furiously along, and the wind keeping up an incessant roar. It was truly fearful; and even now, whenever my thoughts are set on the memorable storm, I experience a feeling of terror. The wind was so peculiar. It was different from any I have ever known before or since. It usually came in gusts, or with tremendous force for a few moments, and then lulled a little, keeping up these variations. But with this storm there seemed no easing up for a moment, but one uniform awful force for three days and four nights, and through the minutest crevice the fine particles of snow found their way. . . . In all the years since that time there certainly has been nothing that could be compared with it. Coming as it did after the settlers had commenced the spring sowing and planting—what little there was done—no one would even dream that such a storm could possibly be, so no one was prepared to meet such an extreme emergency. But even if such a thing had been expected, or known for a certainty, the time had been far too short for the settlers to have made any kind of adequate preparations in such a case. Had the country been more thickly settled, as in later years, and with more stock scattered about, bad as it proved to be under existing conditions, it must have been a hundred-fold worse. . . .

We have already stated that we opened the east door and looked out; for the wind, coming from the north, had kept that side of the house clear of snow. "What can we do?" we said; "for the oxen are out there tied to those old trucks, and have been in that awful situation all night, and if they remain there longer they must certainly perish. In fact, this may already be the case." It was the greater surprise that it was not so. I am telling this more than twenty-nine years after the occurrence, and as I think of those poor dumb brutes out there all through that long night in that awful situation, my flesh feels as though myriads of some minute animal were crawling all over me; and, as my scalp contracts and draws tight about my head, my hair stands up straight. . . . I stepped out into the blinding snow, and Edgar followed. As soon as we got outside, the wind struck us in our faces, and it seemed as though our breath would be taken, and we had to turn our faces from the wind. It seemed more from instinct, than anything else, that we found our way to the oxen, for we could not even see the ground at our feet. . . . We succeeded, however, in finding the oxen, and still alive, but shivering and shaking like a leaf. I tried to untie the ropes, but could not, they being frozen stiff as a stick of wood. So, taking my pocket-knife, I quickly cut them, . . . and we managed, some way, to find the house. The reader, doubtless, is wondering what we were going to do with them. What could we do? There was no other way than to take them into the house, if we expected to have the use of them some other day when the storm should be over, for they certainly could not endure the fierceness of such a storm but a little while longer. . . . Being wet from the rain that came first, the snow had stuck to them, and as it accumulated it froze on them, so that they were covered completely with a coating of ice. As they walked along they looked as though they were encased in a coat of mail, prepared for battle. We put them in one of the small rooms, the one occupied by the boys as a sleeping-room. There was no door to the room, so we put a pole across the opening. . . .

Having got the oxen sheltered from the cruel storm, now the cow, "Nellie," must have our attention. But dare we venture so far away? For she was down in the dugout, nearly two hundred yards off. Of course, all this kind of thing being entirely new to us, we did not realize the extreme peril we were subjecting ourselves to when we took the shovel and started out to find the dugout. . . . The way we got down there and back again seemed almost a miracle. There was a passage-way leading up to the door cut in the bank, the walls being up level with the roof, and this, of course, was filled up with snow. We shoveled and shoveled, and the whirling of the snow in our faces seemed as though it would suffocate us. After shoveling for some time, and making no headway, the snow drifting as fast as we shoveled it out, though loath to do so, we abandoned poor Nellie to her fate, little dreaming that the storm would continue to rage with such fury so long. . . .

As the hours and days and nights wore drearily away, we looked out occasionally to see if there was any abatement in the storm. One day had passed, and night had come, but with no change in the elements. Another night had given place to day, but they were so much alike that the difference, if any, could not be discerned. Tuesday morning had come, but still that never-ceasing roaring and raging haunted us. It was indeed a wearisome time, for the air outside was so densely filled with fine snow that the light was obscured. Moreover, the large window on the south being completely blocked, and there being but one small sash in each of the other two smaller rooms, we could scarcely see about us. We were afraid to use up the little oil that we had in the daytime, and so remained in semi-darkness. And thus another day passed and still no signs of a change. Wednesday, the third day, had come, but bringing with it no relief, and we began to wonder if the storm would ever cease. And when looking into the nearly empty flour-barrel, and remembering the otherwise scanty provision, we were more than ever forced to a realization of the perilous situation in which we found ourselves. Many were the messages that from time to time were sent heavenward, petitioning the Almighty to stay the raging of the storm. Some time during the night, as we lay there listening, we fancied that we could discern a slight change taking place; and, as time wore away, it was evident that the roar of the wind was growing less, and in a few hours more it had died away entirely, and all was still as death.

. . . After getting the oxen out of the house and giving them hay from the little stack close by, we hastened with all speed to the dugout to ascertain if we had a cow still alive. Everything was covered completely out of sight, and the bank of snow extended some distance out beyond the entrance. The snow had packed so solidly that we had to dig it out in blocks. When we took away the door, O, what a sight! Could this be our "Nellie?" If we had seen her in any other place than her own dugout, we would hardly have recognized her. She was lank and pinched up, and altogether a pitiable-looking object.

Considerable snow had drifted in at the door, and she had tramped it down till her head almost touched the roof, which was quite high.

Looking around at the other places, we found that the chickens were all right, except that they seemed to be starving for food. But Bessy! What had become of her? The snow had filled up the outer pen to the top of the rails, and naturally supposing that she was buried under it, we went to work digging it out. But finding that she was not there, we gave her up as lost. There was but little snow on the level prairie, but wherever there was any little obstruction it had gathered into high banks and ridges. Dugouts and barns, in many instances, were buried out of sight. All the deep and broad ravines were full, level with the prairie, and the snow was packed so firmly that teams with heavily-laden wagons passed over it for weeks afterwards. Some time during the morning my wife was looking out at the south door . . . across the prairie to the southwest, and all at once exclaimed: "Look! What's that coming up there? It can never be our pig!": But, to our great surprise, surely enough it was our "Bessy." She was sauntering along just as leisurely as you please, but I presume it was on account of being too weak to get up any other kind of a gait. We traced her track, and found that she had been lying on the open prairie, as I suppose, through the greater part of the storm. . . .

The country at that early day was very thinly settled, but still there was a good deal of stock that perished, and many of the people suffered. It is altogether impossible to describe the nature of the storm in a way that any one could realize what it was; experience could be the only instructor.

Pioneers of the West: A True Narrative. Cincinnati: Jennings and Pye, 126–36.

DEVOURING THE LAND: THE GRASSHOPPER PLAGUES OF THE 1870S

When Jim Burden first arrives at his grandfather's farm in Nebraska, he finds it fascinating that the garden is a quarter-mile away from the house. On one of his trips there with his grandmother, he remains in the garden after she begins her long walk back to the house, contemplating the new land into which he has been transplanted. A "new feeling of lightness and content" (724) comes over him, and he gives a thoroughly romantic description of his surroundings: "There were some ground-cherry bushes growing along the furrows, full of fruit. I turned back the papery triangular sheaths that protected the berries and ate a few. All about me giant grasshoppers, twice as big as any I had ever seen, were doing acrobatic feats among the dried vines. The gophers scurried up and down the ploughed ground. There in the sheltered draw-bottom the wind did not blow very hard, but I could hear it singing its humming tune up on the level, and I could see the tall grasses wave. The earth was warm under me, and warm as I crumbled it through my fingers" (724).

Embedded as they are in this picturesque pastoral setting, the grasshoppers, "twice as big" as Jim had ever seen, seem benign enough—even charming. They are part of what adds to his sense of contentment. However, the real pioneers of the 1870s, who suffered through grasshopper plagues of nearly biblical proportions, hardly saw them in this way. Grasshoppers were the enemy during that time, devouring crops and even invading homes. Some farmers tried burning rubbish at the edges of their fields in an effort to smoke them out, a method that was largely ineffective. For the most part, the homesteaders were forced to watch helplessly as the voracious creatures stripped every particle of foliage on which they settled.

Of the three documents that follow, the first, by Albert Watkins, describes the extent of the destruction caused by grasshoppers and reports on the numbers of families left destitute after the infestation. The second is an excerpt from *Pioneers of the West*, John Turner's personal memoir of life on the frontier. Like all of Turner's accounts of prairie life, this one is written from firsthand experience, in vivid and horrific detail. The third document is an unsigned newspaper article from the *Weekly Review* of Madison, Nebraska, that ran on August 6, 1875. It is a deliberately exaggerated story about grasshoppers that devour not only crops but also structures, home furnishings, and even people. It is an example of the kind of humor that seems to poke fun at people who are suffering from the effects of the grasshopper plague. John Turner mentions this kind of newspaper story in his memoir; he and the other victims of the infestation did not find it amusing.

FROM ALBERT WATKINS, *HISTORY OF NEBRASKA* (1913)

The Rocky Mountain locust during the three years from 1874 to 1876 threatened the practicability of carrying on agriculture in Nebraska, inasmuch as there seemed to be plausible reason for fearing, if not believing, that the invasion by this pest might be continuous. A thorough acquaintance with the history of Nebraska, however, would have largely allayed this fear because it discloses that the immigration of these insects was not regular but at periodical intervals. In his famous Ash Hollow campaign of 1855, General William S. Harney and his command, when in camp near Court House Rock, now in Morrill county, observed that the air was full of grasshoppers; and they were an inch thick on the ground. Of course they destroyed "every blade of grass." W.A. Burleigh, in his report as agent for the Yankton Indians for 1864, says that crops were promising in that part of the country until the grasshoppers came in the latter part of July and destroyed every vestige of them throughout the territory. The air was filled with the insects so thickly as to produce a hazy appearance of the atmosphere, and every tree, shrub, fence, and plant was literally covered with them. In many places they carpeted the ground to the depth of from one inch to two inches. They appeared in a cloud from the northeast extending over a belt some 275 miles wide and passed on towards the southwest, leaving the country as suddenly as they came after an unwelcome visit of three or four days. Mr. George S. Comstock made the statement in 1910 that grasshoppers did great damage on the Little Blue river, where he resided, in 1862 and 1864. Captain Eugene F. Ware relates in his history of the Indian War of 1864 . . . that in August, 1864, at Fort Laramie—then within Nebraska territory [now Wyoming]—the air was filled with grasshoppers. They bunched together in swarms like bees. He saw a cluster of the insects as big as a man's hat on the handle of a spade. Indian women were roasting, drying, and pounding them into meal to be made into bread. William M. Albin, superintendent of Indian affairs at St. Joseph, Missouri, reported in October, 1864, that "in consequence of the extreme drought, the backwardness of the spring, and immense swarms of grasshoppers, the crops in Kansas have been a partial, and in Nebraska and Idaho, a total failure." In his report for the same year, Benjamin F. Lushbaugh, agent of the Pawnee Indians, said that, "swarms and myriads of grasshoppers" came to that part of the territory in August, and they had not left a green thing. . . .

In his annual message to the legislature of 1877 Governor Silas Garber said that, contrary to scientific theories as to the habits and nature of grasshoppers, they had again visited the state in the months of August and September, 1876; and although no serious damage was done immediately by the insects, yet they deposited great quantities of eggs from which there was apprehension for the safety of the crops. It was estimated that 5,000 persons in eleven frontier counties were almost wholly dependent upon charity during the winter of 1874–75. . . .

Professor A.D. Williams was sent out by the *State Journal* to investigate conditions in the Republican valley, and his letters to the paper contained many harrowing stories of want and suffering. For example, an elderly woman said that she lived on a homestead near Rockton, Furnas county, with her husband who was sixty-eight years old. They had lost all their stock, except one yearling, by cattle fever. When she left home a few days before, there was flour enough to make not more than five loaves of bread. "When that is gone we do not know how or where to get more except as aided." Her son (living near) had a wife and six children. They had one cow, one horse, and two yearlings, of the Texas breed, which he could not sell for anything, and two pigs, but nothing to feed them. Fifty pounds of flour was his total supply for the winter. His children were nearly destitute of clothing and he could get no work to do. Another man had a family consisting of mother, wife, and six children. The mother had been sick for a year. He had a team, two cows, and three pigs, but nothing to feed them. He had raised no wheat and only nine bushels of rye. He had 120 pounds of flour left and no meat, and could not get work. . . .

A statement of the Harlan County Aid Society showed that in Republican precinct there were 313 persons—186 adults and 127 children. There were 4,150 bushels of wheat, but mostly owned by a few persons; 55 bushels of corn; 490 bushels of oats; 432 of potatoes; 89 cows; 46 oxen; 121 horses; 9 mules; 213 hogs; young stock, 149; poultry, 2,311. Seed was needed for 2,796 acres, seventeen families needed help and seven were entirely destitute. In Spring Creek precinct eleven families were destitute and eight more would need help within a week. In Sappa precinct eleven families were destitute and there were thirteen more with but a single sack of flour a week ago. In Prairie Dog precinct nine families were entirely destitute, three others would need help within thirty days and seven others within sixty days. . . .

A convention to consider the grasshopper pest and to take action thereon was held at Omaha, October 25 and 26, 1876. An account of the ravages of the insect, in considerable detail, was prepared by John S. Pillsbury, president of the convention, and Professors C.V. Riley and Pennock Pusey, secretaries. A memorial asking the federal Congress to establish a commission composed of three entomologists and three practical men of experience with the locusts, for the purpose of investigating the plague, and that the signal service be required to take observations of the movements of the insects, was signed by the governors of Missouri, Illinois, Iowa, Nebraska, Minnesota, and Dakota. . . . The memorial set forth that the grasshoppers overran sixteen states and territories in the year 1876; that many settlers in that section had suffered a total loss of crops for four successive years; and that the ravages of the insects had rapidly increased during the last twenty years.

Lincoln: Western Publishing and Engraving, 321–25.

FROM JOHN TURNER, "GRASSHOPPER PLAGUE AND AID TO SUFFERERS" (1903)

[The year of 1874] will always be remembered more particularly, and known all over as the "grasshopper times in Nebraska" and surrounding States. Grasshoppers had visited us more or less all along up to this time, destroying most of the little crop of corn that we had been trying to raise. But this year they came down upon us in mighty armies. . . . The little wheat crop was damaged considerably; but it was a pretty fair crop after all, so we thought, at least, compared with some years; for when we threshed it we found that we had a hundred and twenty bushels from ten acres of ground. Some advised smoking out the grasshoppers by placing green weeds . . . along the edge of the field, and setting fire to it. Glad to try almost any method that might be suggested, we gave this plan a trial; but it seemed all a waste of time. The only effect that it had was to scare a few of them off a few rods along the edge of the field, only to alight a little further on. And more than that, we came near seeing the whole field go up in a blaze.

The grasshoppers did not appear in full force till after most of the small grain was cut. But everything else—corn, beans, and vegetables of all kinds, all except about fifteen bushels of potatoes, of which we had planted quite a large piece of ground, were destroyed. This indeed was a trying time for the settlers; for they had been able to raise almost nothing up to this time, and now that there was a little prospect, to have almost everything destroyed in a few hours was very discouraging. This of itself was hard enough to bear; but the burden pressed down still heavier when we read in the Eastern papers—as we did sometimes—remarks made in a mirth-provoking way about the "poor grasshopper sufferers of Nebraska." They seemed to insinuate that the whole affair was a good deal exaggerated, and that the settlers were making a great ado about a small matter. . . . [The grasshoppers] drifted over in such dense clouds as to blacken the whole heavens, and with such a buzzing, roaring noise that it could be heard quite a long time before they came up over us. Sometimes they would fly very low, and at other times they would be far above us, drifting along by the myriads, their gauzy wings glistening like tiny bits of silver. And as they would gently fall to the earth, like a skylark with outstretched wings falling out of the heavens, the sight was much like that of large snowflakes in a gentle storm. When they settled down, the corn and other vegetation would be so completely covered as to be black with them, one over another. But the corn was their first choice to feed upon. When they had stripped it of every particle of foliage—which they would do in a night—they would stick so thickly on the stumps of stalks, and crawling over one another, that no room would be left to stick the point of your finger. I have seen them in the potato-patch and everywhere about, so thick that hardly a speck of ground could be seen. They would swarm in the roads, and be crushed under the wheels of the wagon, and be so thick everywhere that we would be obliged to tie our pants round with a string at the bottom to keep them from trespassing on forbidden ground. For the sensation was just about as pleasant as the crawling of a snake would be, with a gentle waking up with their finely-adjusted forceps in the bargain. As we walked along, they would rise up from the ground in such clouds and swarm about us that we had to fight our way through them. It was a time, too, when nobody needed to be admonished to "keep his mouth shut."

Severe as was the calamity, there was yet more to follow in the years to come. It is well, I think, that we are kept in the dark as to what the future has in store for us, else how deep the despair, and how much more unhappy this life would be for many, by the anticipation of sorrow and suffering yet in the future.

Pioneers of the West: A True Narrative. Cincinnati: Jennings and Pye, 207–209.

FROM "A GRASSHOPPER STORY" (1875)

A gentleman who has just returned from Cherokee County, Kansas, is full of remarkable reminiscences of the grasshoppers infesting that vicinity. He will stand around for an hour, relating the hair breadth escapes of the people whom the grasshoppers have overrun, and who are leaving their homes and fleeing from the fearful scourge. The traveler is inclined to think that many of the crimes attributed to the James boys are to be traced to the hardened and dissolute grasshopper, many of whom, he says, are arming themselves with shot guns and organizing a sort of home guard for offensive and defensive purposes.

One of those creditable stories is to the effect that, a few weeks ago, a woman dug up a panful of dirt in which to plant some flower seeds. She put the pan under the stove, and went out to see a neighbor. Upon her return, after an hour's absence, she found 7,000 bushels generated by the heat, literally eating her out of house and home. They first attacked the green shades on the windows, and then a green painted dustpan. A green Irish servant girl, asleep in one of the rooms, was the next victim, and not a vestige of her was left. The stove and stove pipe followed, and then the house was torn down so they could get at the chimney. Boards, joist, beams, plaster, clothing, nails, hinges, doorknobs, tinware, everything, in fact, the house contained, was eaten up, and when she arrived within a mile of the house she saw two of the largest hoppers sitting up on end and playing mumblety-peg with the carving knife. . . .

The way the matter leaked out was on a suit brought against the insurance company which refused to pay the policy, on the ground that the building was not destroyed by fire; but the court rendered a verdict for the plaintiff, as she had proven that the grasshoppers were generated by the fire in the stove.

Madison, Nebraska, *Weekly Review*, August 6, 1.

PIONEER REMINISCENCES

I felt the old pull of the earth, the solemn magic that comes
out of those fields at nightfall. I wished I could be a little boy
again, and that my way could end there.

My Ántonia, 910

One of Cather's mentors in her early writing career was the already
well-established Maine writer Sarah Orne Jewett (1849–1909), to
whom Cather dedicated *O Pioneers!* Going through some of Jewett's papers after her death, Cather found a letter that contained
the following sentence: "Ah, it is things like that, which haunt the
mind for years, and at last write themselves down, that belong,
whether little or great to literature" (quoted in *The Kingdom of
Art* 448). Cather agreed with Jewett's opinion and advice on this
subject, and she followed it faithfully in both *O Pioneers!* and *My
Ántonia*.

The facts of the Nebraska terrain and the people who inhabited
it are unquestionably among the things that haunted both Cather's
and her characters' minds. Jim Burden's memories of the land and
of Ántonia bring him back to Nebraska after a twenty-year absence.
Alexandra Bergson's mind also was haunted by the land: "For the
first time, perhaps, since that land emerged from the waters of
geologic ages, a human face was set toward it with love and yearning. It seemed beautiful to her, rich and strong and glorious. Her
eyes drank in the breadth of it, until her tears blinded her" (170).
Cather herself felt the "pull of the land," even after she had lived
away from it for decades.

For many pioneers besides Cather and the characters she created, memories of the land itself, the people who settled it, and
the struggle to survive on it were largely positive ones. The following two documents were published as part of a series called "Pioneering in Boone County," which ran in the Albion, Nebraska
newspaper, the *Argus*, in 1922–23. Both were written by men who
had homesteaded in Nebraska years before and who, despite the
hardships and struggles they endured in the process of making a
frontier home, look back lovingly on those early days, just as

Cather herself did and many of her characters do. In the first, by George W. Slade, we are reminded of Jim Burden's encounter with the rattlesnake in *My Ántonia*. Mr. Slade's "hand rake" recalls Jim's grandmother's "rattlesnake cane." In the second, J.E. Green's discussion of the suicides in his area calls to mind the suicide of Mr. Shimerda, Ántonia's father, which itself was based on a real incident from Cather's Nebraska childhood. From some of her neighbors in Nebraska, Cather heard the story of a Mr. Francis Sadilek, a Bohemian immigrant who had lived nearby and had committed suicide two years before Cather and her family arrived in Nebraska. Later, Cather was given an account of Mr. Sadilek's death by his own daughter, Annie Pavelka, who became the model for Ántonia. While the character Mr. Shimerda kills himself because of homesickness, the "epidemic of suicides" that J.E. Green talks about were caused by "grinding poverty." The scarcity of fuel and food, for example, sometimes convinced people that they could not survive no matter how hard they tried. Because trees were practically nonexistent on the plains, something besides wood had to be used for fuel. Many people used corn cobs, but before a corn crop had been planted and harvested, none were available. People had to resort to weeds and sunflowers, both of which were hard to gather and less than satisfactory as fuel.

Food was as about as scarce as fuel. Green tells the story of one man who lived through a blizzard with nothing to eat but sorghum molasses—that is, molasses made from the coarse cereal grass (sorghum) that many people on the frontier planted. Green also briefly speculates that drinking water straight out of the Beaver River might have caused a kind of mental instability that could have resulted in the rash of suicides. Although he does not explain exactly how drinking the river water might have caused mental problems, he probably thought there was a chance it was contaminated in some way. In any case, the far more likely explanation for the suicides is that some people were unable to cope with the lack of so many of the necessities of life and that they were unable to accept the reality of life on the frontier, different as it was from the life they had visualized when they had decided to file claims on their homesteads.

It is worth noting, however, the nostalgia the following pioneers feel as they look back on their experiences as homesteaders, despite the hardships and poverty they had to endure.

FROM GEORGE W. SLADE, "PIONEERING IN BOONE COUNTY"
(1922)

I first got the big idea of going west when I was 16 or 17 years old when we plowed with a big team and an old heavy chilled plow, on my father's farm [in New York], in a field covered with stumps, roots, huckleberry brush and stone. I made up my mind then if there was a place in this U.S.A. that was free from these elements I was going to find it as soon as I could earn the money to get there. I had been reading of vast tracts of land in Kansas and Nebraska that was nearly level and free from stones and stumps, that could be taken as homesteads. So as soon as I was 21 I hired out to a farmer by the month. I worked about eighteen months when I thought I had enough money to get somewhere west.

On the 28th of October, 1878 two other young men and myself bought tickets from Norwich, N.Y. to Omaha. We arrived at Council Bluffs on Oct. 30 about 4 p.m. and inquired of the agent when the next train went west over the Union Pacific and he told us at 9 the next morning. . . .

The next morning we decided to buy tickets to a little town on the Union Pacific called Silver Creek and look at the country near there and inquire about government land. We landed there some time in the afternoon. . . .

That evening after supper I asked a man that came in with wheat, if all the land in Nebraska was like that around Silver Creek. He said, "Oh, no. I live up in Boone County. Some of the finest land under the sun up there," and he said that he thought some homesteads were left. "Put your trunks in my wagon and go up with me in the morning, it will not cost you anything." . . . We told him we would be ready in the morning by the time he was. . . .

I remember passing one house on the way until we got over the line in Boone county and that was at the Loup river bridge, and they called it 25 miles. After we left the Loup valley we began to see some fine country along up the Beaver. . . . We crossed the Beaver at Abbott's bridge, then followed the creek. After tramping through the grass and weeds we came to some sod buildings and straw barns. . . .

I found out there was a land agent named Downs at St. Edward and he told me there were two quarter sections up the creek about six miles. We got him to go up with us and show us the land. We thought it was better than old New York stump lots so we filed on them.

A few days later . . . [a neighbor] sent word to come up. He wanted to

rent us his farm of 114 acres to wheat. Two of us took the farm, and . . .
the land was all plowed ready for seed in the spring, so we each bought
a yoke of oxen. I also bought a breaking plow, harrow and stubble plow,
which took about all my money. Had to get through some way until we
raised a crop. . . .

In February, 1879 we began to sow wheat. Got it all in that month.
Then in April I had to build a house on my claim. How to get the timber
for roof and windows bothered me. I did not have a cent. After awhile I
heard of a man that would sell the material from his old sod house and
would take work in exchange. So in April I borrowed a wagon and started
a sod mansion on my claim. When I was through I did not have any door
but thought I could hang a blanket up where the door belonged until I
could get a board to make a door of.

In May I went up to break prairie. I used a box for a table and a sack
of feed for a chair. A pile of hay in one corner served as a bed. I built up
a sod arch outside for a stove stuck to an old piece of stove pipe in the
top and laid some pieces of iron on top of the sod to hold up my frying
pan and coffee pot and rustled sunflowers for fuel. That arrangement
worked very well except when the wind blew, and the ashes found lodge-
ment in the frying pan. At any rate I kept the old oxen humming all the
breaking season. [Instead of trying to cut a hundred acres of wheat by
hand, we hired a neighbor] to cut it with a drop reaper, and two other
men, one to shock and the other to help us bind the grain. I remember
carrying a hand rake to turn over the bundles, for rattlesnakes had the
habit of getting under them and we did not want to start any trouble
with them.

There was some talk in '79 of a railroad coming up the Beaver valley,
but nothing certain developed until the next year. Then the prospects
began to look brighter. We had only 1020 bushels of wheat and after
paying all expenses had but little money left. We hauled our part to Silver
Creek and Columbus with oxen and sold it for 62 cents a bushel. The
first crop on my claim was very short on account of dry weather and
cinch bugs.

I moved onto the claim along in November '79. I bought a little stove
from the other boys and got two or three boards and made a table, bed-
stead and door. My house did leak some, . . . but I did not have anything
the rain would spoil. I had to go 1½ miles to the Beaver for water for
the oxen.

I worked many days for the neighbors at 50 cents a day for expenses
until I raised the second crop of corn which turned out good and the
price was 40 cents. A neighbor and I loaded a car together. That crop
started me along alright. I traded the old oxen for horses and harness,
bought a wagon, paid my little debts and from that time on the prospects
were much brighter. . . .

. . . Mrs. Slade appeared on the scene in 1899 and then I thought I had just begun to live like other folks. But about 1905 our health began to fail and I knew that I would have to rent or sell. A man came along and offered me my price. In 1907 we came to Unadilla [in New York]. We have both been very sorry we did not stay in Boone county, but I get the *Argus* every week, and that seems like getting a good letter from home.

Albion, Nebraska, *Argus*, March 23, 2.

FROM J.E. GREEN, "PIONEERING IN BOONE COUNTY" (1923)

The earliest history of Boone county, so far as I am concerned, begins with 1871 and 1872, and there was precious little then to make history out of. The Beaver flowed, as it has from prehistoric times, on its way to the Loup and coyotes sang even more melodiously then as now, but such things are not very historical. There were no bridges on the Beaver, but we did have a foot log. . . . A few rods beyond the end of the log, A. Dresser had a sod house and into it the U.S. mail arrived occasionally. The site of this P[ost].O[ffice]. is [now] Wolf Bros. Big Belgian horse barn. Nothing left to even remind us now of Dresser, sod house, P.O., or foot log.

Water was almost as scarce as booze in 1871. Oh, the Beaver carried its hogsheads of it in its mad rush down the valley, but we didn't all live close to the Beaver. Then there were those curious freaks of nature called water holes, but we were not all fortunate enough to have one of these on our farm, so that in the absence of the Beaver and the holes it was dry, very dry. There was plenty down in the earth, but we were not down there and our machinery for going down was not the latest improved. A spade, a home made windlass and anything but smooth and not so very powerful rope and bucket constituted machinery. With this sort of an outfit assembled, a strong man seized the spade and started downward. . . . I had worked the process and had struck water on my place about 30 feet down, [but] it came near being my undoing. I had gone beyond my neighbors a little in that I had displaced the old hand over hand bucket process, for drawing water by a suction pump. Something went wrong down in the well so it became necessary to go down [into] it. There was an opening in the platform about 2 feet square. We leaned the pump against one side of the hole. . . . As the well was only about 3 feet in diameter, I, ordinarily, could have gone down and up on my own steam, but tho't best to have a guardian angel at the top, lest something might go wrong. We had let the short ladder down so I could stand on it to work. Then I made a loop in the rope, set my foot in it and started down, with [Charley] Downs playing out the rope, holding firm against the side of the platform. But since the well was finished, gas, or damps, as it is called, had developed. I soon became faint and called for help. Downs hauled away on the rope, but was unable to move me. In vain did he and my wife struggle with the rope, but I was too heavy for him. I was so weak I could not help myself. Just as their hope had almost died within them, a man rode up and lent his kindly assistance. They say when my head came above the platform my face was ghastly white and I was limp and helpless. . . .

We had an epidemic of suicides. I have never figured out the cause. It might have been drinking too much Beaver water—we have all quit this practice now, maybe it was too much anxiety, grinding poverty, and a wonder about the next meal, maybe too much wild hay and too few California oranges—my, but they were scarce in those days. But the fact remains that three families came from Wisconsin and the three men suicided. One cut his throat. Next hung himself. He used the lines of his harness. Made a regular hangman's knot. His intention was sure strong, because the joist in the stable where he hung himself, was not higher than his head, so that when he was found his knees touched the ground. The third man drank himself to death. It took him a few months longer, so what's the difference? The result was just the same. So that whether by knife, line or booze they all went out by their own volition.

Speaking of grinding poverty and the struggle for food reminds me that in 1872 I took my team and drove down a little north east of Fremont where I worked to earn some wheat and corn. This I took to the mill on the Elkhorn and when ground I had 6 barrels and a sack of flour, 1,300 pounds, and 10 sacks of meal, about 1,000 pounds. I sent this by [United Pacific] freight to Columbus and then hauled it out home from there. As I had no house yet it was stored with Charley Downs, joining my farm. . . . The 10 sacks of meal were stored up stairs, on the floor, strung around next to the eaves. The barrels of flour were stacked against the sod stable wall and covered with hay. In this little house 5 of us wintered, the coldest winter I have ever seen in Boone County. We all seemed to get along fine.

Fuel was a great object in those days. Coal was almost unknown and heating stoves about as scarce. Some would go to bed to keep from freezing. Would get up and manage to get a little something to eat and then turn in again. One time George Huntly was caught at home in a three day blizzard, with nothing to eat the entire three days but sorghum molasses. He was a cheerful old soul, small and lame, but the sorghum had nothing to do with this. We haven't had any of those old time blizzards for several years. Hay and weeds were the chief articles of fuel in those early days. Young people who have three square meals daily and revel around a good Round Oak stove filled with good western coal, and then sit around and grumble about evils mostly imaginary, go away back and sit down and repent in sack cloth and ashes.

Suffering together as we did we learned to overlook the faults of each other. As our memories go back to those old neighbors we are inclined to forget their imperfections and regard them as brothers and sisters. But they were not all saints in those days. One fellow had built his sod house, and not the best either. He got in debt and either could not, or would not, or both, pay up. He had a wife and 7 children and didn't do a thing but pull out and leave them to starve as far as he was concerned. . . . This poor Christian woman struggled along some way and raised her family. . . .

Charley Downs and I were helping a fellow put up his hay. . . . He had only a sod stable on his claim. In one end of this he was living, or perhaps it would be better to say existing. Away out from human habitation and far into the night, [his wife] was confined [for childbirth]: Just we three men were there; no doctor, no nurse, no midwife and no grandmother. She brought forth a son. I suggested she call his name Jesus, but this mother, a devout woman, was very indignant. She thought my suggestion bordered close on blasphemy. But how could I help the thought? I had heard the story of the babe in the manger all my life and this was the first one that ever came to my knowledge. It was long years before this good mother ever forgave me for this break. That babe, born that night in all that dire poverty, under such unfavorable circumstances, now has 5 children of his own, is a leading man where he lives and has the confidence and esteem of all who know him. . . .

As I think of those pioneer days I sometimes wonder how we did get along. But we did and seemed to enjoy life about as well as people do today. I am thankful for those early day experiences and all the blessings God has given me.

Albion, Nebraska, *Argus*, April 5, 1, 4.

TOPICS FOR WRITTEN OR ORAL EXPLORATION

1. If you have ever had to move away from a place you loved, write an essay describing how the experience affected you.

2. The people who moved to the prairies and plains to homestead did so with very high hopes and a great deal of optimism. Is having such high expectations good or bad, wise or foolish? Defend your position.

3. Many homesteaders built sod houses because there was no other choice. Timber was often unavailable. Describe a situation in which you had to make do with what you had.

4. Does it seem fitting that in *O Pioneers!* Ivar lives in a dugout rather than in a sod house? If so, why? If not, why not?

5. Even among the pioneers, status markers existed. A log house was admired more than a sod one, and a sod one more than a dugout, for example. Write an essay on one or more status markers of today. You may choose to focus on cars, clothing, homes, educational credentials, or any number of other things.

6. If sod houses symbolized the industry and endurance of the first plains settlers, what would you say symbolizes the industry and endurance of people today? Write an essay describing one or more such symbols.

7. Cather takes great pains to describe the hardships caused by the harsh Nebraska winters. Write an essay in which you describe a time when the weather—in any season—created great hardship for you.

8. Support or refute the following assertion: Jim Burden loves the land as much as Ántonia does.

9. Compare and contrast Alexandra's relationship to and feelings about nature with Crazy Ivar's.

10. Grandmother Burden explains, and to some extent excuses, Mrs. Shimerda's behavior on the grounds that the effect of poverty on people is deep and unpredictable. Do you agree with Mrs. Burden's assessment of Mrs. Shimerda. Why or why not?

SUGGESTIONS FOR FURTHER READING AND WORKS CITED

Bennett, Mildred R. "The Childhood Worlds of Willa Cather." *Great Plains Quarterly* 2 (Fall 1982): 204–209.

———. *The World of Willa Cather*. New York: Dodd, Mead, 1951.

Cather, Willa. *The Kingdom of Art*. Ed. Bernice Slote. Lincoln: University of Nebraska Press, 1966.

————. *My Ántonia*. New York: Literary Classics of the United States, 1987.

————. "Nebraska: The End of the First Cycle." *The Nation* 117 (1923): 236–38.

————. *O Pioneers!* New York: Literary Classics of the United States, 1987.

Dick, Everett. *The Sod-House Frontier, 1854–1890*. New York: Appleton-Century, 1937.

Foner, Eric, and John A. Garraty, eds. *The Reader's Companion to American History*. Boston: Houghton Mifflin, 1991.

Garland, Hamlin. *Son of the Middle Border*. New York: Macmillan, 1925.

Hine, Robert V. *Community on the American Frontier: Separate but Not Alone*. Norman: University of Oklahoma Press, 1980.

Nelson, Paula M. *After the West Was Won: Homesteaders and Town-Builders in Western South Dakota, 1900–1917*. Iowa City: University of Iowa Press, 1986.

Norris, J.E., ed. *History of the Lower Shenandoah Valley*. Chicago: Warner, 1890; repr. Berryville, Va.: Virginia Book, 1971.

Smith, Henry Nash. *Virgin Land: The American West as Symbol and Myth*. Cambridge, Mass.: Harvard University Press, 1950.

Stouck, David. *Willa Cather's Imagination*. Lincoln: University of Nebraska Press, 1975.

3

The Coming of the Railroad

By the middle of the nineteenth century, the idea of railroads con-
necting the plains and prairies with the East was attractive not only
to the private capitalists who wanted to build them, but also to the
homesteaders who wanted the opportunity to sell their crops to
markets far away. Plains farmers wanted assurance of access to a
reliable but relatively inexpensive method of transporting their
goods over long distances before they invested vast amounts of
money in increasing the size of their farms and producing ever
larger crops. Without assurance that they would be able to ship
their crops to eastern markets, they were simply unwilling to take
such a large risk with their money. At the same time, the railroad
moguls did not have much incentive to lay track through areas that
were not developed enough to assure them a profitable volume of
freight and passengers. Simply put, without the railroads the development of the plains and prairies would be slow and sluggish,
and without such development, there would be no railroads.

The dilemma was at least partially resolved when the federal
government agreed to provide land grants to railroad companies
who were willing to construct lines to the West. The first such
grant was awarded to the Illinois Central–Mobile & Ohio route in
1850, and by 1871 the railroads had received "more than 131 million acres of land for nearly 19,000 miles of line" (Foner and Gar-

raty 907). In exchange for this free land, the railroads were required to provide lower rates for all "federal traffic, and these sav-
ings to the government were roughly equal to the value of the land
grants" (Foner and Garraty 907).

Although the government's action provided the necessary incentive for railroad tycoons to start building the lines, it was not uni-
versally appreciated by all the settlers on the plains. In certain
places, squatters had settled on land subsequently awarded to the
railroads and for various reasons had neglected to file claims.
When the railroad companies attempted to take possession, the
squatters refused to relinquish their property. In Allen County,
Kansas, one of these disputes erupted into violence. The squatters
argued that they had settled on the land first and that it was illegal
for the railroad to take it over. Eventually they banded together to
form an early antirailroad organization, the Settlers Protective Association, the members of which were generally referred to as
"Leaguers":

> The Leaguers attempted, by intimidation and threats, to drive buy-
> ers away from railroad land which had never been occupied. Those
> who had bought railroad land accordingly organized the Anti-
> leaguers. The Leaguers built small structures that could be pulled
> by horses. These shacks were moved onto a piece of land and the
> jumpers took possession during the night. The League hired clever
> lawyers and kept the cases in litigation for several years while they
> farmed the land and harvested the prairie hay which grew so lux-
> uriantly there. . . . During this war blood was shed. (Dick 354)

Arguments over who had legitimate rights to certain tracts of
land were not the only sources of friction. Most settlers were of
the opinion that the railroads should pay heavy taxes for public
conveniences and improvements. The settlers had taken possession of virtually free land under the Homestead Act and began
immediately to form local governments and establish schools. Until
the homesteads were patented, homesteaders were exempt from
paying taxes and instead relied on the railroads to pay the taxes
needed for various improvements (Dick 355). The railroads, however, argued that they should be subject to the same rules as the
homesteaders—that is, they should also be tax exempt until the
land was patented (Dick 355). As the bickering continued, it be-

came clear that some settlers, who had once welcomed the arrival of the railroad with intense enthusiasm, were beginning to wonder whether the iron horse was not more curse than blessing.

Nevertheless, most homesteaders continued to see the railroads as a boon and set about trying to secure the building of lines through their areas. Local newspapers maintained that no effort or expense should be spared in the quest to secure railroads through their regions. Meetings of all settlers in a given area were held, where speakers would exhort audiences to do everything in their power to convince railroads to build through their sections. Delegates from various towns were selected to meet with railroad officials and implore them to build in specific places, often offering to fund local bond issues as part of the inducements. Thus, many small plains towns found themselves vying with each other, and sometimes this competition became bitter and volatile. Often savage debates raged over whether or not to vote bonds for constructing a railroad. In one Nebraska county, the local newspaper in the town that stood to gain the most from having a railroad published the following list of arguments, among others, for voting bonds in order to secure one:

1. The railroad would not come unless the bonds were voted.
2. The railroad would open up the country, establish manufacturing, and draw trade to the towns near it.
3. If a railroad did not come the towns would lose their trade to towns along railroads.
4. Farmers could not have profitable markets until the railroad came through.
5. The lands of the county would lie unimproved until a railroad came. (Dick 359)

The opposition refuted these claims by maintaining that the railroads would do precisely what they intended to do without the lure of bonds, that they allowed towns to bribe them in this way just to obtain more money, and that in any case there was not enough benefit to be gained to make the cost to the community worthwhile (Dick 359–60).

There was, indeed, some truth to the suggestion that the railroads were not always above accepting financial incentives from frontier towns or using scare tactics to convince the locals to vote bonds. Once during the late 1800s, Jay Gould, a Union Pacific Railroad financier, pulled his private car into the town of Columbus, Nebraska, and told the assembled crowd that because the people there had not voted bonds, he would make grass grow in the streets—that is, turn Columbus into a ghost town (Barns 131).

Regardless of the impressive evidence marshaled by their opponents, however, the bonds usually carried. Most of the locals were simply too afraid that they would become one of the many once-successful towns that eventually died because railroads chose not to build through them. In some cases, and perhaps as retaliation for a town's lack of cooperation, the railroad would build a depot just far enough away from a thriving community to strand it; in time a new town would grow up around the depot. In one such instance, "the citizens of Ladore, Kansas, failed to come to terms with the Missouri, Kansas and Texas Railway. As a result the railroad built through Parsons instead of Ladore. Not long afterward the people of the little town placed their houses on rollers and moved them to Parsons, leaving the once promising town to die" (Dick 360).

Because railroad officials were well aware that their best interests would be served only if the population on the frontier increased rapidly and consistently, they launched a massive advertising campaign to attract immigrants to the West. Often the claims they made concerning the profitability of the land and the ease of farming were wildly exaggerated. Railroad agents issued literally millions of circulars, spreading them over the eastern states and Europe. In these circulars, Nebraska and the West in general were depicted as fertile new Gardens of Eden, free for the taking. The Burlington Railroad even offered rate discounts and free temporary lodging at certain depots along the way to people who promised to buy land. Not surprisingly, this crusade to "sell" the West was tremendously successful. In fact, it was largely responsible for populating entire states, Nebraska being one of them.

THE RAILROAD IN CATHER'S FICTION

Cather begins *O Pioneers!* with a description of the small fictional town of Hanover, Nebraska: "The main street was a deeply rutted road, now frozen hard, which ran from the squat red railway station and the grain 'elevator' at the north end of town to the lumber yard and the horse pond at the south end" (139). Mentioning the depot thus early in the narrative tells the reader several things: that the story takes place no earlier than the late 1800s; that the town of Hanover will probably survive because the surrounding farmers are able to ship their crops to eastern markets; that those settlers who fail as farmers and land managers and subsequently give up the whole enterprise, as Carl Linstrum's family does later in the novel, have an easy way to get back to the East; and that in general the plains farmers are not as isolated as they once were.

The small towns in both *O Pioneers!* and *My Ántonia* are based closely on Cather's own Red Cloud, Nebraska, where the real Burlington depot was situated exactly as she describes the fictional ones of Hanover (*O Pioneers!*) and Black Hawk (*My Ántonia*). It was at this depot that Cather, her siblings, and parents stepped off the train in the spring of 1883 after their long trip from Virginia. It was from there, seven years later, that Cather left Red Cloud for Lincoln in September 1890 to attend the University of Nebraska, never again to live permanently in Red Cloud. She arrived at the Burlington depot in Lincoln just as Alexandra Bergson does when she goes to see Frank Shabata in prison.

Jim Burden and Jake Marpole, too, arrive at the Black Hawk depot after their long westbound journey. Jim describes their trip:

Jake's experience of the world was not much wider than mine. He had never been in a railway train until the morning when we set out together to try our fortunes in a new world.

We went all the way in day-coaches, becoming more sticky and grimy with each stage of the journey. Jake bought everything the newsboys offered him: candy, oranges, brass collar buttons, a watch-charm. . . . Beyond Chicago we were under the protection of a friendly passenger conductor, who knew all about the country to

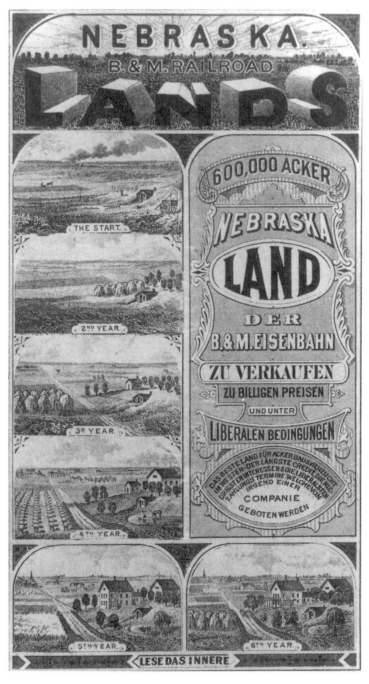

An example of railroad propaganda meant to lure immigrants, in this case German speakers, to the frontier. Courtesy Nebraska State Historical Society.

which we were going and gave us a great deal of advice in exchange for our confidence. He wore rings and pins and badges of different fraternal orders to which he belonged. Even his cuff-buttons were engraved with hieroglyphics, and he was more inscribed than an Egyptian obelisk. (715)

The description of the passenger conductor as savvy, well traveled, and worldly suggests that the railroad is the great connector of the frontier to all things modern and bustling—the promise of access to the great world that lay beyond the sod houses, steel plows, and fields of wheat and corn.

Indeed, the railroad did bring the modern world, with all its newness and conveniences, into the homes on the frontier. The home of Jim Burden's Black Hawk neighbors, the Harlings, for example, contains many lovely furnishings, including a piano, all of which had to have been brought by rail from the East. Significantly, Mr. Harling "controlled a line of grain elevators in the little towns along the railroad to the west of us" (807). The railroad, then, had helped to make Mr. Harling comfortable enough to buy a piano and the other appurtenances of a more urban, "civilized" life.

Like everyone else on the plains, Cather realized that the railroad had put an end to the isolation of the western farmers. Once homesteaders had the ability to ship their grain and livestock over long distances, they began to view farming as big business and to ponder how to fatten their cattle more quickly, how to grow more wheat, produce more milk, cream, and butter, and, ultimately, how to make more profit every year. The more profit they made, the more new machinery they could order and have shipped to them by rail; the more machinery they had, the more profit they could make; and so the cycle continued.

Profit and the acquisition of material goods, however, were not without their problems. With the railroad came certain kinds of corruption and abuse: "Discrimination, high rates, and stock watering," the practice of selling more and more shares of stock, thus reducing the value of all shares already owned by investors (Dick 307). In addition, "the general attitude of the railroad managers toward shippers led to organized opposition" (Dick 307). The sharp growth in population on the plains resulted in increased competition, which in turn resulted in a crop surplus. Excess grain had to be shipped by the railroads, which were charging such high freight rates that much of the farmers' profit was being eaten up. The railroads also created opportunities for corruption among their own employees; in other words, while the railroads were exploiting the farmers, their own workers were sometimes exploiting them. Ántonia's seducer in *My Ántonia* loses his job as a conductor and is blacklisted by the railroad for "knocking down fares" (903). When Ántonia returns home after he leaves her, pregnant and alone, she tells Mrs. Steavens that he has "gone to Old Mexico. The conductors get rich down there, collecting half-fares off the natives and robbing the company. He was always talking about fellows who had got ahead that way" (903).

Cather herself was ambivalent about the effects of the railroad. She appreciated the fact that its presence brought to the area the kinds of people who could add a level of sophistication and grace that the frontier otherwise lacked. It also helped her farmer neighbors acquire the kinds of goods, like pianos, books, and furniture, that they certainly deserved. Despite these real advantages, however, the railroads also created undeniably negative effects. They changed the character of frontier people in ways that Cather found heartbreaking. The earliest pioneers, like Cather's own grandparents, aunt, and uncle, had come to the West with dreams of land ownership and real love of the land itself. Cather subscribed to the somewhat romantic belief that the isolation of the early farmers, her relatives included, had been healthy and noble, that the more separated they were from the depravity of big cities, the more virtuous they were likely to be. They had tilled the soil, fought the elements and grasshopper infestations, and built their sod houses not in order to gain huge profits but simply to survive, to hold tenaciously to the spot on the earth they had claimed as their own. The money-grubbing, materialistic, profit-obsessed farmer had not existed in those early days; he was created along with the railroads. The first pioneers, in Cather's imagination at least, had prized independence, honesty, and selflessness above money and material goods. With the coming of the railroad, however, they became "progressive." They turned into businessmen, too busy to pine nostalgically for the good old days; their minds were occupied instead with how much new machinery, clothing, and how many buggies they could afford to buy and have shipped to them by rail. Furthermore, wealthy easterners saw the frontier as an easy opportunity for land speculation, and they poured vast amounts of money into it for the sole purpose of turning a profit. The land came to be seen increasingly as nothing more than a means to an end.

For many of the sons and grandsons of the early pioneers, the lure of the big, new cities at the end of the railroad line proved stronger than they could resist, and as more and more of them left the prairies and plains, the character of the frontier changed even more. Like Jim Burden, they asked, "What was there for me to do after supper? . . . I couldn't sit and read forever. . . . There was the depot, of course; I often went down to see the night train come in, and afterward sat awhile with the disconsolate telegrapher who was always hoping to be transferred to Omaha or Denver, 'where there was some life'" (850).

The change in the character of the West was, for better or worse, permanent. The "new" farmer might grumble legitimately about the abuses of the railroad, the markets, and the pressure to buy more and more machinery, but in the final analysis, the railroads were part of a whole complex that he had come to embrace and that had placed him among the wealthiest and most comfortable farmers anywhere in the world. The railroad, of course, was not the sole cause of the "materialism and showy extravagance" that in Cather's opinion had supplanted the first pioneers' determination, physical exertion, and love for the land. Nevertheless, the coming of the railroads did signal the beginning of what Cather saw as the decay and eventual collapse of the once noble culture of the West.

THE UNION PACIFIC

The first railway track in Nebraska was laid by the Union Pacific at Omaha on July 10, 1865. It marked the beginning of a vast expanse of lines that crisscrossed the state by the late 1800s. In his *History of the State of Nebraska* (1882), A.T. Andreas explains the beginnings of the line, which was crawling eastward through Nebraska and would eventually meet the Central Pacific line, which was building eastward from Sacramento, California. The convergence of these two lines near Promontory Point, Utah, in May 1869 was one of the great events of the nineteenth century.

FROM A.T. ANDREAS, "RAILROADS" (1882)

In 1838, Lewis Gaylord Clarke wrote to the *Knickerbocker* [*Magazine*]: "The reader is now living who will make a railway trip across the continent." In 1846, Asa Whitney began to urge the project of building a line from the Mississippi to Puget Sound, if Congress would donate public lands to the width of thirty miles along the entire road. . . . [T]he question which recurred to all was that relating to the public lands and the power of the General Government to ex-appropriate them for this purpose. The original thirteen States, without reserve, threw all of the State sovereignty under the keeping of the Federal Congress for the exclusive purposes of public safety and national defense. Immediately [after the Revolutionary War], the people, ever true to their interests and jealous of their rights, withdrew their delegated powers from Congress, and distributed them, by the articles of confederation, among the States comprising the Union as it then existed. . . . [As more and more western territory was ceded to the United States, Congress began donating certain tracts] for schools, railroads, the Indians, and other beneficent purposes, and [this action by Congress], concluded proponents, . . . not only conformed to constitutional provisions, but relieved the public from taxation and managed the public lands for the good of the whole Union. . . .

In all ages, mankind has sought the shortest, most . . . economical route to market, . . . and a like cause impelled the construction of the Union Pacific. The work was demanded in a national point of view, and across the State of Nebraska must the road be built. . . . In 1851, the Hon. S. Butler Kind submitted a plan which received the verdict of a universal approval. It was . . . that the Government should guarantee to any company or persons who would undertake and complete the road a net dividend of 5 per cent for fifty or one hundred dollars; the road to be constructed under the supervision of an engineer appointed by the Government, the cost of the road not to exceed a certain sum, and the guaranty not to begin until the road was completed and equipped for operation. . . . [The work] should be committed to companies incorporated by States, or to agents whose pecuniary interests would be directly involved. Congress might assist them in the work by grants of land or money, or both, under such conditions and restrictions as might be imposed. . . . Such a road would be a powerful bond of union between the East and the West. Commercially, it was rapidly becoming indispensable, and the peculiar geographical position of California and the Pacific possessions invited American capital and enterprise into those fruitful fields. . . .

In June, 1857, a number of distinguished gentlemen from various portions of the United States visited Omaha and conferred with interests and corporations having in view the construction of the Pacific road by way of Platte Valley and South Pass. . . . While in Omaha, they examined the city and vicinity, visited the Platte River, and united in recommending that an appeal to Congress be made for such reasonable grant of land and other aid as would give an impulse to the building of the road. . . . [From 1858 until 1862, several such appeals, in the form of bills introduced in Congress, failed consistently. The bill that finally passed in 1862] provided for the laying-out and construction of a continuous railroad and telegraph line . . . from a point on the 100th Meridian of longitude west of Greenwich, between the south margin of the Republican River and the north margin of the valley of the Platte River in the Territory of Nebraska to the western boundary of Nevada Territory. . . .

At the same time there was no inconsiderable anxiety throughout the West . . . as to what place on the Missouri River the President [of the United States] would select as the initial point of the road, and Omaha or Council Bluffs, it was insisted upon, offered superior inducements in that connection. . . . The preliminary surveys had demonstrated that it was wholly impracticable to construct a railroad west from the parallel [meridian] designated in the Republican Valley [in Nebraska, south of Omaha and Council Bluffs, Iowa, on opposite sides of the Missouri River, about twenty-five miles north of the mouth of the Platte River], while it could not be gainsaid that the eastern terminus at the 100th parallel [west meridian] would not be in the valley of the Platte. . . . Such being the facts, the main branch must be located from Omaha . . . unless in the decision of the matter all geography and all topography should be set at naught.

These arguments and considerations undoubtedly weighted the balance in favor of Omaha, for on the morning of Wednesday, December 2, 1863, the Engineer of the road received a telegram from New York announcing that the President of the United States had fixed the initial point of the road on "the western boundary of the State of Iowa," opposite Omaha, and directing him to formally "break ground" and inaugurate the great work of that day. . . .

[By July 1866,] 135 miles were announced as ready for the "cars" west of Omaha, and 305 miles of the road and its various branches as finished, stocked and in operation, with machine shops, depots and water stations in good supply and order. Its fine bridges spanned all the principal streams which were the terror of emigrants in the days when the slow, toiling team carried him and his household goods to the mountains of gold or the green valleys and plains of the Pacific Slope. The North Platte was thus rendered the superior route for emigration, whether to the gold fields of Montana, Idaho, Colorado, Nevada and California, or the fertile lands of Utah, Oregon and Washington. Its formidable obstacles had been overcome and . . . [t]ravel westward increased astonishingly, and Omaha at once became the great point of departure for emigrants tending in that direction.

While the Union Pacific had nearly crossed the plains of Nebraska and was rapidly approaching the Rocky Mountain Range, the Central Pacific was [building from west to east]. During the fall of 1867, the last and greatest of the tunnels on the western link was opened and the crossing of the Sierra Nevada Mountains into the Great Salt Lake Basin was effected. This achievement of hewing and blasting a pathway through primæval barriers, although included within 150 miles, was equivalent to more than 600 miles of ordinary railroad in cost and resistance to overcome. Early in 1868, the national highway pierced the rich mineral regions of the mountains and continued its movement to the Pacific. . . .

[When the Union Pacific met the Central Pacific in 1869,] a revolution was accomplished in the commerce of the world. . . . California shook hands with New York and New England, and the mingled screams of steam whistles upon engines constructed at points 3,000 miles distant waked the echoes of the mountains. Fruitful as has been the present century in important discoveries and useful inventions, varied and multiform as have been the improvements wrought out by patient toil and unequaled energy of the men of the age in which they lived, no single achievement will compare in its immediate and ultimate consequence to the material prosperity of the people. . . .

Marking, as it did, a new era in commerce, is it surprising that the people of Omaha, situated, as it is, midway between the two oceans and at the initial point of the route, united their rejoicings and congratulations over the spiking of the last rail? Omaha owed all she was to the

Union Pacific Railway. When the great enterprise was commenced, her population scarcely exceeded five thousand, and her commerce with the West was transported on ox and mule trains, subject to the delays and dangers incident to high waters, treacherous quicksands and hostile Indians. Limited as was this Western trade, it was divided between Leavenworth, Omaha and the intermediate river towns. Upon its completion, Omaha counted a population exceeding twenty thousand, and a commerce with the West embracing the trade of Colorado, Wyoming, Utah, Idaho and Montana, carried forward by the iron horse and undisputed by former business rivals. No wonder, then, at the rejoicings that were heard on every side; that a procession of almost unlimited dimensions, made up of the civic and military, embracing alike the merchant and the laboring man, the professional and the artisan, turned out en masse to swell the throng of ten thousand souls who assembled on Capitol Hill to witness and participate in the ceremonies of the day. To Omaha, the completion of the work possessed a peculiar and significant importance. Here through trains [that is, trains that go all the way] to the Pacific are made up; here is collected the commerce of the converging lines which form connections with the Grand Trunk [the transcontinental line formed when the Union Pacific and Central Pacific railways were linked together], are billed through to that proud city by the blue waters of the bay which flow outward through the Golden Gate to the Pacific; and here the returning commerce of California, Nevada, Oregon and the far-off trade of the Western Hemisphere is distributed to the various quarters of America and Europe.

History of the State of Nebraska. Chicago: Western Historical Company, 187–98.

THE BUILDING OF THE BURLINGTON

The Boys' Home was the best hotel on our branch of the Burlington, and all the commercial travelers in that territory tried to get into Black Hawk for Sunday.

My Ántonia, 821

The path of the Union Pacific took it across northern Nebraska. Cather's own Red Cloud, however, was located in extreme southern Nebraska, not far from the border of Kansas. That area of the state was never served by the Union Pacific. Instead, it was the Burlington & Missouri River branch of the Burlington Railroad System that finally built to Red Cloud. It opened for business in November 1878 (Overton 167), a mere five years before that line brought Cather and her family there from Virginia.

One of the most prominent figures in the building of the Burlington was John Murray Forbes of Boston. In the following document, Lloyd Lewis and Stanley Pargellis outline the history of the line and the part Forbes and the men he hired to work for him played in it.

FROM LLOYD LEWIS AND STANLEY PARGELLIS, *GRANGER COUNTRY* (1949)

The citizens of the little prairie town of Aurora, Illinois, in 1849 wanted a railroad to Chicago. . . . For Aurora the solution was not too difficult. Leading citizens put a charter through the State Legislature authorizing them to build the "Aurora Branch Railroad" twelve miles to Turner Junction, where they could meet and run over the rails of the new Galena and Chicago Union Railroad that had begun operations in the preceding October. Money was subscribed; the twelve miles of road were built in 1850. Building railroads . . . was expensive; those twelve miles cost $125,868.77, and Aurora all told numbered 1,200 souls.

If Aurora was to become a station on any through route, especially one joining the Great Lakes to the Mississippi River, more capital than the Aurora citizens could command must be found. It came through the foresight and activity of one of the two men who, within the next fifty years, were to transform these twelve miles of track into a great railroad system. John Murray Forbes of Boston had made money in the Oriental shipping trade. In the mid-1840's a couple of Detroiters, J.F. Joy and J.M. Brooks, sketching for him the excitement and the possibilities in Western railroading, persuaded him to raise funds to buy from the State of Michigan the semi-moribund Michigan Central Railroad, and to complete it—first to Lake Michigan, and then to Chicago. Having embarked on this venture and having beaten a rival, the Michigan Southern, into Chicago by one day . . . in 1852, Forbes perforce had to think of finding a road westward to the Mississippi, since the rival already was building the Chicago & Rock Island in that direction. Casting about for a course, he lighted first upon the fairly prosperous and ambitious little Aurora Branch. "It runs through a fertile and easy country to build," he wrote, "and has no expensive ends, as it runs over the Galena to Chicago and has a very favorable contract for thirty years." Citizens were willing, Forbes found Boston investors to advance funds, and control passed into the hands of Eastern capital. The charter was altered to permit construction westward to Mendota, and the name of the road changed to the Chicago and Aurora Railroad.

That same year Forbes and his Eastern investors acquired a controlling interest in three other Illinois roads that needed funds to complete their building plans: the Central Military Tract Railroad from Galesburg to Mendota, the Peoria and Oquawka . . . and the Northern Cross from Galesburg to Quincy. In 1855 the Chicago and Aurora changed its name to the Chicago, Burlington & Quincy Railroad.

Even before the fulfillment of one of his aims, the extension of the road to the Mississippi, striking the river both above and below the rapids at Keokuk [Iowa], Forbes had been interested in another struggling little railroad, which had been launched as early as 1847 by the citizens of northern Missouri, the Hannibal and St. Joseph, the first road to connect the Mississippi with the Missouri. Through his activity money was found for its completion in 1859, and although the Hannibal and St. Joseph did not formally pass under Burlington management until 1883, it was run during most of these intervening years under much the same board of directors as the Burlington, with Forbes always a figure of weight.

Still again, Forbes, one of those voracious but canny builders who made the West, persuaded the Burlington stockholders in 1857 to buy the control of another unstable little railroad, the Burlington and Missouri River, which, founded in 1852, had managed to advance a few miles west from the Mississippi. In 1856, however, with a land grant from the federal government as inducement, it could look for buyers. "I had vowed to touch nothing new," wrote Forbes, "but the Iowa Road with its rich and populous country and its 300,000 acres of *Free Soil* [that is, not in a slave state] seems to me so very important an extension of our lines that I can't help taking rather more than my share there."

The outlines of the Burlington System, therefore, had been laid by Forbes before the Civil War. That the Burlington and Missouri River Railroad should eventually reach the Missouri, as it did within a few years after the war, was a foregone conclusion when he took over its direction. . . .

"It is impossible for any of the great stem lines of railroad to stand still," . . . Forbes told his stockholders when, in 1878, he formally assumed the presidency of the Burlington, whose finances he had controlled so long.

"The point to aim at," he continued, "is one in which our interests are identical with those of the people around us—namely, to meet the natural and healthy wants of the country just as fast as it is ready to pay a fair return for capital with reasonable safety from unjust legislation."

Forbes was facing a situation in which all railroads, whether they were operated efficiently and honestly or as pawns of stock-market gamblers, found themselves. Being the first great corporations in the nation and situated closer to the people than any others, the railroads were the first to meet the rising demand for government regulation. All across the West the railroads were under attack for an "evil" born of ruthless competition—the practice of charging lower freight rates for long hauls where lines vied with each other and with waterways, and higher rates for short hauls where a road had a monopoly—and the secret "pooling" agreements made between roads reducing incentive to ruinous rate cutting. Demand for state and federal laws enforcing uniform rates and curbs on speculation agitated both Republican and Democratic parties and caused the rise of the Granger Movement, which, when it could not capture the old parties, threatened to form a new one. Hard times added fuel to the flames. The fact that most roads were controlled by Eastern capitalists made it easy for critics to blame Wall Street for railroad ills, a situation dramatized in 1882, when William K. Vanderbilt reputedly said, "The public be damned!"

Although Forbes never permitted the Burlington to become involved in the financial antics of such speculators in railroad stock, . . . he saw the reform agitation as an unwarrantable interference with the sober necessity of maintaining his lines and buying new ones to keep up with his strenuous competition. He built and pieced together so many branch lines that "the Burlington's cat-tails" became a common phrase among railroaders. Between 1870 and 1900 the Burlington pushed through to Denver, to St. Paul and the wheat fields, to the coal mines of South Dakota and Wyoming, to Billings, gateway of the minerals and lumber of the Pacific Northwest, and it began the extension which was to reach the coal regions of southern Illinois after the turn of the century. In the

1880's the Burlington System grew from 2771 to 5160 miles, and by 1900 was operating 7545 miles of its own and controlling 736 more.

For all that Forbes feared the public trend toward governmental control—a tide that in 1887 produced the federal Interstate Commerce Act—his management enabled the Burlington to pay dividends steadily through the . . . 70's and the difficult years following '87, rarely letting them fall below 6 per cent and once, in 1880, raising them to 11¼ per cent—a record of continuous payment that would also be preserved by the road thereafter.

Boston: Little, Brown.

LURING PEOPLE WESTWARD: THE RAILROADS "SELL" NEBRASKA

All railroads employed agents to encourage the flow of population into Nebraska and other western states. These agents distributed stories about the lush, fertile, virtually free, and easily profitable railroad land that was available to them for the taking. They spread the word not only in the eastern United States but also throughout Europe. In Nebraska alone, foreign immigrants "made up nearly 20 per cent of the state's increase in population in the decades of the 70's and 80's, an increase of almost a million souls" (Lewis and Pargellis, n.p.).

The first of the following four documents is by John Ross Buchanan, who was an agent throughout most of his adult life for various railroads, including the Iowa & Nebraska, the Chicago & Northwestern Chicago, the Missouri, Iowa & Nebraska, the Sioux City & Pacific, and the Fremont, Elkhorn & Missouri Valley. He explains his own advertising techniques in a January 14, 1902, address to the Nebraska State History Society at Lincoln, a presentation that was thereafter published in the proceedings of the Nebraska State Historical Society. The railroads and their agents often gave themselves sole credit for peopling the West, and Mr. Buchanan was no exception.

Another method the railroads employed to attract people to Nebraska and lands west was to extol the virtues of those areas through their own publications. The letters that follow Mr. Buchanan's speech are examples of the kind of propaganda printed in one such publication, *The Pioneer*, a journal of the Land Department of the Union Pacific Railway Company. The paper had obviously solicited letters from settlers who had only success stories to tell. The paper's call for letters had clearly asked writers to tell whether or not they had ever had a crop failure since moving to the West and to respond to questions about infestations of grasshoppers and other pests. Grasshopper invasions and bad weather are consistently described by the writers who answered the call as being the very rarest of occurrences and nearly insignificant in effect. These "Letters from Old Settlers" are accounts of only the most thoroughly positive experiences of prairie farming.

FROM JOHN R. BUCHANAN, "THE GREAT RAILROAD MIGRATION
INTO NORTHERN NEBRASKA" (1902)

In the fall of 1880 I came to the road. I found all that northern portion of the state very sparsely settled or wholly unoccupied, and in fact but little known about it. I found there were millions on millions of acres of government land which was available under the "homestead," the "preemption," and the "tree claim" or "timber culture acts," whereby a man could procure 160 acres, and after living on it fourteen months could commute the remaining four years by paying $1.25 per acre and get patent. . . .

These conditions, with some knowledge of human nature, gave me the inspiration on which I promptly acted, advertising in flaming posters and seductive, but more modest, folders—"free homes for the million." That was my slogan, or rallying phrase. It headed every circular, folder, and poster which I issued, and I issued them by the million. I spread them over Iowa, Missouri, Illinois, Wisconsin, Michigan, and Ohio, and even worked some in New York and Pennsylvania. Everywhere, and in every possible publication and newspaper, printed in black, blue, and red ink, in the English and German languages, this sentence of—"free homes for the million."

There seems to be an inherent desire in human nature to get "something for nothing," and here I was offering *free homes*—160 acres of good American soil—by the million. It took with the people, and the tide of immigrations started to north Nebraska. There was a very sparse population in the counties upon our line as far as Antelope county. This will appear from an old folder which I issued, probably in 1883 or 1884 (it was not dated), which states in English and German that there were—

"free homes for the million"
"The above invitation is to all who come early."

Then, for those who have money and want a home nearer by, I say—

"In Washington county there are 150,000 acres of unimproved land available at from $10 to $20 per acre.
In Dodge county were 190,000 acres unimproved land at from $7 to $20 per acre.

In Cuming county there were 240,000 acres unimproved land at from $3 to $7.50 per acre.

In Stanton county there were 225,000 acres unimproved land at $2.50 to $5 per acre.

In Madison county 200,000 acres at $2 to $7 per acre.

Antelope county 500,000 acres at $1.25 to $6.50 per acre.

Holt county 300,000 acres at $1.25 to $6.50 per acre.

Pierce county 200,000 acres at $2.50 to $6 per acre.

Knox county 160,000 acres at $1.25 to $6 per acre."

Over 2,000,000 acres in these counties at $1.25 to $20 per acre. It is perhaps needless to say that now no land can be purchased in Dodge county on the east at less than $45 to $60 per acre, nor in Holt county, the farthest west of the counties named, for less than $20 to $40 per acre. I rode over a farm in Antelope county a few weeks ago for which $50 per acre was offered and declined, and which I know at the time of the above advertising could have been bought at $5 or less per acre. . . .

There is an increased population in Holt county and the counties east of our main line, of about one hundred thousand.

There are half as many more, or an increase of at least fifty thousand, in that territory west of our main line and along and west of the branch line since built, which leaves the main line at Scribner, passing through Colfax, Platte, and Boone counties, and joining the main line again at Oakdale.

The extension of the Fremont, Elkhorn & Missouri Valley R.R. enabled me to continue this, as it pierced that wholly unoccupied section. The railroad was extended in 1880 from Norfolk to Plainview; in 1881 from Plainview to Creighton, and from Neligh to O'Neill, and to Long Pine; in 1882 from Long Pine to Thatcher; in 1883 from Thatcher to Valentine; in 1884 the Fremont, Elkhorn & Missouri Valley R.R. was purchased by the Chicago & North-Western Ry. Co., and its future extension directed under that ownership. In 1885 it was extended from Valentine to Chadron, and from Chadron to Buffalo Gap, at the base of the Black Hills; in 1886 from Buffalo Gap to Rapid City, South Dakota, and the same year another line was constructed starting from . . . a point now called "Dakota Junction," which is five miles directly west of Chadron, whence it ran through Nebraska to the Wyoming state line, and thence through Wyoming in succeeding years to Casper, in Natrona county.

This railroad had no land grant, and the Union Pacific and the Burlington & Missouri R.R. both having large grants, out of which they could pay for liberal advertising, and offer other liberal inducements, drew people to the South Platte. I was at a great disadvantage; our company was running into an unoccupied country, and had little business comparatively; and I trust I may be forgiven for having resorted to the only method within my means and at my disposal to attract attention to the north Nebraska country. At any rate, it clearly resulted in adding at least two hundred thousand people to the population of that portion of the state, and the section is now, I believe, recognized as the very best in the state, and the people are prosperous, thrifty, and contented.

When I commenced advertising "free homes for the million," I knew the land and conditions in all the northeastern part of the state and as far west as Holt county were superb, and would respond bountifully to good farming. . . . Then, too, I shared the common belief that turning up the moist soil would add moisture to the atmosphere, resulting in added precipitation, and so that each such effort and growing crops would aid in redeeming that portion of the so-called arid belt, and I accordingly encouraged—even piloting some—colonies to go well westward, where I knew there was excellent soil. Those who confined themselves to crop raising exclusively in these western sections proved to themselves and to me that it was a mistake, and I quit advising farmers to go so far out. Those who acquired the free land and put a little [live]stock on it were delighted and prosperous, and all who have gone since and pursued the same plan have prospered. The raising of vegetables, especially potatoes, proved successful and profitable, but corn, wheat, and general cropping were unprofitable. The "farmers" proper ultimately moved eastward into that section east of about the one hundredth meridian, and they, too, have prospered.

It was the advancing railroad and the "free homes for the million" advertising which accomplished the result and peopled north Nebraska. This, not only immediately along the line of the Fremont, Elkhorn & Missouri Valley R.R., but the population spread out to the north boundary of the state on the north, and covered two and more counties to the south of the line of our railroad, and the entire north part of the state is fairly well settled.

Lincoln: Nebraska State Historical Society, 29–34.

FROM "LETTER FROM WILLIAM HAGGE" (1875)

Grand Island, Hall County, Nebraska, January 1875

Dear Sir:—In reply to your inquiries, I will say that I came to this State in 1857, in company with some 20 persons, from Scott county, Iowa. We settled in Hall county, Nebraska, and were known as the German settlement. The country was entirely new and we had many disadvantages to contend with that are unknown to the new settlers at the present time.

I took a pre-emption on Section 28, T. 11, R. 9, W., where I have lived and farmed ever since. I have followed what is termed "mixed farming," and have never had reason to complain. Taking one year with another, corn and oats have averaged 50 bushels and wheat 20 bushels to the acre. I have raised as high as 25 bushels of wheat. Cabbage, potatoes and root crops have always done well. We have never had a failure of crops from any cause. The grasshoppers have been here some two or three different years, and during as many seasons, perhaps we have had more or less drouth [drought], but the crops were never seriously affected by either cause until 1874, when the corn crop was almost entirely destroyed. The Colorado beetle injured potatoes for one of two years, but has disappeared. The Chinch bug we have never been troubled with. I consider this one of the best farming countries in the world. The soil is rich and deep, of a quick, warm nature. The climate is remarkably healthful. During my 18 years residence I have never had occasion to call a doctor. I came here poor, with not more than $25 in money. I have now a good farm of 210 acres, 100 acres of which are in cultivation; have a good comfortable building, with a complete set of farming implements. I have made money every year since I came here. All the older settlers are well off. In 1858 and '59 I planted considerable timber, consisting of cottonwood, black walnut, box elder, maple and locust, all of which have done well. Some of my cottonwoods measure more than twenty inches through.

Land Department, Union Pacific Railway Company, *The Pioneer*, June, 2.

FROM "LETTER FROM R.W. HAZEN" (1875)

Fremont, Dodge County, Nebraska

Sir:—In reply to your letter requesting me to give you my experience in this county, I have to say that I emigrated from Ohio to Nebraska in 1858, and have resided here ever since. Corn, wheat and oats have been my principal crops—wheat, averaging one year with another, about 20 bushels to the acre, and corn and oats about 40 to 60 bushels. I have never had a failure of crops. Seasons have varied here as in other countries, but no failure.

In September, 1867, the grasshoppers made their appearance in great numbers, coming from the west, but did no damage, except to garden vegetables. They stayed only a short time, but deposited immense numbers of eggs, which were hatched the next spring, and great injury to crops were anticipated; they soon disappeared, however, and the crops that year were very large. The Colorado potatoe bug came in 1869, and for a year or two damaged the potatoe crop to some extent, but has now entirely disappeared. The Chinch bug has never been known in this country. My farm contains 270 acres, about 100 acres under cultivation. This year I raised 400 bushels of wheat, 700 bushels oats and about the same of corn. The soil is a black, sandy loam . . . suitable for all kinds of crops, but especially adapted to vegetables which reach deep into the ground and grow very large. Grapes and small fruits generally do remarkably well. The soil nearer the Platte river is more sandy, but the growth of grass is very luxuriant. On the uplands it contains more clay, but possesses very productive qualities. The upland has proved better for wheat and the valleys better for corn. I know of no country that has made more rapid and steady improvement. Many people that I know who came here penniless and commenced living in "dug-outs" and holes in the ground, with no stock but a few chickens and a cow, now have good comfortable homes, well improved farms, with their horses and stock around them. Very few who have settled here have any desire to return to their old homes to live. In healthfulness our climate is not excelled anywhere. I know persons who have come here in feeble health, some with strong tendencies to pulmonary complaints, that have entirely recovered and become strong and healthful. The atmosphere, particularly during fall and winter, when it is usually damp in the Eastern and Southern States, is here dry and bracing.

Land Department, Union Pacific Railway Company, *The Pioneer*, June, 2.

FROM "LETTER FROM JAMES JACKSON" (1875)

Wood River, Hall County, Nebraska

Sir:—In answer to your request, I would say I came to Hall county 15 years ago. I spent my first five years in farming and raising stock. At the end of this time I found myself in possession of $1,000 in cash, fifty head of cattle and a farm well under cultivation. This is not doing very bad, considering I started with less than $300. I am often asked, does farming pay? I should think the above would show. I cleared $1,800 off my farm in one year, over and above expenses. For the last ten years I have been in the mercantile business, with a cash capital of $10,000, but I have never abandoned my old farm which has ever been profitable to me. I am often asked if grasshoppers damaged crops before this year. To this I would say, not to exceed thirty per cent, and that only one year before. Chinch bugs never damage crops here. There is not a State east of Nebraska that can compare with Hall county for wheat and oats, of which we had a good crop this year, notwithstanding the grasshoppers.

In conclusion I would say, our county cannot be beat, and as for farming paying, it has paid me better than any business I have been in yet, as my first five years show.

Land Department, Union Pacific Railway Company, *The Pioneer*, June, 2.

CONTROLLING RUNAWAY PROFITS: RAILWAY REGULATION

The railroads consistently charged extremely high freight and passenger rates and at the same time gave free passes to government officials and many other people who had in some way contributed to the building of the roads. These practices were oppressive both to the farmers, who were forced to use the railroads to ship their stock and grain, and to the common passengers, who held no position that would warrant free passes.

The local newspapers were full of calls for government regulation of the railways as a way to end this abuse. The following letter to the editor in the *Omaha Bee* is a typical example.

FROM "RAILWAY REGULATION: THE NECESSITY OF ENACTING A STRINGENT STATE LAW" (1884)

To the Editor of the bee,

. . . It gives me great pleasure to see that this great subject of railroad extortion is not to be neglected by the people or the press. The railroad corporations have attained so great power that nothing but the most strenuous compulsion will induce them to treat the people of this state and country with justice. From motives of greed common to human nature, they will not, and from evils inherent in the system under which railroading has progressed for the past twenty years, they cannot give the people fair rates for transportation. A fair rate would pay cost of carriage with a fair profit added. Excessive stock watering, making a fictitious capital equal to the amount of real capital invested, makes this impossible without bankruptcy. . . .

In the face of all the agitation of the past five years—in the face of two national conventions, and an effort to form a national party upon this issue—in the face of a depression of farm products unknown since 1873, the roads, instead of granting any relief to the farmers [continue to increase their rates]. As far as the transportation of farm products [is] concerned, superabundant crops, which means low prices, and hard times, only add to the revenue of the roads. The crops have to be moved. If they are double [in size], and their price only half as much as usual, the roads still charge the same, and thus their revenue is largely increased.

But they invariably make hard times an excuse for cutting the wages of their employees, and in every manner reducing their expenses.

There are some very essential points which should be aimed at in any legislation, to which I wish to invite your attention:

First. A reduction of rates, both local and through, is one of the primary objects. But to make any such reduction either possible or permanent, stock watering must be stopped, and railroad building be brought down to an actual cash basis; exorbitant salaries must be prohibited, and the employment of non-laborers, such as political attorneys and strikers, must be stopped. . . .

Second. The corporations should be rigidly restricted to the business for which they were chartered—that of common carriers. . . . [A]ll speculative enterprises which railroad officers are enabled by virtue of their superior advantage to engage in, should be rigidly suppressed. This would be in the interest of economy and in the interest of the men and places along the lines, and is fully within the scope of the law-making power.

Third. A rigid law regulating the location of stations, making it impossible for roads to pass towns . . .

Fourth. All discriminations between persons and places should be prohibited.

Fifth. Free passes of all kinds should be prohibited and every means taken to destroy the power of the corporations over the legislative, judicial, and executive members of the government.

Sixth. In all cases penalties adequate to the enforcement of the laws should be provided, and authority vested in some state officer to enforce the law. This duty should be made mandatory, under the severest penalties, and adequate means appropriated to perform it.

It may not be entirely within the power of a state legislature to accomplish all this. But national legislation has got to be reached through state legislation and agitation; and nothing less than an attempt in good faith to accomplish them will be accepted by the people.

The farming industry is greatly depressed compared with the railroading industry, and in fact most other industries, except perhaps those of the poor . . . laborers of our great manufacturing and mining cities. Farmers can raise their own bread and meat, and so can live, no matter what betides. But I will state a fact within my own knowledge and experience, that a farmer owning a quarter section farm free from debt, and himself frugal, temperate and industrious, cannot raise and maintain an average family in comfort and give his children an education at all adequate to the advanced ideas of the times and lay by anything for adversity and old age. I hope all readers will take this cool and true statement in, and compare it in their minds with the accumulations of two hundred millions in thirty years by one family in railroading. . . .

Omaha, Nebraska, *Omaha Bee*, December 17, 2.

THE GLAMOUR OF THE RAILROADS: BRINGING POLISH TO THE PLAINS

Cather's ambivalence about the commercialization of the plains, caused to a great extent by the railroads, can frequently be felt throughout her work. Cather appreciated sophistication and refinement, however, and whatever else they brought with them, the railroads did deliver those things. One of the best descriptions of this new "plains aristocracy" and the way it changed the class structure of the frontier is found in the opening chapter of one of Cather's later novels, *A Lost Lady* (1923). It is a description of the grace and style in which the railroad men often lived.

FROM WILLA CATHER, *A LOST LADY* (1923)

Thirty or forty years ago, in one of those grey towns along the Burlington railroad, which are so much greyer to-day than they were then, there was a house well known from Omaha to Denver for its hospitality and for a certain charm of atmosphere. Well known, that is to say, to the railroad aristocracy of that time; men who had to do with the railroad itself, or with one of the "land companies" which were its by-products. In those days it was enough to say of a man that he was "connected with the Burlington." There were the directors, the general managers, vice-presidents, superintendents, whose names we all knew; and their younger brothers or nephews were auditors, freight agents, departmental assistants. Everyone "connected" with the Road, even the large cattle- and grain-shippers, had annual passes; they and their families rode about over the line a great deal. There were then two distinct social strata in the prairie States; the homesteaders and hand-workers who were there to make a living, and the bankers and gentlemen ranchers who came from the Atlantic seaboard to invest money and to "develop our great West," as they used to tell us.

When the Burlington men were travelling back and forth on business not very urgent, they found it agreeable to drop off the express and spend a night in a pleasant house where their importance was delicately recognized; and no house was pleasanter than that of Captain Daniel Forrester, at Sweet Water. Captain Forrester was himself a railroad man, a contractor, who had built hundreds of miles of road for the Burlington,— over the sage brush and cattle country, and on up into the Black Hills.

The Forrester place, as every one called it, was not at all remarkable; the people who lived there made it seem much larger and finer than it was. The house stood on a low round hill, nearly a mile east of town; a white house with a wing, and sharp-sloping roofs to shed the snow. It was encircled by porches, too narrow for modern notions of comfort, supported by the fussy, fragile pillars of that time, when every honest stick of timber was tortured by the turning-lathe into something hideous. Stripped of its vines and denuded of its shrubbery, the house would probably have been ugly enough. It stood close into a fine cottonwood grove that threw sheltering arms to left and right and grew all down the hillside behind it. Thus placed on the hill, against its bristling grove, it was the first thing one saw on coming into Sweet Water by rail, and the last thing one saw on departing.

To approach Captain Forrester's property, you had first to get over a wide, sandy creek which flowed along the eastern edge of the town. Crossing this by the foot-bridge or the ford, you entered the Captain's private lane, bordered by Lombardy poplars, with wide meadows lying on either side. Just at the foot of the hill on which the house sat, one crossed a second creek by the stout wooden road-bridge. This stream traced artless loops and curves through the broad meadows that were half pasture land, half marsh. Any one but Captain Forrester would have drained the bottom land and made it into highly productive field. . . . But he had selected this place long ago because it looked beautiful to him, and he happened to like the way the creek wound through his pasture, with mint and joint-grass and twinkling willows along its banks. He was well off for those times, and he had no children. He could afford to humour his fancies.

When the Captain drove friends from Omaha or Denver over from the station in his democrat wagon [a multi-seated cart, usually drawn by two horses], it gratified him to hear these gentlemen admire his fine stock, grazing in the meadows on either side of his lane. And when they reached the top of the hill, it gratified him to see men who were older than himself leap nimbly to the ground and run up the front steps as Mrs. Forrester came out on the porch to greet them. Even the hardest and coldest of his friends, a certain narrow-faced Lincoln banker, became animated when he took her hand, tried to meet the gay challenge in her eyes and to reply cleverly to the droll word of greeting on her lips.

She was always there, just outside the front door, to welcome their visitors, having been warned of their approach by the sound of hoofs and the rumble of wheels on the wooden bridge. If she happened to be in the kitchen, helping her Bohemian cook, she came out in her apron, waving a buttery iron spoon, or shook cherry-stained fingers at the new arrival. She never stopped to pin up a lock; she was attractive in dishabille, and she knew it. . . . [W]hatever Mrs. Forrester chose to do was "lady-like" because she did it. They could not imagine her in any dress or situation in which she would not be charming. . . .

New York: The Library of America, 1990, 3–5.

TOPICS FOR WRITTEN OR ORAL EXPLORATION

1. The railroads changed the pioneers' way of life drastically. Pick a modern invention—airplanes, computers, or the Internet, for example—and describe how it has changed modern life, for better or for worse.

2. Instead of a farmer or a writer or a teacher, Jim Burden becomes a lawyer for one of the railroads. His job requires him to travel often, and all over the country. Does he seem well- or ill-suited for this job? Debate this question as part of a class discussion.

3. Research the life of the nineteenth-century railroad magnate Jay Gould. Write a paper explaining how he rose to the top of the railroad industry.

4. In the character of Crazy Ivar (*O Pioneers!*), write a letter to the editor of a newspaper, commenting on the effects of the coming of the railroad to his area of the countryside.

5. What do you assume Alexandra's attitude toward the railroad is? Mostly positive or mostly negative? Defend your opinion with evidence from *O Pioneers!*

6. By the middle of the twentieth century, trains had been largely replaced by cars, trucks, and airplanes as a means of transporting both freight and passengers in the United States. Many people say that this change has been a negative one, that the cost of relying almost exclusively on non-rail transportation has been too high. The costs these critics point to include pollution, depletion of natural resources, dependence on foreign oil, and destruction of the land for superhighways and airports. Where do you stand on this issue? Write a paper in which you define and support your position.

7. Railroad agents often used exaggeration and propaganda to entice people to move west so that the railroads would have a market for their services. Do salesmen of today use the same methods to persuade people to buy the goods or services they are selling? Describe such sales tactics that you have experienced, or someone you know who has.

8. In *My Ántonia*, how is the railroad presented both as a link to the larger cosmopolitan world and as a link to the dangerous and immoral world of the big city?

9. At the beginning of *My Ántonia*, Cather's narrator tells us that the germ of the story is her conversation with Jim Burden during a railway journey. Discuss how that setting for the story's genesis is symbolically appropriate.

10. One reason the railroads were so important on the plains was that
    they owned a great deal of land. How does the fact that so much
    prime land had already been taken by the railroad influence Cather's
    characters in either *O Pioneers!* or *My Ántonia?*

SUGGESTIONS FOR FURTHER READING AND WORKS CITED

Barns, Cass G. *The Sod House*. Lincoln: University of Nebraska Press,
    1930.

Bertolini, Luca. *Cities on Rails: The Development of Railway Stations &
    Their Surroundings*. New York: Routledge, 1998.

Cash, Joseph. *Working the Homestake*. Ames: Iowa State University Press,
    1973.

Dick, Everett. *The Sod House Frontier*. New York: Appleton-Century,
    1937.

Fahey, John. *The Inland Empire: Unfolding Years, 1879–1929*. Seattle:
    University of Washington Press, 1987.

Fleisig, Heywood. "The Central Pacific Railroad and the Railroad Land
    Grant Controversy." *Journal of Economic History* 35 (1975):
    552–64.

Foner, Eric, and John A. Garraty, eds. *The Reader's Companion to Amer-
    ican History*. Boston: Houghton Mifflin, 1991.

Gifford, Colin T. *And Gone Forever*. Hersham: Oxford, 1996.

Harley, C. Knick. "Western Settlement and the Price of Wheat, 1872–
    1913." *Journal of Economic History* 38 (December 1978): 865–78.

Lewis, Lloyd, and Stanley Pargellis, eds. *Granger Country*. Boston: Little,
    Brown, 1949.

Overton, Richard. *Burlington Route*. New York: Alfred A. Knopf, 1965.

Riley, C.J. *The Golden Age of the Passenger Train: From Steam to Diesel
    & Beyond*. New York: Michael Friedman, 1997.

Schmollinger, Steve. *The Feather River Canyon: Union Pacific's Heart of
    Stone*. Pasadena, Calif.: Pentrex, 1996.

Soloman, Brian. *Along the Rails: The Lore & Romance of the Railroad*.
    New York: Michael Friedman, 1999.

Vranich, Joseph. *Derailed: What Went Wrong & What To Do about Amer-
    ica's Passenger Trains*. New York: St. Martin's Press, 1997.

Willson, Jeff. *Burlington Route across the Heartland: Everywhere West
    from Chicago*. Waukesha: Kalmbach, 1998.

4

Another Country, Another Language: Foreign-Born Pioneers

During the nineteenth century the population of the United States was increased considerably by people from outside its borders. The story of the masses of people who immigrated from foreign shores to help build America is well known. We are a nation created almost entirely by people born elsewhere. Some came for religious freedom or to escape political persecution, but by far the majority came because the economic situations in their home countries were bad enough to leave them hungry and destitute. Their occupations and the degree of their success in their newly adopted country varied widely: "Some became farmers and others toiled in factories. Some settled permanently and others returned to their homelands. Collectively, however, they contributed to the building of a nation by providing a constant source of inexpensive labor, by settling rural regions and industrial cities, and by bringing their unique forms of political and cultural expression" (Foner and Garraty 533).

Of the five million people who came to the United States between 1815 and 1861, nearly half were from Ireland (Foner and Garraty 534). From the end of the Civil War to 1890, ten million more immigrated, mostly from Germany, Ireland, England, Wales, and Scandinavia; from 1890 to 1914, fifteen million more arrived, "Poles, Russian Jews, Ukrainians, Slovaks, Croatians, Slovenes,

Hungarians, Romanians, Italians, and Greeks," for the most part (Foner and Garraty 534).

Leading Sources of Immigrants to the United States, 1820–1975

Country of Origin	Numbers (in millions)
Germany	6.9
Italy	5.2
Ireland	4.7
Austria-Hungary	4.3
Canada	4.0
Soviet Union/Russia	3.3
England	3.1
Mexico	1.9
West Indies	1.4
Sweden	1.2

Source: Foner and Garraty 534.

   The foreign-born immigrants who chose to settle on the plains did so for many of the same reasons native-born Americans living in the East did: they were lured west by promises of cheap, fertile land that the Homestead Act had made available, and by railroad representatives' and land speculators' stories—often highly exaggerated—of a promised land, a utopia where success and the "good life" came easily to anyone willing to put in an honest day's work. The railroad agents from Nebraska focused their advertising campaigns mostly on Scandinavians, Germans, French-Canadians, Czechs, and Russians, and as a result "more Czechs, Swedes, and Danes settled in Nebraska than in any other Great Plains state" (Pers 7). These were the people who became Cather's new neighbors after her move from Virginia, and they helped make her own transition to a "new" country more bearable: "Coming from the homogeneous Anglo-Saxon culture of white settlers in the Shenandoah Valley—where the sharpest divisions were those between Baptists and Presbyterians, supporters of secession and Union sympathizers—she was excited by the discovery of difference and volunteered to deliver mail to the immigrant settlements, an imaginative pretext for entering the homes of her neighbors" (O'Brien

71). From the very beginning of her transplantation to Nebraska, Cather appreciated the difference between the bland uniformity of Virginia and the rich diversity of the multicultural plains of Nebraska: "On Sunday we could drive to a Norwegian church and listen to a sermon in that language, or to a Danish or Swedish church. We could go to the French Catholic settlement in the next county and hear a sermon in French, or into the Bohemian township and hear one in Czech, or we could go to church with the German Lutherans" (Cather 237).

Biographers and other serious readers of Cather have long taken note of how much more interested Cather is in foreigners than in native-born Americans. Nearly all of her Nebraska-based stories and novels, including *O Pioneers!* and *My Ántonia*, have foreign immigrants as their main characters. Almost without exception, Cather portrays them as stronger, more vibrant, more refined, and even more noble than their American counterparts.

While Cather's description of the vivaciousness and integrity of foreign immigrants is convincing, the American characters in the novels are often portrayed as nearly blind to those qualities. The fact that many Americans were unreasonably prejudiced against the foreign-born was not lost on Cather, and she takes great pains to reveal that prejudice in her novels. In *My Ántonia*, for example, the Scandinavian and Bohemian girls—"hired girls," as they were called—were considered by many of the upstanding Americans in Black Hawk as "a menace to the social order. Their beauty shone out too boldly against a conventional background" (840). As narrator, Jim Burden expresses Cather's own exasperation concerning the Black Hawk merchants' "uninquiring belief[s]" about the hired girls: "I thought the attitude of the town people toward these girls very stupid. If I told my schoolmates that Lena Lingard's grandfather was a clergyman, and much respected in Norway, they looked at me blankly. What did it matter? All foreigners were ignorant people who couldn't speak English. There was not a man in Black Hawk who had the intelligence or cultivation, much less the personal distinction, of Ántonia's father. Yet people saw no difference between her and the three Marys; they were all Bohemians, all 'hired girls'" (839).

One explanation for Cather's sympathetic view of people from foreign cultures is that she herself felt like an alien in an unfamiliar land. Because the foreign-born homesteaders shared her feelings of displacement and uprootedness, she felt a closer kinship with them in some ways than with her own family. They, like her, were also acutely aware of the need to adjust to their new surroundings and culture as quickly as possible. But this assimilation was not always easy, either for Cather herself or for her European neighbors. In *O Pioneers!* we learn that Alexandra Bergson's father had "the Old-World belief that land, in itself, is desirable" (148), yet neither he nor his neighbors knew exactly how to farm it; in fact, his neighbors "knew even less about farming than he did. Many of them had never worked on a farm until they took up their homesteads" (148). John Bergson, for example, had worked as a shipbuilder in Sweden, Mr. Shimerda (*My Ántonia*) as a weaver in Bohemia, and farming turned out to be a more difficult occupation than either had imagined. The land was "an enigma," we are told in *O Pioneers!* "It was like a horse that no one knows how to break to harness, that runs wild and kicks things to pieces" (148). Adjusting to a new land and a new way of life, then, proved to be precisely as difficult a task for the Swedes, Russians, Danes, Bohemians, and French-Canadians as it was for the nine-year-old Willa Cather from Virginia.

Another reason Cather generally admired her foreign neighbors more than her American ones is that she believed they were more cultured and refined than her countrymen. They appreciated art and manners more fully than Americans did because they came from countries steeped in artistic and cultural traditions unknown in the United States. Although his family is nearly destitute by the time they arrive in Nebraska, Ántonia's father remains elegant, dignified, and proud. It is important to him that his new American neighbors know that back in Bohemia "they were not beggars; he made good wages and his family were respected there" (760). Jim Burden, the narrator, tells us that "everything about this old man was in keeping with his dignified manner. He was neatly dressed. Under his coat he wore a knitted gray vest, and, instead of a collar a silk scarf of a dark bronze-green, carefully crossed and held together by a red coral pin" (728). Even when homesickness overcomes him and he takes his own life, he does so in the most orderly and formal way possible: "When we found him, everything was decent except . . . what he couldn't nowise foresee. His coat was hung on a peg, and his boots was under the bed. He'd took off that silk neckcloth he always wore, and folded it smooth and stuck his pin through it. He turned back his shirt at the neck and rolled up his sleeves" (776). This obvious refinement, which was characteristic of so many of the European immigrants Cather knew, made the condescending attitude many Americans held toward them even more deplorable to her. That so many Americans were clearly culturally inferior to the European immigrants to whom they felt superior was a constant source of annoyance to her (Pers 20).

All her life, Cather believed that native-born Americans were culturally, and even intellectually, inferior to most immigrants. She made this opinion the theme of several of her Lincoln and Pittsburgh newspaper reviews after she had moved away from Red Cloud. In one such review of an American opera, which she wrote for the Pittsburgh *Leader,* she asserts that "taken as a class American operas are very much the worst in the world. They are a good deal like American wines, and they lack body, richness, traditions—everything that wines and music should have" (15 December 1896). Similarly, describing a very talented singer in an article for the *Nebraska State Journal* that same month, she says that because of Americans' inability to recognize and respect quality or to distinguish the excellent from the ordinary, it is possible for mediocre singers, artists, and actors to rise to the top, while the truly talented must struggle merely to survive (13 December 1896). Thirty-seven years later, on the occasion of winning a French literary prize in 1933 for *Shadows on the Rock*, one of her later novels, she was still expressing the same view. In her acceptance speech she said, "The loyalty of people far away in a rude society to manners and customs and gentler behavior they knew and practised in an older society is something very thrilling to me. Of many human virtues, it seems to me the most beautiful" (quoted in "French Prize Presented to Willa Cather" 13).

Lest Cather be charged with shallow, sentimental, or romanticized portrayals of foreign immigrants or of simply falling prey to the simplistic notion that Americans are bad and Europeans good, it is important to point out that not all her depictions of immigrants are positive. As Cather scholar Bernice Slote points out,

It is only fair to say that in [*My Ántonia*] she has a Bohemian villain, too—Peter Krajiek, who had cheated and deceived his own countrymen, the Shimerdas, [because he was the only person around who could speak their language and so could tell them anything he wanted to and get away with it]. And there were conflicts between national groups, just as there were between "Americans" and "Foreigners": "Bohemians has a natural distrust of Austrians," says one of the hired men in *My Ántonia*. When asked to explain, he simply lays it on politics, something too long (and, we know, too long ago) to explain. Bohemian Ántonia, too, has a warning to Jim Burden: "You won't go and get mixed up with Swedes, will you?" (Slote 100)

In addition, both Ántonia's mother and her brother Ambrosch are portrayed as ungrateful and grasping, and her brother as somewhat lazy as well. Otto, one of Mr. Burden's hired men, reveals his own ethnic prejudice when he says, "You can't tell me anything new about a Czech; I'm an Austrian" (797). Cather also takes great care to describe the Norwegians' refusal to allow Mr. Shimerda's body to be buried in their cemetery as uncharitable at best and cruel at worst. Frank Shabata of *O Pioneers!* is also cast in a negative light. He is jealous and gloomy, and he consistently tries to destroy the joy and vibrancy of his wife, Marie.

Furthermore, in Cather's work there seems to be an erosion over time of the immigrants' "high values of the rising years on the plains. There is a turn downward. In *O Pioneers!*, for example, Alexandra's brothers grow up to be quarrelsome about money, politics, [and] position" (Slote 104). Cather suggests that the second and succeeding generations of immigrants are somewhat less noble than the first. The implication is that insofar as they love money more than they love the land, they are becoming more Americanized.

In general, however, it must be admitted that Cather treats her foreign characters with much more respect and admiration than she does her American characters. Almost all the social life in her Nebraska fiction takes place in the communities of foreign immigrants; little, if any, is described as initiated by Americans. She consistently associates delight in life and in the land with foreigners rather than with Americans. Her attitude is perhaps best summed up in one of her articles, first published in *The Nation* in 1923: "Colonies of European people, Slavonic, Germanic, Scandinavian, Latin, spread across our bronze prairies like the daubs of color on a painter's palette. They brought with them something that this neutral new world needed even more than the immigrants needed land" (237). Her love for that beautiful palette was obvious in her fiction throughout her entire career.

The documents that follow provide information about the immigrant groups that appear in Cather's novels. Of all her foreign neighbors in Nebraska, the ones that figure most prominently in her fiction, especially in *O Pioneers!* and *My Ántonia*, are Scandinavians and Bohemians (that is, natives of Bohemia—then part of Austria-Hungary, later of Czechoslovakia, now of the Czech Republic—and known, along with the Moravians, as Czechs): Alexandra Bergson and her family are Swedes; the Shimerdas and the Shabatas are Bohemians. Other ethnic groups, however, also play important, although smaller, roles: the French-Canadians in *O Pioneers!*, the Norwegian Crazy Ivar, and the Russians Peter and Pavel of *My Ántonia*, for example, all contribute to the "beautiful palette" of characters in the novels.

The first three of the following documents are written by Czech-American historians. The first offers a general overview of Czech history and of life in the old country. It also describes some of the forces that drove so many of the Czech people to immigrate to America. The second explains in detail the religious differences among the Czech immigrants and the reasons for these differences. The third describes the social life generally pursued by Czechs in the United States.

The next set of documents concerns the two most important Scandinavian groups in Cather's work: Swedes and Norwegians. The first provides a general overview of Swedish immigration to the American West. That account is followed by a series of letters written by two Swedish immigrants to family members back in the old country. The last document in the set describes the precise Norwegian settlement Cather knew as a child, the inhabitants, cemeteries, and churches that she very likely used as models for the Norwegian characters and places in *O Pioneers!* and *My Ántonia*.

Just as there was a Norwegian settlement near Cather's Nebraska home, there was also a French—more accurately, French-Canadian—community in the vicinity. It was this colony that gave Cather the model for characters like Amédée Chevalier and the "French country" in *O Pioneers!* The document following those describing the Scandinavian communities provides historical information about French-Canadian migration to the Great Plains, mostly from the Canadian province of Quebec.

The final document in this chapter helps illuminate the characters of Peter and Pavel in *My Ántonia*, by outlining the pattern of German-Russian immigration to the American frontier. It suggests that the German-Russians, like so many others, came to America to escape oppression and poverty in their home country.

BOHEMIAN BACKGROUNDS: ROSE
ROSICKY'S *A HISTORY OF CZECHS*
(BOHEMIANS) IN NEBRASKA

My papa sad for the old country. He not look good. My papa,
he cry for leave his old friends what make music with him.
My Ántonia, 771–72

One of the earliest histories of Czechs in Nebraska was compiled
by Rose Rosicky, whose 1929 work is still consulted today by people interested in investigating the real immigrant communities on
which so much of Cather's work was based. Rosicky provides
information about the Eastern European country from which
Cather's Bohemian neighbors came and explains the origin of the
word *Bohemian* as it was used in Cather's time. She also discusses
the reasons for the animosity between Austrians and Bohemians,
which Mr. Burden's hired man, Otto, refers to in *My Ántonia*. At
one point she mentions the Hussite movement, which was named
for John Huss, to whom Emil alludes in *O Pioneers!* He asks Marie
Shabata, "What did you ever burn John Huss for, anyway? It's made
an awful row. They still jaw about it in history classes" (176). Huss
(1372–1415) was a Bohemian religious reformer whose attacks on
the Catholic Church in Bohemia aroused that church's hostility
even before the Protestant Reformation. He was excommunicated
in 1411 and burned at the stake for heresy in 1414.

FROM ROSE ROSICKY, *A HISTORY OF CZECHS (BOHEMIANS) IN
NEBRASKA* (1929)

Nebraska, of all our states, contains the largest number of Czech farmers
of the first generation (born in Europe), or one-fifth of all who live in
the United States. This is in accordance with the report of the Immigration Commission. . . . Of late years Bohemians are being called, more and
more, Czechs. . . . However, to call a Bohemian a Czechoslovak is mis-
leading, the Slovaks being another branch of Slavs. Bohemians are Czechs
of Czechoslovakia. Moravians are practically Czechs, so we class them
with the latter. . . .
When immigrants from Bohemia and Moravia came to Nebraska, and

for many years prior thereto, these countries were part of the Austro-Hungarian Empire. Geographically they formed the northwestern corner of it, being bounded by Saxony on the northwest, Bavaria on the southwest, Prussian Silesia on the northeast, Austria and Hungary on the south and east. [World War I] changed these boundaries. . . .

In the first century b.c. a Celtic people called Boii settled in Bohemia. They were compelled by the Germans to emigrate and Bohemia was then occupied by the warlike tribe of Marcomanni, who moved westward at the time of the great migration of nations. The Slavic immigrants appeared in the sixth century and called themselves Czechs . . . because their leader was so named. Therefore the name Bohemia, given to that country by Latin historians, is antiquated and geographically and racially incorrect, for it is derived from the name of a Celtic people. Besides, in more modern times, the word Bohemian is used also to describe artist life in its irresponsible and even immoral phases. It has its origin in the French word *bohème* (gypsy) and uninformed people even look upon Bohemians (Czechs) as possible gypsies. So for one reason and the other, Bohemians prefer to be called Czechs. For a brief period Bohemia formed a part of the great Moravian realm under Svatopluk. The Moravians, also a Slavic people, took their name from the river Morava, the largest river in Moravia. Svatopluk's rule (870–894) was followed by onslaughts of Hungarians (Maygars) who devastated the country and from 1029 Moravia was united with Bohemia, either as an integral part of that realm, or as a fief ruled by margraves [a German title given to the governor of a border province]. In 1526 Moravia, with all the other Bohemian lands, passed under the rule of the House of Hapsburg.

By the close of the ninth century the princes who ruled the Czechs had been converted to Christianity, mainly introduced by the Germans, while the Moravians were converted by the apostles Cyril and Methodius of the Eastern Church. In the tenth century Bohemia was under the rule of the dukes of Premysl, who acknowledged the overlordship of the kings of Germany. These dukes or princes elevated themselves into the rank of kings by the close of the twelfth century and were thus recognized by the German sovereigns, their state forming part of the Holy Roman Empire of the Germans. . . . The Premysl dynasty ended in 1306 . . . and from that date to 1439 the house of Luxemburg was in power. During this time the Hussite movement began and a large part of the succeeding history is concerned with religious struggle. . . . [F]ew countries have been so torn by religious wars. . . .

Bohemia and Moravia are rich agriculturally, although their industries are many and varied. However, it may be said that the people inclined towards farming are in the majority, but the country is densely populated. This fact and another, Austro-Hungarian militarism and despotism, . . .

were the two chief factors why so many emigrated to [the United States]. . . .

Czech newspapers were a great force in aiding immigrants to find new homes. These papers in those days . . . had a department devoted to communications from subscribers, and such communications often dealt with the subject of good locations. Their importance . . . can easily be appreciated, when we consider that their readers knew little or no English. The history of the counties most heavily settled by Czechs shows that they began coming [to Nebraska] between 1865 and 1880. Prior to 1871 there was no Czech paper [in Nebraska] and the leading journal was the weekly *Slavie*, Racine, Wisconsin, published by Charles Jonas [or Karel Jonás in the Czech language], considered the most distinguished Czech-American of his day. . . . The first pioneers wrote letters to friends, or for publication in the *Slavie*, for the purpose of attracting others, and it was but natural that immigrants, not knowing English, placed utmost reliance in their own people and readily followed them into newly-established colonies.

Omaha: Czech Historical Society of Nebraska, 20–21, 26.

RELIGIOUS DIFFERENCES AMONG CZECHS: IVAN DUBOVICKÝ'S "CZECH-AMERICANS: AN ETHNIC DILEMMA"

The Bohemians, you know, were tree worshipers before the missionaries came. Father says that people in the mountains still do queer things, sometimes,—they believe that trees bring good or bad luck.

O Pioneers!, 212

Maria Shabata of *O Pioneers!* obviously knows a good deal about "Free-thinkers," though she herself is a Catholic, as we see from her response to Emil's question about why the Bohemians burned John Huss at the stake: "We'd do it right over again, most of us. . . . Don't they ever teach you in your history classes that you'd all be heathen Turks if it hadn't been for the Bohemians?" The following article by Ivan Dubovický spells out the reasons for the existence of at least three distinct religious groups among Czech-Americans: Catholics, Protestants, and Freethinkers. As he makes clear, one of the most important reasons for anti-Catholic sentiments among some Czechs is their historical resistance to, and everlasting resentment of, the Habsburg rule. The Habsburg family established a hereditary monarchy in Austria in 1282 and gradually extended its power, and thus that of the Catholic church, over surrounding areas, including Bohemia.

FROM IVAN DUBOVICKÝ, "CZECH-AMERICANS: AN ETHNIC DILEMMA" (1993)

Many authors have tried to attribute the roots of the main antagonism within the Czech minority in the United States—the tensions between Catholics and freethinkers—to a freethought "spirit" brought from the homeland, where it had grown out of centuries-old Czech Hussite and Protestant traditions. Such a general assumption is untenable, however, without considering the social structure of immigrant communities, the differences between cities and farming areas, and historical developments in the Old Country. For the first two decades of Czech immigration, this assumption is almost completely wrong. More correct were authors . . .

who considered the deeply rooted anti-Catholicism among Czechs to have been a symbol of Czech resistance to Habsburg rule. . . .

A majority of Czech immigrants were Catholics, at least in a formal sense. Up to the 1860's, the number of immigrants with definite free-thought convictions was very small, and their activity did not have a great impact in any Czech community, where Czechs, regardless of their religious views, typically participated in cultural life and sometimes joined the same societies. . . . Non-Catholics did not offend Catholics and vice-versa. . . .

A marked change seems to have occurred in the second half of the 1860s. Zealous freethinkers began to attack the Catholic church to the extent that editor Karel Jonás finally refused to publish their inflammatory statements in his *Slávie*. Instead, in 1868 he decided to issue a new paper, *Pokrok* (Progress), in which militant freethinkers had free reign. . . . This newspaper may have laid the foundation for the future disintegration of American Czechs into two opposing ideological groups, freethinkers and Catholics. Later, Jonás was said to have felt sorry for having published this journal. . . .

Why did the ideological division of the Czech immigrant community occur in the 1860s? At that time many Czech intellectuals ceased entirely to believe in the possibility of fostering any sense of Austrian nationality as a political, supraethnic identity that would be embraced by all cultures residing in the Empire. The Czechs, as well as other non-Germans, were not considered by the Habsburg authorities as independent, sovereign nations but only as ethnic and linguistic groups within the political German nation.

On the other hand, when the Habsburgs instituted constitutional rule in 1860–61, Czech political representatives began to claim the sovereignty of the Czech nation within the framework of the Habsburg Monarchy on the basis of historical Bohemian states' rights. When the Habsburgs refused to recognize these claims after 1867, the Czech political leadership began to define as its enemy not only the Habsburg dynasty—with its tradition of Germanization and administrative centralization—but the dynasty's main supporter, the Catholic church. Thus, Czech patriotism was penetrated by anti-Catholic or even atheistic attitudes, which were soon disseminated throughout the country by the Young Czech party or through mass patriotic meetings . . . held outdoors at actual and legendary historical sites. . . .

For many Czech peasants, their Catholic faith did not automatically mean they were pro-Austrian as some Czech-American freethinkers or socialists mistakenly [state]. In many villages Catholic priests had been leading advocates of the Czech National Revival. Peasants did not consider their Catholic faith to be an obstacle to patriotism as is evident in southern Bohemia, the least Protestant part of the Czech lands, which was a main center of . . . [patriotic] meetings and an increasing adoration of [John] Huss. . . . Nevertheless, few Czechs converted to Protestantism, and the resurrection of Hussitism would not come until 1919. . . . All these developments testified to a weakness in religious enthusiasm among Czechs no matter whether they were Catholics, Protestants, or freethinkers.

Moreover, belonging to the Catholic church was not just a result of religious persuasion. The church filled various functions, especially in the countryside. It provided education, and its customs, celebrations, and feasts gave a rhythm to peasant life. This "practical" importance also helps explain why the stereotype of Catholicism as being anti-patriotic did not lead to the decatholization of Czechs in the Czech lands to the same extent and at the same time as it did among Czech-Americans.

In the 1860s emigration to the United States increased rapidly: during the three years after 1866, the same number of people emigrated to America as in the entire previous decade. Among them was a small but influential group of intellectuals, . . . who had already been influenced by the new idea of Czech patriotism based on anti-clericalism that *Pokrok* immediately started to disseminate. *Pokrok* was said to be the first Czech newspaper to abandon definitely the "old-fashioned programme of [Czech] nationalism" and at the same time *Pokrok* "struck out boldly and openly against clericalism." . . .

The change in the character of immigration brought immigrants to America from those social categories that in Bohemia and Moravia had stood in the forefront in the spread of freethought ideas. They included [people] who were recruited from [among] craftsmen, artisans, small tradesmen, and partly from industrial workers, occupational groups that were steadily increasing among emigrants at the expense of wealthy and middling farmers, traditionally the main supporters of Catholicism. . . . Immigrants in the former occupational groups, though originally Catholics, believed the Church was unprepared to meet their practical needs and they joined fraternal societies . . . whose members had embraced freethought. . . .

Freethinkers by now presided over much of the social and cultural life of Czech-American communities, as well as over the leading newspapers and magazines whose editorial policy was consistently anti-clerical and sometimes hostile to all organized religion. Czech-American freethinkers exported their opinions back to Bohemia, where some of them were listed as "traitors" by the Habsburg authorities. Whereas the first free-thought newspaper . . . was established in 1860, the first Czech Catholic newspaper in the United States did not appear until 1867–68. Not until

1872 did Father J. Hessoun of St. Louis start regular publication of *Hlas* (The Voice).

The Catholic church in the United States also began to understand the great importance of patriotism for Czech-American believers. The "Czech" character of Catholic parishes and societies is often evident from their having been named for Czech saints. Catholic publishers, too, tried to attract their readers by the patriotic names of their journals. . . . As far as Czech-language education is concerned, Catholics gave it equal or even more attention than did freethinkers.

The more the freethought movement was atheistic, the deeper it penetrated among Czech socialists, whose numbers in the United States steadily increased as a result of their persecution in the Habsburg Monarchy, especially after the 1870s. Among the increasing number of workers were many outstanding socialist leaders. . . . Angered by their persecution by the Habsburgs, these immigrant socialists held strong anti-Austrian attitudes and in the United States organized their socialist party on the basis of ethnicity. By 1913 there were fifty-two branches of the Czech Section of the Socialist Party in America, with 1,400 members in sixteen states. . . .

The impact of Czech freethought in the United States should not be over-estimated. Many American Czechs were ideologically indifferent. The typical Czech worker in Chicago or farmer in Nebraska put aside the problems of his old homeland in taking care of his job or his farm. Culturally he had been transplanted to new surroundings in which he tried to find a new strategy for ethnic survival. If Germanization had been the main threat to Czech national identity in the Habsburg Monarchy, in the United States the danger came from the very attractive American way of life. This new way of life was not spread [forcibly], but it attracted immigrants and especially their children by its liberal political atmosphere, material prosperity, and technological sophistication. Its attractiveness best explains Czech-Americans' willingness to assimilate.

Nebraska History 74 (Fall/Winter), 195–208.

THE SOCIAL LIFE OF BOHEMIANS: SARKA B. HRBKOVA'S "BOHEMIANS IN NEBRASKA"

The aspect of life on the plains that Czechs found hardest to adjust to was the isolation. In their home country, they were accustomed to many more communal gatherings, complete with music, dancing, dramatic performances, and food. Cather's portrayal of Czech characters in both novels is consistent with this description of the real Czech immigrants. In *O Pioneers!*, Marie Shabata thrives on what little social life is offered to her on the plains. In fact, her love of music and gaiety is one of the things that keeps her from falling into utter despair over her marriage to the sullen and temperamental Frank Shabata: "She's too young and pretty for this sort of life. . . . But she's the kind that won't be downed easily. She'll work all day and go to a Bohemian wedding and dance all night" (196–97). Frank's bad humor itself might be blamed on his own inability to adjust to the loneliness associated with a plains farmer's life. The Shimerdas (*My Ántonia*) clearly suffer from a lack of communal and cultural engagement as well—especially Mr. Shimerda. We are encouraged to view his suicide as at least partly a result of the sense of loss he experienced when he exchanged the much more social existence of Bohemia for the solitude—one might even say desolation—of the American homestead.

In the following excerpt, Sarka B. Hrbkova, a professor of Slavonic languages at the University of Nebraska during the early twentieth century, describes the efforts of Czech immigrants to create a social and cultural life for themselves in America. One of their most common strategies was to establish fraternal organizations that would sponsor regular social events and activities, one of their most important purposes. Czechs joined these societies in great numbers.

FROM SARKA B. HRBKOVA, "BOHEMIANS IN NEBRASKA" (1919)

The Bohemian people in the United States are unusually strong on organization. Judging alone by Nebraska's Bohemian lodge membership one might easily believe they were inveterate "joiners." It is well known that as members of labor unions they are "stickers." They believe thoroughly in the adhesive value of organization to gain a point. However, it is as organizers of social and fraternal protective societies that the Bohemians excel. Practically every man of Bohemian birth or parentage belongs to one or more associations which have for their object insurance, protection in sickness and death, as well as the development of social life. There are also a number of organizations offering no insurance but, instead, opportunities for education along gymnastic, musical, literary or related lines.

The lodges of the fraternal class afford cheap insurance, the assessments in nearly every instance being much lower than in other [lodges]. . . .

Among the social institutions which do not have any insurance feature but devote themselves directly to the betterment of social and educational conditions are the Sokol societies and the Komensky clubs. The first Komensky education club, whose purpose is the cultural development of Bohemian communities, was organized . . . in 1906. [It and subsequent clubs] have established libraries and reading rooms, organized evening schools, and provided good, clean entertainment for the community.

The Sokol societies . . . provide physical training, wholesome sports, and the use of libraries for members. The high national ideals which characterized the organization of the original Sokol or Falcon societies in the mother country actuated all the early enthusiasts who plunged into the rough pioneer conditions after life in Bohemia where they had all the accessories of the highest civilization. . . . [In some frontier towns] a very popular and typical Bohemian amusement, amateur theatricals, reached a high state of development. [One example is Wilber, Nebraska, where] there was no tragedy too difficult for the Wilber Thespians to attempt, [under the direction of] J.K. Schuessler, the grand old man of the Bohemian American state. . . . Mr. Schuessler . . . was a professional actor in Bohemia and a man of deep patriotic feeling who gave of his ability and strength to the artistic upbuilding of the community which he adopted after he had renounced allegiance to Austria. Under his direction the first successful singing societies were organized, and great indeed was the pride and pleasure of each community in the rendition of those fine Czech folk songs, whose lingering melodies haunt and charm and most appealingly hold united all Bohemian hearts.

The earliest performance of a Bohemian play and concert in Saline county [Nebraska] was in 1869, in the first log schoolhouse of the district about midway between Crete and Wilber. The building . . . was used as a meeting place for the Bohemian Reading Society, which was organized in June, 1869. . . .

It is especially significant that this oldest organization of Bohemians in Saline county, and which was among the oldest in the state, was effected for the purpose of meeting to read and discuss books and magazines. Even in those difficult times, when life was mainly a matter of preserving existence in the hard, rough conditions of the day, these recent immigrants from a foreign land to the prairies of Nebraska held to the social and educational ideals of the mother land, bringing into the sordid commonplace of existence the rosy poetry of song, music, the dance, the theatre, and communion with books.

Music, either vocal or instrumental, always had to be present in any gathering of Bohemians, whether it were a meeting of neighbors or a formal session of a lodge. The Czechs are not without warrant called "the nation of musicians." . . . If a wager were to be made that every Bohemian community in Nebraska today had its own band or orchestra, it is safe to say that the [bettor] would win.

Publications of the Nebraska State Historical Society, vol. 19, 195–208.

SWEDISH IMMIGRATION TO THE AMERICAN FRONTIER: JOSEPH ALEXIS'S "SWEDES IN NEBRASKA"

On the sidewalk in front of one of the stores sat a little Swede
boy.

O Pioneers!, 139

Probably the most famous of all Cather's characters based on the
actual Swedish immigrants she knew as a child is Alexandra Bergson of *O Pioneers!*, but there are many others. The entire Bergson
family in that novel is Swedish, as is Carl Linstrum's family. The
arrival of Swedish immigrants in Nebraska began in the mid-1800's,
and their farms dotted the countryside where Cather spent a good
portion of her childhood. These were the real-life models for the
memorable Swedish characters in her work.

Joseph Alexis, professor of Germanic languages and literatures
at the University of Nebraska in the early 1900s, was interested in
the history of Swedish immigration, specifically their immigration
to Nebraska. The main sources of the following, which resulted
from this interest, were church reports, general immigration histories, and newspaper articles. He delivered his findings to the
United States, and to Nebraska in particular, in an address to the
annual meeting of the Nebraska State Historical Society on January
22, 1914. The speech was published in 1919.

FROM JOSEPH ALEXIS, "SWEDES IN NEBRASKA" (1919)

The Swedes left the old country for the same reason that their forefathers
in the Viking age set out for foreign shores. The fatherland was not productive enough to support a large population. Since the founding of the
Swedish colony on the Delaware in April, 1638, Swedes have been emi-
grating to America, though the number of immigrants was wellnigh insignificant until the middle of the nineteenth century. The colony on the
Delaware was short-lived, and the Swedish Lutheran churches erected
there fell into the hands of the Episcopalians.

There have always been people of an adventurous spirit who struck
out over the western seas for America, and there are traces to be found

of individuals from Sweden who roamed about as far south as Texas and Mexico. These adventurers founded no settlements in the early years of the last century, but they doubtless [made their friends back home interested in America]. . . .

It is not known at what time the first Swede arrived in Nebraska. In the [1860s] considerable numbers reached Omaha either directly from Europe or from the eastern states. Some remained in Omaha, while others took homesteads or bought cheap railway land and then settled down on the lonesome prairie. The building of the Union Pacific shops in Omaha, in 1865, afforded work for many newcomers, and at this time the Swedes began to come to Nebraska in great numbers. There was a great demand for machinists, blacksmiths, carpenters and other tradesmen. The building of the railroad bridge in 1871 also called for laborers. Ever since that time there has been a large colony of Swedes in [Omaha, and] the stream of migration [continued west from there]. . . .

In 1871 a committee was sent out from Altona, Illinois, to study conditions in Nebraska, in the hope that a colony might be founded somewhere in the state. The committee came by railroad to Lincoln and then went, partly by wagon and partly on foot, to the vicinity where Stromsburg is now situated. The land was to their liking, and they took homesteads and urged their friends to do likewise. Stromsburg was founded in 1872, and a steady stream of migration to Polk county followed. The town is strikingly Swedish, as the number of Swedish churches indicates. The Lutherans, the Mission Friends, the Baptists, the Methodists, and the Free Mission are all represented. . . .

When the branch of the Union Pacific railroad was extended westward to Central city, the name Hordville was given to a Swedish settlement, where the pioneers had taken homesteads in the early seventies.

In 1864 immigrants from Dalsland, Sweden, settled on homesteads along Logan Creek in Burt county. The town of Oakland was named for John Oak, not of Swedish descent, who had previously settled there. In 1867 another party arrived. . . . There are now no less than six Swedish churches in the settlement. . . . Through the Swedish paper *Hamlandet* the opportunities of this country were made known among the Swedes east of the Missouri river.

In 1872 Peter Matson and Bengt Olson, from Galva, Illinois, settled, with their families, in what is known as Platte county [Nebraska]. Arriving in the fall, they built their sod houses and prepared for the winter. Columbus, their nearest town, was thirty miles distant. In 1874 still more people came from Galva. They had belonged to the Methodist church in Illinois, and naturally they organized Methodist churches in their new homes. [The] Rev. Olin Swenson, who came to the valley about 1876, built two churches. A few miles westward a large Lutheran congregation grew up. Newman Grove, in the southwestern corner of Madison county, is about ten miles from the settlement just mentioned. In 1878 a party settled northwest of the town, and two years later others took land to the north. The first company of settlers to reach Boyd county arrived in 1890, from Oakland. The Bonesteel branch of the Northwestern railroad was not built at this time. The nearest railway station was O'Neill, thirty-five miles distant. . . .

There are many other places that might have been mentioned in connection with Swedish immigration to Nebraska, but time and space forbid. I have named only the most important points. As time goes on our interest in the beginnings of our state will be all the keener, and we shall all be the more desirous to know who our pioneers were. We are yet so near the beginning that we may not grasp full the significance of pioneer days. I hope, however, that our state may succeed well in preserving the records of the past and that there may be written on the pages of history at least a few chapters dealing with the Swedish element in Nebraska.

Publications of the Nebraska State Historical Society, vol. 19, 78–85.

SWEDISH IMMIGRANTS' LETTERS HOME: OLE OLESON AND JOHN THOMPSON

The immigrants Cather knew on the plains and the characters she modeled on them often maintained their connections to the old country, either by carrying on its traditions in America or by their relentless homesickness for the old ways. The following letters provide a realistic glimpse into the joys and sorrows of certain Swedish immigrants in Nebraska, both about their homeland and about their new lives as American farmers.

Ole Oleson immigrated to the United States in the 1880s with his brother Nils and sister Malena (Erickson 141). Both of the letters that follow were written to his brother John, who had stayed in Sweden along with another brother, Pehr (Erickson 141). In the first letter, Ole enlists John's help in procuring Nils's inheritance money from their father so that Nils and Ole will be able to buy a farm together (Erickson 141). In the second, he expresses relief that Nils's money will be sent and reports the best and worst of news about family matters.

The next set of letters home to Sweden were written by one John Thompson to his mother. His letters are typical in that they reveal a certain degree of homesickness, report family news, give reports about the weather, and ask for news from home. In one letter he mentions his marriage to his second wife, but not his first wife's death. It is reasonable to assume, however, that Thompson was not divorced but had been widowed when he married his second wife. In this same letter, he mentions hunger in Sweden, a subject that was evidently introduced by his mother in one of her previous letters to him. In contrast, his descriptions of life in America are positive almost without exception.

FROM OLE OLESON, LETTERS TO HIS BROTHER
IN SWEDEN (1890)

Ceresco [Nebraska], Jan. 22, 1890
  Brother John!

Happiness throughout the New Year, as well as a good and much sought after fiancee, many children, and all else pleasant.

That letter addressed to Weeping Water has already come, and as you probably know, I have quit my place up there. Nils and I will try to farm or rent land together, and for the sake of that goal, we have each written a letter to the old man.

We wait each day for a coming yes, an affirmative reply. And I don't doubt but that he could send it right away. He is surely good for it one way or another. I think that if there is no other way, Pehr should know that we feel this way, thanks be to his smart head and good fortune. What is more natural than that we should need money when we wish to farm, and besides, I have just as much use for his money as he himself ever would, since we will be farming together.

Both of these letters were sent on November 19th with the request that Nils' money be sent here, but we have not received an answer yet. Nils even wrote a letter in the middle of September trying to get it, and very rightly [Father] replied with the next letter that Nils would receive it in several years. But naturally we can not wait for that. I don't understand why he is waiting with his answer for so long. It has been over two months since we sent our letters. Nils has now sent another on January 19th. It doesn't take more than 40 days at the most for a letter to go back and forth.

Kind brother John, be so good as to answer my letter, and also say if anyone has exaggerated anything there. For my part, I think that one is entitled to his right just as well as the other. We have a bunch of things that we need to buy and it would be nice if he would hurry up and send it.

Dear brother John, be so good as to do what you can for us and hurry, hurry. Be good and answer immediately, and then I will tell you some news in the next letter.

Requested sincerely by your brother,
Ole Oleson
Ceresco, Saunders Co.
Nebraska

• • •

Dear Brother,

I received your letter as well as one from Father with great pleasure. It was good to hear that Nils' money will finally be sent here. We will try to use it in the best way, for money is always welcome and badly needed whoever one is, and in whatever part of the world one is.

We received a letter yesterday, the 17th, from our cousin, Nilla Nilsson. She is in Chicago and has with her some things from home for us, which our old mother has woven and crocheted for us. They have not come to us yet, but are coming soon. They will be treasured momentos from home, Brother John. Tell our old mother that, dear brother.

I will tell you, just between you and me, that I have heard that sister Malena is dead. I knew nothing about that until Father told me. We have since then written to her husband, so that we can find out how things stand. I wrote several letters to her as well as to him, but never received any replies. She must have been sick a long time and perhaps not strong enough to go to the post office and fetch any letters. From his part, I don't believe he would have given her any of my letters. I could journey there and find out how it is, but that would cost around $25, and that is too much money to put out uselessly.

Actually it was not this terrible news which I have just written about which I meant to tell you about. No, there was a whole other matter. On the 16th of December, 1889, we received a little Christmas present, a little daughter, who is named Hilma Oleson, everything went quickly and well.

We find ourselves all in health and hope the same for all of you there at home. Now I shall end my letter for this time, hoping to hear from you again soon, as well as to hear many good tidings from the old home.

We have good weather here now and if it continues to hold on like this, spring will soon be upon the land.

Hope to hear from you soon again, I remain your faithful brother,
Ole Oleson
Ceresco, Saunders Co.
Nebraska

FROM JOHN THOMPSON, LETTERS TO HIS MOTHER IN SWEDEN (CA. 1890)

My beloved mother,

. . . I shall now write a few lines to you for it has been a long time since I have written you. But I shall first thank you for the letter which I have received from you in answer to my last letter. It is very pleasant to hear from my old home for it is a long time since I was there with you. It surely would be a great joy if all of us were to meet there at home with Jesus, where no separation shall ever occur.

I can tell you that we are healthy and feel well. We wish that you have the same fortune. I can also tell that we have moved since I last wrote to you. We now live in Ceresco. We have been here since April 1892 when I bought a place here and paid $40. For 160 acres, which lay right to the town itself. The girls now go to school in town. That place which

I had in Swedeburg I rented out for 5 years. It is only 4 English miles from here to where I used to live in Swedeburg.

I have heard about the hunger at home from Thelander Bengtson. He works for us and he says that he has been around there for many years. I also talked to Ake Svensson since he has come back.

I can also tell you that I am married. Nils Johnsson and Thelander Johnson are married to my wife's sisters, so I am now brother-in-law to both Nils Johnson and Thelander. Also, since my wife is my first wife's niece, then my girls and my new wife are cousins

I shall now end my letter for this time with many dear greetings from all of us to you. First and foremost you are greeted from your son,

John Thompson
Ceresco Saunders Co.
Nebraska North America

* * *

My dearly beloved Mother, God's peace.

I shall now write a few lines to you again in order to let you know that we are healthy and feel rather well and we wish you the same. We talk of you many times a day. We wonder so much how you got along this winter when there was so much snow and cold weather. It would be really nice if you could get someone to write a few lines for you to us so we might know if you have received the letters which I have written to you and how things go with you these days.

I have written a letter to Johannes and one to Martin Andersson and some to Per Niklasson in Hjortaröd. I have not gotten a reply to a single one. They must have all sunk to the bottom of the sea or they have blown away, for I can not understand what has happened to them. Perhaps the folks back home have become angry with me so that they don't want to answer my letters. Nevertheless, I must wait until I receive an answer. You may now write to us and let us know how you and the rest of my relatives are.

We have had a very light winter. Here there has not been any snow. We have had a few cold days so that we were chilled but now we have beautiful weather, so that we can begin to be out some days. I don't have much to write. I don't know any news, but I can send greetings from Nils Jönsson. They are healthy and feel well. We get together for the most part every Sunday, and they come here and visit us. When we are to-gether, then I talk about Old Sweden for them. It would be so pleasant then if Mother were also with us. We are not together a single time but that we talk of you.

I shall now end my letter for this time with many dear greetings from us to you. Greet Johannes and family. Greet Per Nicklasson and family.

Don't forget to greet Little Hilda so much from me. But first and foremost I and my beloved wife and children greet you warmly.

Penned fondly by your son.

John Thompson

Ceresco, Saunders Co. Neb.

U.S. of America

Susan Jean Erickson, "From Stories to History: Letters and Documents—Swedes in Saunders County, Nebraska, 1867–1914." Thesis. University of Minnesota, 1989. [All four of the above letters are taken from this thesis and included here courtesy of the Svenskaemigrantinstitutet in Vasjo, Sweden, where the letters are on file.]

MABEL COOPER SKJELVER'S HISTORY OF A NORWEGIAN SETTLEMENT IN CATHERTON PRECINCT

When Willa Cather's grandfather and uncle and their families first homesteaded in Nebraska in the 1870s, they were among the very first people to arrive in that particular area of Webster County. Thus, the area became known as Catherton, and the name stuck. When Cather and her immediate family immigrated from Virginia to Nebraska in 1883, Catherton, not the town of Red Cloud, was their destination.

A short distance to the west of Catherton was a settlement of Norwegians, some of whom Cather almost certainly used as a models for her fictional Norwegian characters. Cather, her siblings, and her mother and father lived with grandfather Cather in Catherton only eighteen months before Charles, Cather's father, decided that farming did not suit him, moved his family into Red Cloud, and went into business selling insurance and real estate, and making farm loans (Woodress 43). Nevertheless, a year and a half in Catherton was enough to supply the young Cather with many of the characters that would later appear in her fiction, just as her subsequent years in Red Cloud did. Many of her first neighbors on the plains were foreigners—Norwegians among them—and all these foreigners created the strongest and most lasting impressions on her imagination.

Mabel Cooper Skjelver's history of Webster County includes a section on the Norwegian settlement in the Catherton precinct. One of the most illuminating sections of Skjelver's work is her description of the Norwegian Zion Lutheran Church and cemetery. It is possible, perhaps even likely, that this cemetery is the one that became the model for the Norwegian graveyard in *My Ántonia* that "could not extend its hospitality to Mr. Shimerda" after his suicide (785).

FROM MABEL COOPER SKJELVER, *WEBSTER COUNTY: VISIONS OF THE PAST* (1980)

The Norwegian settlement in Catherton precinct was along Thompson Creek in Franklin and along the west branch of Farmers Creek in Webster

County. The upper part of the west branch of Farmers creek meandered along the county line. There were also a few Norwegians and Danish settlers farther east on Indian Creek

It was in the spring of 1872 that Erick Erickson, Dahle and G.O. Lee and other Norwegians homesteaded at the head of Farmers Creek, while [later several other Norwegians arrived, including two brothers, named Hans and Otto Skjelver].

The two Skjelver brothers . . . filed on homesteads, Hans on May 18, 1873 and Otto in the fall of 1876. Both brothers worked in the lumber camps of Wisconsin before coming to Webster County. Otto came to America in 1869 and Hans came in 1871; however, it was Hans Skjelver who first decided to join a group of Norwegians in Webster County. Both men helped to establish the Norwegian Zion Lutheran church and a religious school that was eventually to be District 66, "North Star," a name selected because of the many Scandinavians within the community. Otto Skjelver was the first teacher of District 66, and the Otto post office was named for him. Both brothers were well educated, but Otto, who had a more outgoing personality, became the spokesperson between the Scandinavian and English-American community. He helped interpret American laws, customs and their usage to his fellow countrymen. . . .

Settlement along the creeks was desirable, for both water and wood were vital needs on the uplands. Dug outs and log houses were their first dwellings, to be replaced by sod houses and later by frame houses. Log houses were preferred by the Norwegians for this was the type of dwelling known in Norway. Hans Skjelver lived in a log house until he was able to build a frame house.

Water was carried or hauled from the creek, upland lagoons, springs or rivers, the Little Blue and the Republican. Such long distance water hauling was very troublesome and the settlers thought a community well would be more healthful and less burdensome. They met to consider the location and to plan the division of labor. It was decided to dig the well on German O. Lee's land, but the exact location where water might be found could not be readily determined. The well would have to be dug with hand tools and no one knew how deep, or whether they would find water. Mr. Lee thought they could be sure of finding water if he used a forked branch or divining rod. Securing a forked branch, he started out over his land. After a great deal of walking, as he neared the west branch of Farmers Creek, the branch began to move in his hands. When he arrived in the middle of the creek bed the twig bent downward. Some thought this a hoax, for of course, there would be water beneath the creek bed, but would it be advisable to dig a well in the loose sand; furthermore, a heavy rain would simply fill it with water and mud. Lee insisted that this was the only place water could be found, and if the well was not dug everyone would have to continue to haul water from long distances and drink the cloudy, tepid liquid. As for a heavy rain bothering the well, they could put up a dike so the high water would flow around the well. Reluctantly, they started to dig and all went well until they struck sand, and it became necessary to shore up the well walls, so that the sand would not cave in on the diggers. They used the cut lumber they had on hand, then it was either make the long journey to Juniata to get more or cut down trees and split the wood into crude usable pieces. It became a long tedious undertaking, more than even Mr. Lee had anticipated, but they persisted. At a depth of some 80 feet, they struck water. There was great rejoicing, and thankfulness. Water was hauled from this community well during the next year until the later spring of 1874 when a heavy rain caused the creek to overflow its banks, washed the dike away, flooded the well, filling it with sand and mud.

Now that they knew water was to be found, these Norwegian pioneers dug a second well on Erick Erickson's land that same year. The following year, a crew of men with a well boring outfit, put down wells for many of these early farmers. A large round wooden tub was sunk, that did away with the laborious and dangerous timber shoring of the side walls. Ropes and buckets still were needed to bring up the water, but soon wind power or hand pumps were employed to lift water to the surface.

A tragedy brought another matter to the community's attention. Edward, the small son of Knut Erickson, was struck by lightning. There was not minister or cemetery. So the neighbors made a crude coffin, organized a simple service for the burial of the child on his father's land. When two other Erickson children died a little later from typhoid fever, a community burial site and a church was a recognized need. Christian Hold donated the land in 1875 and the Norwegian Zion Lutheran cemetery was laid out. The three Erickson children were moved to this location and reburied in one grave—the first grave to be dug in the Zion Lutheran cemetery.

Red Cloud, Neb.: Webster County Historical Society, 62–64.

D. AIDEN MCQUILLAN'S "FRENCH-CANADIAN COMMUNITIES IN THE UPPER MIDWEST DURING THE NINETEENTH CENTURY"

> Emil had more friends up here in the French country than down on Norway Creek. The French and Bohemian boys were spirited and jolly, liked variety, and were as much predisposed to favor anything new as the Scandinavian boys were to reject it. . . . The French boys liked a bit of swagger. . . . Now they carried Emil off to show him the club room they had just fitted up over the post-office, down in the village. They ran down the hill in a drove, all laughing and chattering at once, some in French, some in English.
>
> *O Pioneers!*, 241–42

The French, or more strictly speaking French-Canadian, community nearest to the Cather homestead was called LaPorteville (Slote 97), probably so named because many of the inhabitants were members of the LaPorte family. In December of 1885, LaPorteville's Wheatland Post Office was renamed the St. Anne Post Office, with Jean B. LaPorte as postmaster (Skjelver 14), but the locals may have continued to refer to St. Anne as LaPorteville. The French Catholic church there was also called St. Anne's. Perhaps Cather had this name in mind when she chose the similar sounding Sainte-Agnes as the name of the French community in *O Pioneers!* In any case, the LaPorteville community was almost certainly the place she had in mind when she described all the scenes "up in the French country" (185) in *O Pioneers!* and also where she became acquainted with the people on whom she based the characters of Amédée Chevalier and his wife Angelique in that novel.

D. Aidan McQuillan's essay provides important background information on French-Canadian immigration and farming in the plains states. It explains how the inhabitants of Cather's LaPorteville might have ended up there. In the following excerpt the author focuses on Kansas, but all its information is applicable to Nebraska as well.

FROM D. AIDAN MCQUILLAN, "FRENCH-CANADIAN
COMMUNITIES IN THE UPPER MIDWEST DURING THE
NINETEENTH CENTURY" (1983)

French Canadians had operated on the plains west of the Mississippi
River during the eighteenth and early nineteenth centuries as fur traders
and guides, but there was no connection between the traders and the
beginnings of French-Canadian agricultural settlement in Kansas in the
later 1860s. The location of the new farming communities was a consequence of the location of the railhead at Waterville, in eastern Kansas,
and the availability of homesteads in the Republican River valley when
the first French Canadians came west from Kankakee [Illinois] in 1868.
When these pioneer farmers found that most of the alluvial bottom lands
in the Republican River valley were already occupied, they selected homesteads a short distance south of the river in eastern Cloud and western
Clay counties. Many of them had been born in Quebec, but almost all
had lived in Illinois before coming to Kansas. There was practically no
direct migration from Quebec to Kansas. The new arrivals from Kankakee
took up homesteads that had been abandoned by American farmers and
during the 1870s managed to develop a fairly solidly French-Canadian
settlement.

The Kansas frontier represented a new challenge to the French-
Canadian farmers. The problems of drought and unpredictable moisture
supply were of a different magnitude from what they had experienced in
Illinois. Despite environmental hazards and the severe test of an acute
economic depression from 1893 to 1896, the majority of French Canadians not only survived but eventually prospered. By 1915, they had built
up good-sized farms and were producing large quantities of wheat for a
booming wartime market. They had become successful commercial farmers, and in matters of farming they were indistinguishable from their
American neighbors.

The French-Canadian communities were not assimilated rapidly in Kansas. Although the communities in Kansas were small, they managed to
preserve a distinctive French-Canadian flavor. Indeed, Concordia became
a minor cultural center, although it never achieved the stature that Kankakee did for the French-Canadian communities in Illinois. The sisters of
Saint Joseph established a parochial school and taught 150 children of
both sexes; most of the children came from the hundred or so French-
Canadian families living in Concordia. Elsewhere there were small villages
such as Aurora, Clyde, and St. Joseph that served the needs of the rural
French-Canadian population. The settlers built parish churches in Aurora

and St. Joseph, and there were almost always a few French-Canadian priests to minister in them. French-Canadian doctors had their own medical facilities in Concordia, in Clyde, and in St. Joseph; French-Canadian lawyers were prominent in county administrative positions in Concordia, the county seat. . . . Because of the supportive institutional structures and the leadership provided by French-Canadian priests, a French-Canadian identity survived in these small Kansas enclaves well into the twentieth century. It is impressive that despite the fact that there was almost no direct migration from Quebec, French did not give way to English as the dominant language in the Kansas communities until the 1920s.

In *French America*. Edited by Dean R. Louder and Eric Waddell. Translated by Franklin Philip. Baton Rouge: Louisiana State University Press, 124–26.

RUSSIAN-GERMAN COLONIES IN AMERICA

Of all the strange, uprooted people among the first settlers, those two [Russian] men were the strangest and the most aloof. Their last names were unpronounceable, so they were called Pavel and Peter.

My Ántonia, 733

The characters of Pavel and Peter, who lived "up by the big dog-town" in *My Ántonia* are referred to as Russians throughout the novel. Their real-life models, however, were almost certainly Russian Germans—that is, they were descendants of Germans who migrated to the Volga region of Russia in the mid-1700s. In his study of these Russian Germans, Fred C. Koch traces their places of origin in Europe and provides a history of their settlements on the plains.

FROM FRED C. KOCH, *THE VOLGA GERMANS: IN RUSSIA AND THE AMERICAS, FROM 1763 TO THE PRESENT* (1977)

Mingled in the swelling streams of immigration from Russia to the United States in the early 1880s was a strain of people whom officials generally classified along with other nationals from that country as Russians. But they were not Russians. Despite the fact that their country of origin was Russia, where four and five generations of their people had been born and reared, few save those who had served in the tsar's military forces had any grasp of the Russian language. Though these immigrants' antecedents had lived deep inside Russia since the mid-1760s, their ancestry was wholly German and their language was developed out of the eighteenth-century German dialects with Hessian [the language of the inhabitants of the western German state of Hesse] predominating. These non-Russians had become a markedly growing segment of Russia's contribution to America's melting pot since 1874. From 1890 onward, their movement became a surge that ended with the outbreak of World War I. . . .

This singular group considered itself neither Russian nor German but specifically Volga German. . . . The homeland its members had left was an ethnic enclave larger than the state of Maryland, straddling the lower Volga river. . . . Their ancestors—refugees from the war-tortured Germanies of the Holy Roman Empire—had begun to populate this enclave in the 1760s when it was the undeveloped primitive southeastern frontier of Catherine II's Russia. By the 1870s, as their land-island was growing overpopulated, the inhabitants began abandoning it in turn for greater opportunities and better futures in the Western World. Now politics and events have obliterated both empires. . . .

The Volga Germans were predominantly an agricultural people. From 90 to 95 percent, in some villages more, had always been farmers. When they came to the New World they sought out regions that offered them the livelihood in which they and their forefathers had been engaged on Russia's steppes. They were drawn to the prairies of North America . . . and there was a saying that every hillock on the landscape was a thorn in their eyes.

The earliest arrivals in America found their way to Nebraska and Kansas, from where many of them sooner or later spread to the rapidly opening West on the trail of government homestead, timber, and preemption land or low-cost railroad acreage. They came to the western United States only 13 years after the Union Pacific and Central Pacific joined railheads [in May 1969].

In 1870, building of the Northern Pacific railroad along a northern route to Washington Territory had begun and the lines from west and east were joined at Gold Creek, Montana, on September 8, 1883. But in 1882 a company of 17 Volga German families, some of whom had arrived in Nebraska as early as 1876, had outfitted themselves with covered wagons and joined a 40-wagon train that set out from there for the Northwest over the legendary Oregon Trail. After wintering in Walla Walla, in southwestern Washington Territory, they traveled north in the spring of 1883 toward Ritzville, a dusty, rustic village of about 60 inhabitants on the Northern Pacific's new tracks. Only four years earlier, the first sod had been broken in this vast domain of rolling, treeless prairie covered with bunch grass and sagebrush.

The newcomers immediately filed on government land claims. Five miles from Ritzville, amid the prairie farmlands they broke with heavy iron plows, they established their county's first public schoolhouse and formed its first school district within one year after their arrival. Near the schoolhouse, they built Washington Territory's first German Congregational church. . . .

Completion of the Northern Pacific's rail connection with St. Paul brought more and more settlers to this region, including both Volga Germans and immigrants from German colonies in the Ukraine. . . .

The wagon-train contingent typified the religious and educational interests not only of the immigrants from Russia's Volga colonial region but also those of the newly arriving German-speaking settlers from her Black Sea [shore area]. . . .

By 1920, 11,875 first- and second-generation Russia Germans were living in Washington State. . . . However, this far-northwestern segment was only about 4 percent of the Russia German population in the United States. [The population of Russia Germans in other states at that time is shown in] the following distribution:

Colorado	21,067
Kansas	31,512
Minnesota-Iowa-Missouri	8,124
Montana-Idaho-Wyoming	12,179
Nebraska	22,421
North Dakota	69,985
Oklahoma-Texas	12,368
South Dakota	30,937
Washington-Oregon-California	30,435
East of the Mississippi, fewer than	64,000
Scattered throughout six other states	725

Of a grand total of 303,532, the Volga Germans with 118,493 and the Black Sea Germans with 116,540 constituted the two major groups. . . .

Most Volga Germans entered the New World with little money. Those who arrived before the 1890s were not handicapped greatly thereby because of the available free government acreage and the low-cost railroad lands. Those who came after the middle of the 1890s usually had to find employment as common laborers in urban centers, as farm workers in rural areas, and occasionally as farm renters or sharecroppers. The low-income first-generation members of these later arrivals generally gravitated gregariously into urban ghettos, often lacking sewers, water systems, gas, electricity, street lighting, sidewalks, or even graded streets. Their simple frame houses were furnished with homemade furniture and their crude bedsteads laid with straw-filled mattresses. . . . Austerity often became humiliating and sometimes painful; but these people never felt the world owed them anything, nor did the world as a rule even know they existed.

The poverty in which the landless, unskilled first generation lived was surmounted quickly by the children, who through education, resourcefulness, and industry raised themselves out of their parents' economic and social status. . . .

As a class, these immigrants from the land of the tsars were industrious and hardworking; they possessed physical stamina and spiritual vigor. Generations of their people had been hardened in Central Europe's travails and their adversities pursued them to the Volga where they had to wrest their livelihood from a sparsely populated wilderness, peopled largely by bandits [and] brigands. . . . Hardship had always been their companion. Their word for "to work" was not the German *arbeiten* but rather *schaffen* which means "to produce, to create." They labored. Their livelihood and existence could be sustained only through hard labor. . . . In reclaiming the wastelands along the lower Volga, these people overcame unusually primitive conditions.

University Park: Pennsylvania State University Press, 1–4.

TOPICS FOR WRITTEN OR ORAL EXPLORATION

1. Search out an older person in your community whose parents or grandparents immigrated to the United States from another country. After a personal interview, write a report on the immigrant experiences that have been passed down to the next generation.

2. Prejudicial attitudes toward the foreign born were common in the United States during the great waves of immigration of the late nineteenth century. Discuss a series of examples of xenophobia—that is, contempt toward or dislike of foreigners—in *O Pioneers!* and *My Ántonia*.

3. Ever since the days of the seventeenth-century New England Puritans, American xenophobia included a deep abhorrence of the Roman Catholic Church, partly, perhaps, because of an American suspicion of any loyalty to a foreign leader like the pope. Cather, however, portrays the Catholic Church quite sympathetically in her work. Compare and contrast the depictions of the Catholic Church in *O Pioneers!* and *My Ántonia*.

4. Discuss whether Cather depicts the plains as a "melting pot" or as a "salad bowl" in these two books. Support your opinions with evidence from the novels.

5. Write an essay comparing and contrasting Frank Shabata of *O Pioneers!* and Ántonia's brother, Ambrosch, of *My Ántonia*.

6. Analyze the differences between the "old world ways" of the Scandinavians and those of the Bohemians in these two novels.

7. Pavel tells Mr. Shimerda the horrific story of an old country wedding party. What is the importance of this story to the rest of the novel?

8. America is ambivalent about foreign immigrants even today. In 1996, President Bill Clinton signed a new immigration law called the Illegal Immigration Reform and Immigrant Responsibility Act, which some people saw as discriminatory and unfair to immigrants. Research this law and write a paper arguing its fairness or unfairness.

9. On the Ellis Island website (http://www.ellisislandrecords.org), the immigration records of people who came to this country one hundred years ago are now accessible via the Internet. Try to locate your ancestors' records, if they came through Ellis Island, and write a report on what you find.

10. Jim Burden takes great offense to the prejudicial thinking of some of his countrymen toward immigrants. Despite his flirtation with Lena

Lingard, however, he marries one of his "own kind." Discuss the significance of this choice.

SUGGESTIONS FOR FURTHER READING AND WORKS CITED

Aberle, George P. *From the Steppes to the Prairies.* Bismarck, N.D.: Bismarck Tribune, 1964.

Balch, Emily. *Our Slavic Fellow Citizens.* Philadelphia: William F. Fell, 1910.

Blegen, Theodore C. *Land of Their Choice: The Immigrants Write Home.* St. Paul: University of Minnesota Press, 1955.

Capek, Thomas. *The Czechs (Bohemians) in America.* Boston: Houghton Mifflin, 1920.

Cather, Willa. *My Ántonia.* New York: Literary Classics of the United States, 1987.

———. "Nebraska: The End of the First Cycle." *The Nation* 117 (1923): 236–38.

———. *O Pioneers!* New York: Literary Classics of the United States, 1987.

Erickson, Charlotte. *Invisible Immigrants.* Coral Gables, Fla.: University of Miami Press, 1972.

Erickson, Susan Jean. "From Stories to History, Letters and Documents: Swedes in Saunders County, Nebraska, 1867–1914." Thesis. University of Minnesota, 1989.

Foner, Eric, and John A. Garraty, eds. *The Reader's Companion to American History.* Boston: Houghton Mifflin, 1991.

"French Prize Presented to Willa Cather." *New York Herald Tribune,* 3 February 1933: 13.

Gjerde, Jon. *From Peasants to Farmers: The Migration from Balestrand, Norway, to the Upper Midwest.* New York: Cambridge University Press, 1985.

Handlin, Oscar. *Race and Nationality in American Life.* 4th ed. Garden City, N.Y.: Anchor Books, 1957.

Luebke, Frederick C. *Ethnicity on the Great Plains.* Lincoln: University of Nebraska Press, 1980.

O'Brien, Sharon. *Willa Cather: The Emerging Voice.* New York: Fawcett Columbine, 1987.

Pers, Mona. *Willa Cather's Swedes.* Västerås, Sweden: Märdalen University, 1995.

Rice, John G. "The Role of Culture and Community in Frontier Prairie Farming." *Journal of Historical Geography* 3 (April 1977): 155–72.

Schoepflin, George, ed. *The Soviet Union and Eastern Europe: A Handbook*. New York: Praeger, 1970.

Skjelver, Mabel Cooper. *Webster County: Visions of the Past*. Red Cloud, Neb.: Webster County Historical Society, 1980.

Slote, Bernice. "Willa Cather and Plains Culture." *Vision and Refuge*. Edited by Virginia Faulkner with Frederick C. Luebke. Lincoln: University of Nebraska Press, 1982, 93–105.

Sollors, Werner. *Beyond Ethnicity: Consent and Descent in American Culture*. New York: Oxford University Press, 1986.

Steiner, Edward A. *On the Trail of the Immigrant*. New York: Fleming H. Revell, 1906.

Woodress, James. *Willa Cather: A Literary Life*. Lincoln: University of Nebraska Press, 1987.

5

Women on the Frontier

During all of the nineteenth century and most of the twentieth, pioneering was viewed as a mostly male experience. The trip west was often described as an exclusively male adventure, undertaken by optimistic young men who were out to make a fresh start and create a New Eden far away from the sophistication and refinement of the East. The western land itself sometimes took on masculine features: it was rugged, reluctant to submit to the plow, independent, and brawny, or as Cather says in *O Pioneers!*, "like a horse that no one knows how to break to harness, that runs wild and kicks things to pieces" (148). Women, when they were mentioned at all, which was seldom, were often talked about in stereotypes. Unfortunately, these stereotypes have embedded themselves so deeply in the American imagination that even persistent efforts to correct them have not been completely successful.

One of the most pervasive stereotypes of the female pioneer is that of the reluctant, heartbroken young wife who is forced to leave a comfortable and civilized eastern life to accompany her husband, who has decided over her strenuous objections to immigrate to the crude and punishing West. One early chronicler of frontier life, Everett Dick, contributed mightily to this particular stereotype in his book *The Sod-House Frontier* (1937):

> Courageously the frail girl broke old ties in the East hardly daring
> to hope ever to see her old home and friends again. Resolutely and
> tearfully she turned her back on the comforts of the East, the ex-
> cellent furniture, flowers and garden, to face life on the bleak prairie
> in a dugout with but meager furniture and the monotonous solitude
> of the prairies. (233–34)

Typically, in Dick's stereotype, this female pioneer continues to
toil bravely in the face of overwhelming sorrow and adversity until
she either loses her mind, destroys her body, or forces her husband to take her back home. Dick admits that the number of times
the latter happened cannot be documented; nevertheless, he main-
tains firmly that some pleaded with their husbands to take them
back home no matter what the cost, so desperate were they to
return to the East (234). In this view the woman is weak or even
helpless, an absolute victim both of her husband's choices and of
the untamed land itself.

Like all stereotypes, this one has some slight basis in reality, for
there were indeed certain women who resisted moving west to
homestead and who, once they arrived on the prairie, so yearned
to return home that they became mentally depressed and physically ill. What makes it a stereotype, however, is the fact that the
majority of women did not have anything like this experience. Most
of the wives who accompanied their husbands on the westward
trails did so willingly. They did not, for the most part, come from
eastern lives of middle- or upper-class ease or luxury with "excellent furniture, flowers and gardens" but from situations that made
them dream of something better. The majority of these women
could see the value of moving west as clearly as their men could.
They were perfectly well aware that the land they were leaving was
depleted, that eking out even a meager living on it was becoming
increasingly difficult and would probably soon become impossible.
Furthermore, they believed that if they stayed, they and their children would be more vulnerable to diseases like tuberculosis.

Their reluctance to leave home, then, was moderated by their
hope for a better future on richer, cleaner, and, they believed,
healthier land. One survey of "159 women's trail diaries and reminiscences showed that only a small number, about 18 percent,
were strongly opposed to the westward journey while 32 percent
were strongly in favor of the trip" (Myres 102). The rest evidently

did not express their feelings about being uprooted one way or the other.

Another possible explanation for the enduring stereotype of the heartbroken woman forced to head west is that some historians mistook the grief and sorrow associated with saying goodbye for a strong aversion to the very idea of relocating (Myres 101). The leave-taking itself is consistently described in women's diaries as an unbearably sad experience, but its crushing sorrow is alleviated somewhat by the optimistic vision of the future that most women shared with their husbands. These mixed feelings are articulated in a familiar trail song that one pioneer woman copied into her diary:

> Farewell's a word that breaks my heart
> And fills my soul with woe
> But the fertile fields of Oregon
> Encourage me to go.
>
> (quoted in Myres 101)

Willa Cather's own family is a case in point. Her mother, Virginia Boak Cather, certainly did not want to leave her Back Creek, Virginia, home. Furthermore, when she and her family first arrived in Nebraska and moved in with her father-in-law and mother-in-law on their isolated homestead, Virginia's fears about the loneliness of the plains were likely confirmed. By that time, the elder Cathers had been living in Nebraska for about a decade and had built a comfortable frame house to replace their first sod one. Virginia Cather and her young family had reasonably comfortable accommodations waiting for them when they arrived. Nevertheless, it is significant that Cather's immediate family stayed on the farm only a year and a half before moving to the small town of Red Cloud, twelve miles to the southeast. Most of Cather's biographers, while admitting that the reason for the move into town cannot be documented, believe that Virginia Cather was unhappy enough with the isolation of a prairie homestead to insist on relocating (Woodress 43). Significantly, however, she did not insist upon moving back to Virginia.

There is something of Virginia Cather's attitude in the character of Mrs. Bergson, Alexandra's mother in *O Pioneers!* Virginia Cather insisted on bringing her role of "southern lady" with her to the plains from Virginia. Her effort to maintain the habits and routines she was accustomed to back home was typical of a great many pioneer women, and the fictional Mrs. Bergson is representative of them:

> Habit was very strong with Mrs. Bergson, and her unremitting efforts to repeat the routine of her old life among new surroundings had done a great deal to keep the family from disintegrating morally and getting careless in their ways. The Bergsons had a log house, for instance, only because Mrs. Bergson would not live in a sod house. . . . She had never quite forgiven John Bergson for bringing her to the end of the earth; but, now that she was there, she wanted to be let alone to reconstruct her old life in so far as that was possible. (151–52)

Mrs. Bergson does "reconstruct her old life" to a great degree and thereby creates a satisfactory situation for herself. The only time she becomes intensely unhappy is when her daughter Alexandra begins to talk about moving again. Mrs. Bergson's memories of the way she had to live when she first arrived on her homestead continue to haunt her, and she is afraid that another move will require her to relive those early days: "I don't want to move again; out to some raw place, maybe, where we'd be worse off than we are here, and all to do over again. I won't move!" (167). She describes her first days on the plains as being "much worse" than the present: "Drouth, chinch-bugs, hail, everything! My garden all cut to pieces like sauerkraut. No grapes on the creek, no nothing. The people all lived just like coyotes" (167). The thought of starting over and having to suffer again the privations that go along with a new beginning is simply more than she can bear.

This aversion to the location or the kind of house women were expected to live in when they first arrived may help explain the persistence of the stereotype of the melancholy woman who survives through sheer grit. The brown sod houses, often leaky and full of vermin and dirt, were unattractive and at first sight seemed impossible to transform into homes. Many women broke into tears when they first saw them, and their diaries and letters often record such reactions (Myres 141–42). Yet most of these women eventually succeeded in making their dwellings livable, even comfortable, and they took pride in their ability to do so under very adverse conditions. In other words, in the majority of cases a woman's initial disappointment did not last and therefore should not be used as evidence of deep and abiding unhappiness. Furthermore, by the end of three or four years the improved economic situation of many homesteaders allowed them to build much more attractive and comfortable frame houses, just as Cather's own grandparents and aunt and uncle had done. This pattern was more the rule than the exception.

Another prevalent stereotype, which possibly grew up as an attempt to correct the previous one, is that of the strong, tough, enduring, and capable wife, equal frontier helpmate of her husband. The direct opposite of the image of the reluctant, teary woman, it too was very familiar to both nineteenth and twentieth-century Americans. Robust and stalwart, this woman could and did work the fields with her husband, kill wild animals with a rifle, and at the same time give birth to and raise children, all the while continuing to be a civilizing influence in the domestic sphere. She was the superwoman of the plains, and while this picture is perhaps less offensive than the one of the woman as martyr, it is in most ways just as unrealistic.

While the reality of life on the frontier unquestionably required some women to help in the fields and do other "men's work" when necessary, for the most part women's time was spent working in the domestic realm, as it had been in the East or in the old country. Domestic tasks on the trip west and on the frontier homestead, however, were of a much different character than they had been back home. Much of the work was as physically exhausting as plowing and harvesting. In fact, because women had to make do with few, if any, of the conveniences to which they had formerly been accustomed, even domestic work on the frontier came to resemble closely the kind of frontier work men typically did. When they arrived at their homesteads after long, grueling trips overland in prairie schooners, for example, most women did not have cook stoves. On the trail to the West, many had used small travel stoves, sometimes called "emigrant stoves," flimsy affairs that were usually either utterly destroyed by the time the trip was over or had been thrown out at some point to lighten the load (Myres 147). In the absence of any kind of stove, women had to cook over open fires, a process that often took all day and in some cases only produced a couple of loaves of bread, since the baking process took so long and so little could be baked at one time (Myres 147).

Even more arduous than the cooking was the washing. In her study of pioneer women, Sandra L. Myres includes one woman's outline of the steps involved in completing this chore:

1. bild fire in back yard to het kettle of rain water.
2. set tubs so smoke won't blow in eyes if wind is peart.
3. shave 1 hole cake lie sope in bilin water.
4. sort things. Make 3 piles. 1 pile white, 1 pile cullord, 1 pile work briches and rags.
5. stur flour in cold water to smooth then thin down with bilin water [for starch].
6. rub dirty spots on board. Scrub hard. Then bile. Rub cullord but don't bile just rench and starch.
7. take white things out of kettle with broom stick handel then rench, blew and starch.
8. pore rench water in flower bed.
9. scrub porch with hot sopy water.
10. turn tubs upside down.
11. go put on a cleen dress, smooth hair with side combs, brew cup of tee, set and rest and rock a spell and count blessings. (152)

As Myres goes on to point out, before any of the above steps could be taken, women had to make lye soap, which they did by "pouring water and lime through fireplace ashes carefully preserved for this purpose. Then the lye was combined with the left-over household grease, also carefully preserved in a barrel or can. The two ingredients were boiled together and had to be constantly stirred until the soap 'came' and could be dipped into the soap barrel" (152). Furthermore, if rain water were not available and a well had not yet been dug, women had to haul their water, often over a distance of several miles.

Thus we see that women's work began to look increasingly like men's work in many ways: it was often performed outdoors, and it required enormous physical stamina. However, it remained, strictly speaking, domestic work. Those times when necessity required women to pitch in and do "men's work" were not uncommon, but they were almost always temporary departures from the norm.

A good example of such a departure is Ántonia's time working in the fields alongside her brother Ambrosch after their father commits suicide in *My Ántonia*. Taking care of the farm is too much for Ambrosch alone, and Ántonia's mother must take care of the house and the other children. Also, because the family is poor, hiring a man to help with the plowing and planting is out of the question. Ántonia soon comes to love the work, however, and even becomes competitive about it: "'Jim, you ask Jake how much he ploughed to-day. I don't want that Jake get more done in one day than me. I want we have very much corn this fall. . . . I work like mans now. My mother can't say no more how Ambrosch do all and nobody to help him. I can work as much as him'" (791–92).

Despite her love for "mans" work, it was not considered appropriate for a woman to engage in it for very long. The culture of the American West was as disapproving of the blurring of strict gender roles as was the culture of the American East. Jim Burden's grandmother frets about Ántonia and expresses the conventional wisdom of the day when she says, "'Field work will spoil that girl. She'll lose all her nice ways and get rough ones'"; Jim himself believed she had "lost them already" (794). Ántonia does not seem to mind the disapproval, though, and insists that she likes outdoor better than indoor work: "I not care that your grandmother say it makes me like a man. I like to be like a man" (801). Jim's grandmother, however, has the final say. When Ambrosch starts hiring his sister out "like a man, and she [goes] from farm to farm, binding sheaves or working with the thrashers," Mrs. Burden finally puts an end to it by "getting her a place to work with . . . the Harlings" (806). Working as a "hired girl" in another woman's house was acceptable; working as a thrasher was not. The field work was only an interlude. When Jim Burden sees Ántonia again on his return to the prairie after twenty years, she has become part of the norm. Firmly anchored in a domestic enterprise, she cleans, pickles, preserves, and bakes *kolaches* for her husband and eleven children.

Like Ántonia, Alexandra Bergson of *O Pioneers!* works in the fields for a time but is required to quit when the family can afford to hire a man. Unlike Ántonia, however, Alexandra retains another traditionally male role even after she leaves the fields—that of farm overseer and business manager. Her father, John Bergson, realizes early on that his only daughter has much sounder judgment about farm economy than his sons do, even though they do most of the physical farm labor. The narrator tells us that Bergson's boys "were willing enough to work, but when [their father] talked with them they usually irritated him. It was Alexandra who read the papers and followed the markets, and who learned by the mistakes of their neighbors. It was Alexandra who could always tell about what it had cost to fatten each steer, and who could guess the weight of a hog before it went on the scales closer than John Bergson himself" (148–49).

Mr. Bergson finds it regrettable that this talent had not manifested itself in one of his sons, "but it was not a question of choice" (149). Like other members of the culture, John Bergson sees Alexandra's gift for making sound business decisions as much more suited to men than to women. We are told that Alexandra inherited the ability from her grandfather Bergson, not from her grandmother. Still, as he lies on his deathbed, John Bergson tries to be thankful that he has at least one child to whom he can "entrust the future of his family and the possibilities of his hard-won land," even if that one child is a girl (149).

As farm manager and decision maker, Alexandra succeeds admirably during the twenty years following her father's death, despite often running counter to her brothers' desires. She turns the Bergson farm into one of the most profitable in the country. While such an accomplishment is undeniably associated primarily with men, Alexandra nevertheless does not fit the stereotype of the rugged, somewhat masculinized frontier woman who works the fields along with her husband. Of course, Alexandra does not have a husband, and therefore the equal-helpmate role is out of the question. But she retains a traditionally female position in other ways: she manages the household in much the same way she manages the land. She has help in the form of her "kitchen girls," whom she got "from Sweden, by paying their fare over" (188), but she does not abandon the domestic sphere entirely; she is overseer of the house as well as the farm. In addition, she possesses a good many maternal qualities: she takes note of her niece's musical talent and offers to give her a piano; she sees to it that her youngest brother, Emil, gets a college education; she brings Ivar onto her farm and protects him from those who want to send him to an asylum; she even takes Frank Shabata under her wing after he goes to prison, promising to try to get him a pardon.

To the extent that she does step out of the traditional female realm, however, her work is devalued by some of the men around her, primarily her brothers Oscar and Lou. They are expressing the prevailing view when they tell Alexandra that family property "belongs to the men of the family, because they are held responsible, and because they do the work" (220). Alexandra's indignant response "And what about my work?" seems to have no effect; Lou answers, "Oh, now, Alexandra, you always took it pretty easy. . . . there's no woman anywhere around that knows as much about business as you do, and we've always been proud of that. . . . But, of course, the real work always fell on us. Good advice is all right, but it don't get the weeds out of the corn" (220). Alexandra refutes this argument valiantly, but to no avail:

> "Maybe not, but it sometimes puts in the crop, and it sometimes keeps the fields for corn to grow in. . . . Why, Lou, I can remember when you and Oscar wanted to sell this homestead and all the improvements to old preacher Ericson for two thousand dollars. If I'd consented, you'd have gone down to the river and scraped along on poor farms for the rest of your lives. When I put in our first field of alfalfa you both opposed me, just because I first heard about it from a young man who had been to the University . . . [and] you cried . . . when we put in the first big wheat-planting, and said everybody was laughing at us."
> Lou turned to Oscar. "That's the woman of it; if she tells you to put in a crop, she thinks she's put it in. It makes women conceited to meddle in business." (220–21)

The manual labor of plowing, planting, weeding, thrashing, and all the rest was done by men and was considered the "real work" of the country. Managerial work, especially if done by a woman, was not. No amount of reason or logical argument Alexandra brings to bear changes her brothers' conventional view—a view they shared with the rest of society.

On frontier farms, then, as elsewhere in the United States, work was gender determined: women did domestic work, which included a few tasks outside the house, like tending the garden and the poultry; men "worked the fields, sold crops and livestock, tended the large livestock (hogs, cattle, and horses), butchered

hogs and cattle, and looked after the equipment and farm buildings" (Cherry 230). Most women stayed within their roles, and
most saw their work as an important contribution to the new and
better life they came to the West to obtain. That exceptions existed
is undeniable, however, and it is out of these exceptions that the
stereotypes of women grew.

One area of life that remained closed to nineteenth-century
women, on the frontier as elsewhere, was politics. By the middle
of the nineteenth century the talk of equal rights, especially the
right of the ballot, for women was common throughout the country. As support for equal suffrage grew, however, so did the opposition to it, and many women were as violently opposed to it as
men were. In general, both sexes subscribed to the doctrine of
"separate spheres," the notion that women could exercise their
own judgment and claim authority only in the home or in those
realms that could reasonably be called private, extensions of the
home. For example, women "dominated most of the activities of
the . . . churches and schools, [and] . . . few denied women prec-
edence in promoting cultural activities or maintaining the moral
order" (Cherry 231). Organizations like the Women's Christian
Temperance Union were very active on the frontier, and women
were more than welcome to become involved in such societies.
The WCTU was a political group and as such would normally be
off limits to women, but because its purpose was to civilize men
and to protect the morals of the community, it was viewed as an
exception—an appropriate activity for women. Generally, though,
men were solely responsible for both business and political affairs.

Although rigid sex roles were as firmly in place on the frontier
as they were in other parts of the country, historians are still de-
bating the question of whether or not pioneer life offered women
a better chance of escaping those roles than other types of experience did. The answer that probably comes closest to the truth is
that some women gladly took advantage of the nontraditional roles
and opportunities the frontier offered them, while others rejected
them out of hand:

> Some historians have concluded, based on women's reminiscences,
> diaries, and letters, that the frontier did not offer as many oppor-
> tunities for women as it did for men and that women often failed
> to take advantage of the frontier experience as a means of liberating

themselves from constricting and sexist patterns of behavior. Yet
these same reminiscences, diaries, and letters also contain evidence
to support the contention that women on the frontiers modified
existing norms and adopted flexible attitudes and experimental behavior patterns. For some these changes were easily made and en-
thusiastically accepted; for others they were reluctantly made and
strongly resisted. What has perhaps confused the various interpre-
tations of woman's place and the westering experience is that the
reality of women's lives changed dramatically as a result of adap-
tation to frontier conditions while the public *image* remained relatively static. Image, myth, and stereotype were contrary to what
women were actually experiencing and doing. (Myres 269)

The first eleven of the following documents consist of ten letters
and one diary written by four different women living on the plains.
None of these women are highly educated, as their nonstandard
spelling, grammar, and punctuation shows. However, they collectively present a representative picture of the kinds of lives most
women lived on the frontier. Using an easy, familiar tone and col-
loquial language, the writers describe their daily lives largely in
terms of domestic routine, a routine described repeatedly in both
O Pioneers! and *My Ántonia* as belonging to characters as varied
as Grandmother Burden, Mrs. Bergson, Alexandra Bergson and her
kitchen girls, and to Ántonia herself after her marriage to Anton
Cuzak.

The letters also describe some of the adversities the women were
forced to face: homesickness, blizzards, grasshoppers, deaths, and
in one case the departure of a woman friend whose family in the
East had convinced her to return. In another letter the writer discusses her physical appearance with her sister back home. She emphasizes that although she is living on the frontier, maintaining
her attractiveness remains very important to her. Most real frontier
women seemingly had the same concern about feminine appearance as Jim Burden's grandmother expresses when she worries
that Ántonia's field work will cause her to lose her femininity and
give her the appearance of a man.

These women's own words support the conclusion reached by
one historian of women's lives on the frontier:

The answer to how plainswomen dealt with harsh frontier conditions does not seem to lie so much in women's personal feelings

toward themselves, their situations, and their men; rather it derives from three characteristics of plainswomen themselves: their ability to create a rich social life from limited resources, the tremendous reward they derived from their roles as cultural conservators, and their willingness and ability to bond to each other. (Riley 97)

These personal accounts by frontier women are followed by two documents on the woman suffrage question and one excerpt from the *History of the Women's Christian Temperance Union in Nebraska,* 1892. Both suffrage and temperance were live issues for many women on the plains. Some of the real people on whom Cather based her characters would have been aware of, and were probably involved in, both movements.

THE LETTERS OF REBECCA CULBERTSON HUTCHINSON

The writer of the following personal letters, Rebecca C. Hutchinson, was born around 1837. The date of her death is unknown. In her letters she describes to her family back home what farm life is like on her Fort Niobrara, Nebraska, homestead. In addition to a primarily positive view of her and her husband's prospects, she often mentions her social life, which evidently consisted mostly of church activities, her husband being a preacher. She also makes her need for money clear in her insistence that her brother Cyrus force the tenant who is renting her former home to send her the rent she is owed. Like Jim Burden's grandparents in *My Ántonia*, Mrs. Hutchinson and her husband have created a comfortable home and a bountiful garden despite the hardships of weather and an obvious shortfall of cash.

FROM REBECCA CULBERTSON HUTCHINSON, LETTERS HOME
(1885–86)

Ft. Niobrara June 23 1885

My dear Brother—You will think I have forgotten to write but I have been hearing through Lillie from you all until lately we have not heard. I guess Minnie's [letter] to her was so long going if they did go—she sent with a man and he forgot to put it in the office but said he would soon and send, so tell Lillie that this will account for not getting a prompt answer. Our crops look nice here. Every thing growing nicely. We have near seven acres of each corn and sugar cane besides a fine lot of potatoes on some ground that was broken by mistake so we have a nice garden with plenty vines of all kinds sweet corn in abundance with plenty nice beans so we shall be supplied with abundance of vegitables and corn if nothing happens. Our potatoes are very fine—I still like here would rather be where this wind did not blow so hard some times but can not take a nice farm and health every where. It is misting rain today Mr. Hutchinson is out busy in the field does not pay any time to lose week days Sunday [Mr. Hutchinson] is the only preacher for several miles. . . . We have Sunday School in our house as well as preaching. Have a nice lot of neighbors as one large family of Baptists from northern Ills [Illinois]. With one son in law and two daughters all Baptist[, and] . . . some other Christian neighbors who all want preaching and all will be glad to pay as soon as they can raise to save buying provisions. Some have done well those who were here last year and raised a crop but it cost us to build to move a little but near all the moving here from the river was donated but breaking and lumber we are having so as to get ready for winter and to secure against the rains is costing besides our living a side from what is given, or paid for preaching but no money comes to amount to anything I want $10.00 if you cannot get the rent money and if you can please send it all you can get or the [woman] must move she has not paid only the carpet since first of last November and I should like $25.00 if you can get same of her. I know it is your harvest and you are busy but I would be very glad if you can see to it if she had the money to pay down I would sell my dower for $75.00 but not unless I got the money down and the back rent. Love to all

Your sister as ever

Mr. Hutchinson sends love to all

Tell Lillie to write Rebecca C. Hutchinson

• • •

Ft. Niobrara Neb. Feb 9- 1886

My dear Brother . . .

I promised to write sometime ago, but have been putting it off not recieving any letters reminds me I must answer if I hear. I had hoped to hear through Lillie to Minnie but she has not heard although she wrote a long time ago to her. How are you all doing and Orinda why do you not write? I will answer directly I can assure you. We have had a nice winter so far, not much snow or sleighing either the snow does not lay on the ground long enough for sleighing here often. We have had a few days like spring, but, today the wind is blowing and it is colder but not very cold. We like it here better all the time The people and church are very kind They have helped Mr. Hutchinson in breaking and our wood has not cost us any thing since we have been here. The neighbors and all who would make a surprise wood hauling and got us enough wood to last us all winter and next summer. Our yard looks like the land in front of the old home when we were all there once. You filled the lane with logs only ours is dry pine. They also put a nice overcoat with a nice pair of mittens with $3–75 in one of them on the Christmas tree for Mr. Hutch also some other favors so it seems like old times with my Preacher and plenty around us once more for we have those also. The vacant land is nearly all taken but nice land 160 [acres] or the claim can be had for $300.00 or $400–00 and $600–00 with some improvements one or two close to us will soon be sold at that rate. You have plenty where you are. Where is Lou's man Piper has he got well. Here is the place for sick folks plenty of prairie land with cabins on them only every one wants a good big team of young horses old ones do not do well. Well, yes, Lou come on and bring Lillie along but may be you would not like the new prairie and cabins

Now Cyrus is that old woman in my house yet if so she must send me some rent money or leave it as soon as the weather will permit she has not paid anything since one year or since Oct 1884—only that carpet. I need the money or some at least to get Minnie and myself some clothing and she must pay or get another house. It is the County business to look after such. Now please see to it and tell her she must go or pay some rent as I need it. Please see her and write and oblige Your sister R.C. Hutchinson

Courtesy Nebraska State Historical Society, Lincoln, Nebraska.

THE PERSONAL CORRESPONDENCE OF JULIA BAPTIST

Julia Baptist homesteaded with her husband during the mid-1800s. Her letters home are especially interesting because they record her impressions of the prairie from the time she and her family first arrived in 1885 until after they had been there for over three years. Like Willa Cather and her family, the Baptists immigrated to Nebraska late enough to arrive by train, not by covered wagon. Baptist describes herself and her family as fundamentally happy with their choice to move west, but she also describes in detail the hardships they face and in one letter freely expresses her sorrow over being separated from the people who are dear to her. Nevertheless, she becomes very defensive about her life on the prairie and energetically refutes some of the stories that have drifted back to her relatives about the terrible conditions homesteaders must face. In her last letter she shows how common was the belief that the farther west people moved, the healthier they would be.

Her letters echo the narrator's descriptions of both success and failure in *O Pioneers!* During his last days on earth, John Bergson lies pondering the "things that had held him back": "One winter his cattle had perished in a blizzard. The next summer one of his plow horses broke its leg in a prairie-dog hole and had to be shot. Another summer he lost his hogs from cholera, and a valuable stallion died from a rattlesnake bite. Time and again his crops had failed" (147). Years after his death, however, his fields become lush and productive under his daughter Alexandra's management. When Carl Linstrum asks Alexandra how she did it, she says, "The land did it. It had its little joke. It pretended to be poor because nobody knew how to work it right; and then, all at once, it worked itself. It woke up out of its sleep and stretched itself, and it was so big, so rich, that we suddenly found we were rich, just from sitting still" (194). Such diametrically opposite descriptions are found throughout both Cather's novels, as they are in the following letters, and both are equally accurate.

FROM JULIA BAPTIST, LETTERS HOME (1885–88)

Holdrege Neb.
    April 10th 1885

Dear Sister

We got here Saturday evening about half past Seven oclock Sam was at the depot wating for us he had been in evry evening since Wednesday. We got through all right. Eva injoyed the trip better than Ida or Etta it was fun for Eva she would stand up on the seat and jump sing and run to the watter tank after watter and when we got home she said that it did not look like Nebraska but it looked like home. i think my self that it is a nice country all except the wind it blows prity strong some times but they say that it will not be so bad after while they say that it always blow harder in the spring than any other time i can not tell yet but i think i will like it very well we have close neighbors all around. . . . tell father that we had plenty to eat coming and we did not get away with all of it there was one chicken and some bread and part of the cake and some other thing left tell father that we had a good time coming. . . . my chickens and turkeys are laying the duck and eggs i brought got here all right we are all well the childrin are doing fine. . . .

They are going to start a new rail road here the first of next month and run northwest there 500 men coming in to work on it they say.

Lizzie write and tell me all the news.

I remain your sister

Julia Baptist

                • • •

Holdrege Neb

July 11[?] 1885

Dear Sister

. . . This is a good country for any thing that a person puts in the ground to come up the garden looks fine we have had plenty of rain so far. We put out thirty six apple trees this spring and some small fruit black berries straw berries. Our well is two hundred and ninteen feet deep it cost seventy six dollars besides the wind mill it cost one hundred fifty dollars. The land here is cheep but the improvement costs nearly as much as the land the land here is going up all the time the town is growing fast the new railroad is helping it. grosires and other things here are as cheep as they are back there excep the coal it is terribel heigh but most of the people in the country burn corn cobs . . . some people here that dont even know the prise of coal. . . . tell Father and Mother that ever kind of bugs that is back there is out in Neb to eaven the little squash bugs is out here to. . . .

I remain your sister

Julia Baptist

                • • •

Holdrege Neb
   May 18 [18]86
   Lizzie your letter of Apr. 15 was recieved i am glad to heare that you
are all well. We are far off from each other still we can communacate
with each other and find out how we are getting along it seemes to me
as if wasent but a little while ago since i left there and here one long
yeare has past away and we have raised a crope harvested it have started
in on other new years toils & cares i cant help but to think that procos-
tination is the thief of time when i look back . . . and remmember we use
to go to school togeather it seemes to me as if it was but yesterday but
when i come to think nearly ten long years has past away since i left
home and we are now far apart where we can not see each other but
still i am glad that we can heare and know frome each other . . . we are
all well past the winter well and had a good time at chrismas and have
now started in for another summer work have sowed twenty three acers
of spring wheat ten of oats and are putting in forty acers of corn and . . .
ten acers in clover timethy it has come up fine wheat oats look nice we
are having plenty of rain before we come out we use to heare that it did
not rain here but it is all a mistake we have plenty rain since we have
bin here . . . from what you write in your letter you must think that i
have been exaggerated the country but i have rote nothing to you but
what is so you neadent to beleave what you heare for i know that
_____nor_____ [names omitted] did not say that we did not raise
any thing last year for that is not so you can tell Mrs. Tuke[?] that who
ever said that told a big lie for i positivly say that we raised a better crope
of any thing that we planted then we ever raised back there and i can
fuly say that this is as good a country as illinoise with the exception of
wood and watter but the watter is no draw back to the country for a
person after once get a well he will always have watter and good watter
to the wells never goes drie there never was known of a well going drie
the wind blows little harder here in the spring and faul then it dose back
there but we need the wind for to draw watter. . . . after a person is here
a while he dont notice the wind we think this country can not be beat
for farming of course this is a new country and things are not as convenient as they are back there it takes goodeal to improve a place the only
objections we fine is that things are to cheap corn is 14 ct wheat 50 ct
oats 20 ct potatos 50 ct hogs 3.25 per houndred we raised 55 bu of corn
per acer last year some of our neighbors 65 and 70 some oats went as
heigh as 50 bu per acer wheat 25 bu we also raised larger potatos here
we ever raised back there and ever thing also in perportion. . . .
   Julia Baptist

· · ·

Holdrege Neb
  March 19th [18]88
  Dear Sister
  . . . i recived your letter of Dec 29th and it found us all injoying good
health. . . . Cora is big and fat she can run all over clime chairse and ever
thing we had a very nice winter had some prity cold weather in January
but not much snow febuary was nice but . . . today we are having one of
the worst blizzards we have had this winter in fact we dident have any
blizzard this winter untill today last week was warm and there was goodeal of wheat sowed yesterday was to hot to wear a coat to day we cant
go out side of the doore on acount of the snow and wind the snow comes
wet and it sticks to a person face and eyes so that he cant go against the
wind at all that is the worst thing about the blizzards the snow comes
wet with wind and stick that a person cant see anything they had one in
the northern part of this state . . . in febuary that kill about three hundred
persons about us going back we will not go this spring we may go in the
faul and may never go at all if Sam's folk was settle back there and could
get along with out us we would never go but even as it is we may go
farther west in stead of going back cant tell untill faul comes. I think that
Jess and Grace is going farther west in the faul the Doctor tell them that
they will have to go on acount of Grace She has the start of consumption
and is not able to do any thing now the Doctor tells them that if they
dont go west soon that she will not live over a year she is going back to
visit her folks in Iowa and Minnesota she will stay about three months
and then come back and then they may go out to Colorado where Jessie
is in the faul the Doctor tells them that out there is a better place then
here for it is farther South and the weather is not so changable. . . .
  Yours Truly
  Julia

Courtesy Nebraska State Historical Society, Lincoln, Nebraska.

THE LETTERS OF MARTHA (MATTIE) THOMAS OBLINGER

Mattie Oblinger and her husband Uriah moved to a homestead in Nebraska after having rented a farm to work in Indiana for the first three years of their marriage, 1869–72. Uriah was a veteran of the Civil War and as such was able to claim more land under the Homestead Act than nonveterans were. He, his brother Horace, and his two brothers-in-law, Giles and Samuel Thomas, settled in Nebraska in 1872, and Mattie followed him in the spring of 1873. Her letters display a slightly higher level of literacy than those of the previous two women, but they are similar to the others in tone, style, and content. Their descriptions of sod houses, snakes, gardens, country schoolhouses, and frontier funerals are very similar to those Cather includes in both *O Pioneers!* and *My Ántonia*. In the last letter included here, Mrs. Oblinger reports that one of her neighbors, of whom she was very fond, will likely be persuaded by her family in the East to give up the pioneer life and move back home. Mrs. Oblinger's disappointment at seeing her go echoes Alexandra's own disappointment when, in *O Pioneers!*, Carl Linstrum breaks the news to her that he and his family are also giving up trying to farm a homestead and moving back east.

FROM MARTHA THOMAS OBLINGER, LETTERS HOME (1873–74)

Fillmore County Neb
　　June 16th 1873
　　Dear Brother & Sister & all of Uncle Wheelers
　　Thinking you would like to hear from us and hear how we are prospering I thought I must write you a letter and so fulfill the promise I made when I last saw you
　　The reason I have not written sooner I have not had the time. . . . Sunday is rather a poor day for us to get a chance to write too for we have went to Church and Sunday school every Sunday I have been here two Sundays we went about 9 miles the rest of the time we went to Giles the next preaching will be at Giles which is in two weeks The man that preaches is quite old and is a baptist minister but when he preaches he makes no distinction in denominations. . . .

Most all of the people here live in sod houses and dug outs I like the sod house the best they are the most convenient I expect you think we live miserable because we are in a sod house but I tell you in solid earnest I never enjoyed my self better but George I expect you are ready to say it is because it is somthing new No this is not the case it is because we are on our own and the thoughts of moveing next spring does not bother me and every lick we strike is for ourselves and not half for some one else I tell you this is quite a consolation to us who have been renters so long there are no renters here every one is on his own and doing the best he can and not much a head yet for about all that are here was renters and it took about all they had to get here some come here and put up temporary frame houses thought they could not live in a sod house This fall they are going to build sod houses so they can live comfortable this winter a temporary fram [frame] house here is a poor thing a house that is not plastered the wind and dust goes right through and they are very cold A sod house can be built so they are real nice and comfortable build nice walls and then plaster and lay a floor above and below and then they are nice Uriah is going to build one after that style this fall The one we are in at present is 14 by 16 and a dirt floor Uriah intends takeing it for a stable this winter It will be a nice comfortable stable A little ways from the door is a small pond that has water the year round we use out of it for all purposes but drinking and cooking We have the drinking water cary about 1/4 of a mile and the best of water We have two neighbors only 1/4 mile from us.

I must stop and get supper. . . .

Uriah has 23 acres of sod corn planted it looks real well I tell you it is encourageing to have cut a lot of corn and all your own We have a nice lot of Squashes and Cucumbers & Mellons & Beans comeing on. There was a striped bug worked some on our squashes but did not bother our other vines We have our Potatoes and cabbage up at Giles as they do not do well on sod I set a hundred & thirty cabbages last week they are every one growing We have the nicest patch of early rose potatoes in the neighborhood will not be long until we will have new potatoes We have fared pretty well in the potato line as Uriah bought ten bushel when I cam to Crete [Nebraska] he bought it for seed and to use we will have plenty until new potatoes come If nothing happens we will have a nice lot this fall I have nice Tomatoe plants comeing on I want to set more Tomatoes and Cabbage this week. . . .

Uriah is breaking sod to day he will soon have 40 acres turned over then it will be ready to go into right next spring It looks like it was fun to turn the sod over here there are no roots or stumps to be jerkinking the plows out. . . .

It looks very strange to me to see Crops growing here and no fence around them They have a herd law here and the stock a man has for use about home he must lariett them out his other cattle he puts them in herds in the neighborhood gets them herded for 25 cts per month The prairie looks beautiful now as the grass is so nice and green and the most pretty flowers I can not tell how many different kinds I have noticed. . . .

I thought when I left the timber I would not see any more birds but there are lots of them here some that are entirely different to any I ever saw in Ind. There is more Rattle snakes here than there are garter snakes in Ind[iana] Uriah has killed two on our place there are not so plenty right in our neighborhood as they are three miles east of here near a prairie dog town some men over there have killed as high as 18 & 20. . . .

I wish you would come here I am quite sure you would like the country for it is as pretty and good as it can be of course it has some draw backs as all other places do. . . .

I want you all to be sure and write soon We send our love and best wishes from

U.W. & M.V. Oblinger

• • •

Sunday forenoon Aprile 12th 1874

Fillmore Co Neb

Dear Father & Mother & Bros & Sister

To day finds me conversing with you through the silent medium of the pen What a blessed prvalege that we can converse in this way when we are dprived of converseing with each other varbaly How I would love to see you all to day if it was so that I could. . . . I am looking forward to the time when we will go back on a visit but what changes there will be untill that time When I think of the changes there has been allready and not quite a year It seems like it can not be There has been so many passed a way and so many married it will hardly seem like the same place but I fancy the old homestead will look natural. . . . We are at home to day there is no Church but there is a funeral about five miles from here. . . . The funeral is of an old lady that came here last July from Ill[inois]. She was badly afflicted before she came and has been for several years with Rheumatism and other diseases she has been helpless for a long time the Drs told her they could do nothing more for her with medicine but per-haps if she would come here it would help her although they thought she could hardly live untill she would reach here But she is done with her suffering she was a very religious woman and bore her trials with out murrmuring and seemed as though she was only waiting for the Lord to call her away Her name is Merryman. Their house and farm we can see quite plain The old man is living here and two sons. . . . If we could drive up the gate [back home] I wonder who would be the first on to meet us

Nett [Mattie's sister] I imagine I would see you comeing making about two jumps from the door to the gate Charlie I dont believe you would take time to get your hat and then stick your hands in your pockets and walk out Well I would not care how all of you would cut your extras ["cut up," act silly] if I could only see you Now I am not home sick and have not been since I have been here but you know it is natural for friends to have a great anxiety to see each other after they have been seperated awhile.... Well our schoolhouse is going up quite fast suppose it will be done in time The district south of us have voted to build a school too It will be just one mile south of us while ours will be one mile North The one South will be on the corner of a RR sec They voted to build a frame 18x24 Giles children will have quite aways to go as it isn't in his district and is just two miles from his house I suppose the districts will be divided before his children are old enough to go to school unless he makes a better progress than he has been....

I have not made garden yet will make some tomorrow if it does not rain it has the appearence of rain this evening I would have made some this last week but the ground was not ready and Uriah wanted to finish his wheat I feel like killing my old hens they will not go to setting [laying] I expect when they do take a notion to set they will all want to set at one time I have made two table clothes & two shirts for Uriah & one for my self out of our waggon sheet Don't you think I will have a good time washing them this summer.... I have commenced peicing a quilt I know no name for it it is peiced of dark & light calico did think I would piece an Ocean wave but when I piece that I want it for a nice quilt I have seen some scraps quilts peiced that way here and they look real well.... I tried a new way to make bread custard I use water insted of milk and it does real well If you doubt it why just try it & see If you was living in Neb you would try a great many projects that you would never think of in Ind....

Oh yes I suppose we will live high now as Uriah has taken a step toward the white house He was elected School director last Monday and voted a five dollar sallary for him guess he will not have to work now I torment him considerable about it Nett how do you do up your hair now days Does the boys hurry you as they use to when you go to comb I do mine up just as I use to for Sunday and every day too for my old net is played out if I had a braid I could do my hair up as you use to....

Well I am getting sleepy so I will close and send this to the office if I get a chance tomorrow I am as ever

Yours truly

MV Oblinger

• • •

Fillmore co Neb
   Nov 24th 1874 Tuesday evening
Dear Father & Mother & Bros & Sister
   This is a late hour to commence writing but I thought it about time
we were writing again and I thought that perhaps there might be some
one going up to town tomorrow so that we can send to the office had a
chance this morning but no letter ready for you I was quite sure we
would get a letter from home to day but was disappointed Well we
slaughtered our old sow to day. . . . Our hog was in tolerable good order
was not near as fat as she would have been had we corn to feed her I
tell you wheat does not put the fat on like corn does do not know how
much lard I will have as I have not fried it out yet have two pots full on
the stove now The old sow would weigh close on to two hundred we
have another shoat to kill after while How many hogs are you fattening
this fall and how many are you going to salt down. . . . Well Uriah is
reading & Ella [their daughter] has gone to bed but there seems to not
be much sleep about her for she is singing & cutting all kinds of monkey
shines She had quite a time to day as there was nothing escaped her
notice she was bound to see her Pa kill the old sow when he went out
she wanted to go too I told her she must not as it was too cold so she
went to the north window and climbed up where she could see the whole
performance and she never flinched I guess she would have stood right
by him had I let her when I went to clean the entrails . . . she had more
questions to ask than a Philadelphia lawyer could have answered she
thought the paunch was an awful nice thing for the old sow to keep her
dinner in but she thought the entrails did stink awful bad. . . . She is
better of the whooping cough coughs some yet as she has taken a little
cold and I expect it will be that way all winter with her Did not get any
of that medicine for her as we had no money at the time and she was
getting better thought she would not need it. . . .
   Mr Macbeths buried their babe yesterday died of the whooping cough
was about nine months old and they have another child that is very bad
with it Macbeth is a brother of Mrs Furgison & lives nine miles from here
Furgisons went down yesterday and we sent them that recipe They are
the only children that have been dangerous with it They are very poor
folks and like the rest of us see pretty hard times and it seems hard to
see their child taken away but I suppose it is all for the best as it is the
Lords will to remove those that he sees fit to remove from earth to
heaven. . . .
   I see by the Journal that they were talking of sending help to the Grasshopper region from Cass Co[unty] well all the help that can be sent will
be needed for there are many needy persons that will suffer unless they
are helped west of us they are a great deal worse off than through here

and many in this County have applied for help and they realy need it people in the east have no idea how bad it is for there are so many come here as we did with but little and have had no chance to gather any thing ahead and to help matters along the merchants in Sutton have all combined and will not trust another person [extend credit] if they do it is fifteen dollars fine I think it a little mean of them and they will not pay hardly any thing for what a person has to sell wheat is only 45cts I sent some butter up two weeks ago and Uriah could not find any one a buying at all I suppose they all had a pound ahead he brought the butter back & I was as mad as a wet hen I have about 10 lb packed and Ill bet if we was not compelled to sell it they would pay a good price before they would get it They were paying 20cts to day Ill bet they will pay more than that before three months guess I will send some up and get a little coffee and the rest I will keep awhile. . . .

Our love to all inquiring friends and we are as ever yours truly
MV Oblinger

• • •

Monday evening Dec 14th 1874
Fillmore County Neb
Dear Father & Mother & Bro & Sister
. . . This morning Morgan come by going up after a barrel of things that had been sent them by Mrs Morgans folks so Uriah went with him to get the letter but the barrel has not come yet Morgans barrel wieghed 280 lbs & come from Coshockton Ohio and then only six dollars Uriah went over home with him he said there was lots of nice & good things in it Mrs. Morgan she sent Ella some Chestnuts & 4 large green Apples & sent me a half gallon or more of the nicest dried peaches I do think she is a splendid woman but I guess we will loose her this spring as her folks have been writing & pleading with her to come to Ohio to live ever since she has been here & I guess they have accomplished it I am real sorry of it too She will go back in May or June & Morgan will go next fall and rent out his farm here I dont [think] he will be satisfied there as well as here for her people do not like him very well just because he was a poor boy when he set out for himself He is a man that is well thought of here and could not be any better man to a woman. . . .

I wish you could see [Ella] she is as fat as a little pig and her cheecks as red as roses I guess I can say she is over the Whooping cough & how glad I am last week she had quite a cold that made her cough some & coughs a little yet did not cough any last night & but little to day dont think you ever seen her so fat Indeed if she was there Grandpa nor no one else would get lonesome she would keep you busy answering questions and telling her how to read & reading for her and pronouncing for her when she spells wish you could see her when she reads in her 1ˢᵗ reader she has several peices almost memorized The Lady Sheep and Butterflies she can say with but little telling her Pa thinks she would make a good peddler she will come to her Pa with her book when he is busy reading & he will try to make her wait or go away & the first thing he knows she has him looking at a picture or telling her how to pronounce a word & the first thing he knows she has him reading for her. . . . We went to Fairmont last saturday a week I got some Christmas candies for her I did not want her to be disappointed for she is talking so much about it I took nearly 8 lbs of butter to fairmont got 20cts per lb I got some muslin to make two suits of underclothes for me self got some coffee & matches & thread & needles & a thimble & some soap to wash hands. . . . I am finishing my dress treid to finish it this evening I am making it to fit & do not intend or do not think I will have to make it any larger or any smaller You need not judge me by yourself you say peaches fattened you well I have not had any peaches nor any thing else to eat to fatten me do not know my weight now was going to get weighed in Fairmont but forgot it But it is of no use for me to say any thing for I dont suppose you will believe what I say & you can not see me so we will let time prove these things. . . . It may look to some like we have sunk all that was ever given us but I think we have something to show for it we have a good farm (or think it will be a good farm) and a pleasant home that we can call our own & have a pretty good show for another team [of horses]. . . . I know we have to live close & very saveing to get along but we enjoy health & happiness & a plenty to eat as long as it last will try to make it reach the next crop We could have lived nicely this winter if Mr Grasshopper had not come indeed we are thankful for what they did leave. . . . my love to all we are all well

   M Oblinger

Courtesy Nebraska State Historical Society, Lincoln, Nebraska.

THE DIARY OF MARY MARGARET (PIKE) HARPSTER: A RECORD OF EVERYDAY LIFE

As I entered the kitchen I sniffed a pleasant smell of ginger-bread baking.

My Ántonia, 719

Mary Margaret Pike was born in Iowa on June 26, 1852. She moved to Nebraska in the company of another family in August 1868, and there in 1870 she married William Ambrose Harpster. The diary excerpted below covers the years 1885–89 and is typical of frontier women's diaries of the time. Mrs. Harpster records occurrences that might seem thoroughly mundane to some twenty-first-century American women, but the events she describes—domestic activities, weather, birthdays, deaths, and neighboring farms—were the things that shaped and gave meaning to the lives of nearly all nineteenth-century frontier women. Domestic tasks were much more time consuming then than now, of course, and women were judged harshly if they did not perform them competently. Cather comments on this tendency to be judgmental in her description of Mrs. Bergson in *O Pioneers!*: "She disapproved of all her neighbors because of their slovenly housekeeping, and the women thought her very proud. Once when Mrs. Bergson . . . stopped to see old Mrs. Lee, the old woman hid in the haymow 'for fear Mis' Bergson would catch her barefoot'" (152).

FROM MARY MARGARET PIKE HARPSTER, PERSONAL DIARY
(1885–89)

1885

May 15—Bought pail of coffee . . . and paid $1.00. Jimmie died yesterday from poison [there is no evidence suggesting whether "Jimmie" is a person or an animal]. . . .

• • •

17—Still cloudy and rainy. River is high

• • •

19—Churned and ironed

• • •

22—Finished 8 pieces of sewing for the children. . . .

23—Sold Mr. Munson 2 quarts of milk to make ice cream. Churned and Baked 13 loaves of Bread and 3 pies this forenoon. Heavy thunder storm lightening struck the telegraph post. . . .

• • •

Oct. 7—nice and clear this morning went to the quarry this afternoon. . . .

8—nice and pleas. this morning went to see Abbie [Abbie is either her sister or just a neighbor]. . . . made sweet-pickle for tomato

9—nice and clear this morning at house all day set-up the stove

• • •

13—nice and clear this morning washed for myself and Abbie

14—nice and clear this morning sold frank beans $1.20

• • •

20—. . . . I went to Abbie's, we killed a hog this evening moved the stove in the east room.

21—nice and cool this morning took care of the meat and lard today went to church

22—nice and clear. Am washing got our pictures . . . today

23—nice and clear this morning. Baked . . . 9 loaves. one sack of flour. $1.00. got oil.

24—cloudy looks like rain it is raining so I can't go to Abbie's today. Jesse [Mrs. Harpster's son] went to Abbie's. stayed all night

25—looks like rain this morning went to Abbie's today

• • •

27—nice and clear this morning got oil rained awful hard this afternoon baked and worked

• • •

Nov. 1—nice and clear heavy frost last night

• • •

1886

Jan. 2—Snow snow all the time Mr. Keigh was Buried to day

• • •

5—clear and pleasant today made 2 shirts for Mclain's .50 cts Jesse went to school today

• • •

18—snowing yet nice sleighing here

• • •

25—nice and clear, thawed all day gave Kit 8 pounds of rags

• • •

Feb. 5—very nice and warm went to Hanks. It is his birthday he is 33 years old

Temperance   6—nice this morning

meeting   7—nice and warm

• • •

Apr. 17—Delia Swope left for Cal. This morning got 2 pounds Butter of Mikes 15 cts per pound 30 cts. Paid them $1.00

• • •

22—nice to day I washed and made Will and Jesse a shirt

• • •

May 21—Nice all day. _____ was here paid me 60 cts for sewing I paid Judd $1.30 on the bird cage owe 45 cts yet we had ice cream Jesse went to stay all night with _____ I paid franks wife for the bird. $1.50

• • •

Dec. 26—cold and snowing all day we killed a chicken for dinner

• • •

1887

Feb. 11—cold. I pieced the quilt Mother cut out today and Baked Bread

• • •

13—cold and windy we went to Mrs. Egberts funeral and went to uncle Sauls for dinner. May K. has a boy.

14—rainy and lonesome Will at town got lard

• • •

16—finished the quilt Julia learned me to knit shell work.

• • •

22—Pleaseant we went to grandpa Wanders funeral was at Kits for dinner. . . .

23—Snowing awful hard most all day we went to Hanks to help them Butcher a hog they gave us the head

• • •

28—very nice I washed. Julia was here for dinner. Sam Mowry died tonight at 2 oclock. Clara Larch died at 7 oclock. I went to Kits to help her fix to move

March 1—very nice all day I ironed and went to Claras funeral at 2 oclock. Judds moved on the farm
2—cloudy and cold we went to Sams funeral

• • •

April 9—awful windy the men had to stop work

• • •

12- . . . Hank's mother went to Kansas. Mr. Wilson was here this afternoon I got me a dress at Mclains

• • •

1889

Oct. 26—nice went to Hanks to work he gave me a hog head
27—nice fixed the head

• • •

Nov. 1—snowing like fury all day ironed for Lilly Olds

2—very nice washed and ironed for Reeds $1.25 Will got Johns team and hauled wood

DEBATING THE WOMAN SUFFRAGE
QUESTION IN NEBRASKA

The following two documents center on the woman suffrage question, which was being debated increasingly often during Cather's time on the Nebraska frontier. The first is an article from the Cather's local newspaper, the *Red Cloud Chief*, published around the time Cather and her family moved into the town of Red Cloud from her grandfather's farm a few miles away. The second is an excerpt from an early history of Nebraska, published in 1882. It describes the occasion upon which the subject of women's rights was first introduced in the Territorial Legislature of Nebraska.

Although Cather does not mention the issue of woman suffrage directly in her novels, some of the female characters she creates are described in ways that suggest the right to vote would have been important to them. These are characters who chafe under the restrictions of traditional female roles, preferring a greater degree of independence and self-determination. Ántonia, for example, discovers when she works on her own family's farm and when she is hired out as a farm hand for others, that she very much enjoys the freedom playing a male role allows her. In addition, we are told that Frances Harling, the eldest Harling daughter in *My Ántonia*, "virtually managed [her father's] Black Hawk office during his frequent absences. . . . Grandfather [Burden] said Frances Harling was as good a judge of credits as any banker in the county" (808). Lena Lingard, too, prizes her independence highly, as she makes clear when she expresses her view of marriage to Jim Burden: "I don't want a husband. Men are all right for friends, but as soon as you marry them they turn into cranky old fathers, even the wild ones. They begin to tell you what's sensible and what's foolish, and want you to stick at home all the time. I prefer to be foolish when I feel like it, and be accountable to nobody. . . . [Family life is] all being under somebody's thumb" (892). Alexandra Bergson herself is, of course, perhaps the most memorable portrait of a strong, independent woman in either novel. Willa Cather certainly knew real Nebraska women whose beliefs very closely resembled those expressed by her female characters, women to whom the extension of voting rights must have seemed completely natural and logical.

FROM "THE LADIES" (1885)

The National Woman's Suffrage Association held its second secret session to-day, Miss Anthony presiding. The following officers were elected for the ensuing year: President, Elizabeth Cady Stanton; Vice Presidents, Susan B. Anthony, Matilda Joslyn Gage, Phoebe W. Couzins, Rev. Olympia Brown, Abigail Scott Dumway and acting honorary Vice Presidents from each State and Territory. Reports and letters were then read presenting suggestions as to the future work of the association. Mrs. Stanton presided at the afternoon meeting, which was largely attended. Letters and telegrams were read from friends wishing success to the movement. . . . Resolutions were read and discussed, particularly the one denouncing the religious dogmas teaching that woman was an afterthought in creation, her sex a misfortune, marriage a condition of subordination, and maternity a curse, as contrary to the law of God and the precepts of Christ, and inviting the co-operation of religious teachers in securing recognition of the cardinal point of our creed that in true religion there is "neither male nor female, neither bond nor free, but all are one." The discussion of this resolution was long and spiritual, and . . . it went over for further argument to-morrow. At the evening session addresses were made by Matilda Hindtman, Rev. Olympia Brown, and Lillie Devereaux Blake.

Red Cloud, Nebraska, *Red Cloud Chief*, January 30.

FROM A.T. ANDREAS, "THE WOMAN SUFFRAGE QUESTION" (1882)

The questions of the extension of the elective franchise to women was first presented to the people of Nebraska in the winter of 1855, by Mrs. Amelia Bloomer, the distinguished advocate of the equality of women before the law, and of other noted reforms in social and political matters. On the 29th of December, 1855, that lady, a resident of Council Bluffs, Iowa, received a letter signed by Hon. William Larimer, Jr., and twenty four other members of the Territorial Legislature, requesting her to address that body in the Hall of Representatives on the subject of women's rights. The invitation was accepted . . . and the 8th of January, 1856, designated as the date of the delivery of an address. A correspondent of the *Chronotype*, published at Council Bluffs, thus described the event, and the appearance of the lady on that occasion.

"Mrs. Amelia Bloomer, who had been formally invited by members of the Legislature and others, arrived at the door of the State House at 7 o'clock P.M., and, by the gallantry of Gen. Larimer, a passage was made for her to the stand. The house had been crowded for some time with eager expectants to see the lady and listen to the arguments which were to be adduced as the fruitage of female thought and research. When all had been packed into the house, . . . Mrs. Bloomer arose, amidst cheers. We watched her closely, and saw that she was perfectly self-possessed— not a nerve seemed to be moved by excitement, and her voice did not tremble. She arose in the dignity of a true woman, as if the importance of her mission so absorbed her thoughts that timidity or bashfulness were too mean to entangle the mental powers. She delivered her lecture in a pleasing, able, and, I may say, eloquent, manner, that enchained the attention of her audience for an hour and a half. A man could not have done better. In mingling with the people next day, we found that her argument had met with much favor. As far as property rights are concerned, all seemed to agree with the lady that the laws of our country are wrong, and that woman should receive the same protection as man. All we have to say now is, that Mrs. Bloomer's arguments on woman's rights are unanswerable. We may doubt the policy of allowing woman to vote, but who can draw the line and say that, naturally, she has not the right to do so? Mrs. Bloomer, though a little body, is among the great women of the United States; and her keen intellectual eye seems to flash fire from a source that will consume the stubble of old theories, until woman is placed in her true position in the enjoyment of equal rights and privileges. Her only danger is in asking too much."

The interest awakened by this advanced move resulted in the offering of a bill in the House giving to women the right of the franchise. This bill was drawn, it is said, by Gen. William Larimer, Jr. . . . The local squabbles which engrossed attention prevented the bill from receiving action until the last day but one of the session. Gen. Larimer spoke eloquently in its behalf. A vote was taken, showing that . . . fourteen favored the measure; while . . . eleven were against the adoption of the bill.

Having passed the House, the bill was sent to the Council, where it was twice read; but, owing to the conflict over the fixing of county boundaries and other questions—many of which were spoken upon to "kill time" and defeat legislation—the suffrage bill never reached a vote. The law limited the session to forty days, and the Legislature came to a close before anything definite could be done. It is said that great excitement prevailed when the vote was announced in the House, and that some members of the opposition proposed to present Gen. Larimer with a petticoat as a badge of his devotion to the sex. After the lapse of a quarter of a century, it is safe to remark that such an emblem, had it really been imposed on the General at that time, would now be regarded as an historic garment, worthy of preservation among the valued relics of the State.

It is a fact easily demonstrable from the statute books, that Nebraska has ever been one of the foremost States in the just work of treating women as the equals of men before the law. Step by step the world has moved in this reform, which had as its foundation the truth that mind, not body, was the element endowed with inalienable rights. The accident of sex was no more worthy of consideration than that of physical perfection or imperfection. Man, no matter how feeble in frame, was still regarded as possessed of political rights; and woman, from deductions as consistent as those of mathematics, must of necessity be the possessor of equal rights where equal responsibilities rest upon her. This State, composed, as it always has been, of men of fine intelligence and liberal ideas, was quick to accept this fact, and laws of an equitable character were enacted in behalf of women. . . .

History of the State of Nebraska, Chicago: Western Historical, 183–84.

THE WOMEN'S CHRISTIAN TEMPERANCE
UNION IN NEBRASKA

Pioneer women's voices were for the most part unheard in the political sphere. The public roles required of politicians were deemed inappropriate for women, who were allowed to hold some degree of sway only in the private realms of everyday life. One of the few exceptions to this rule was the Women's Christian Temperance Union (WCTU), an organization that began in 1874 with a women's temperance group in Ohio, where, by means of axes, as well as marches and other public demonstrations, women put an end to liquor sales in certain areas of that state. By 1890, WCTU membership had grown to 150,000 nationwide (Foner and Garraty 1157).

From its beginnings the WCTU was an exclusively female and nearly exclusively Protestant organization, and as it spread farther into the American frontier, pioneer women saw membership in it as a natural extension of their Sunday School and other church work. Protestants far outnumbered Roman Catholics on the western plains, and many Protestant ministers, especially Methodists and Baptists, would have included exhortations to abstain totally from alcoholic beverages, which were viewed as sinful. When Jim Burden was charged with "send[ing] about word that there would be preaching at the sod schoolhouse" (730) in *My Ántonia*, for example, it was Protestant preaching he was announcing. Grandfather Burden was clearly the type of Protestant who would have embraced such a message, for he "didn't approve of dancing," either (851), and it is not possible that he would have disapproved of dancing but not of drinking. People who went to hear these sod-schoolhouse preachers would often have heard temperance messages.

Many women, then, thought of the WCTU as the political arm of their church, and they relished the chance to be politically active in a way that was at the same time socially acceptable. Certainly Mary Margaret Harpster, whose diary is included in this chapter, was one such woman. She makes note of a temperance meeting in the margin of her diary entry dated February 6–7, 1886.

FROM ADA BITTENBENDER, *HISTORY OF THE WOMEN'S CHRISTIAN TEMPERANCE UNION IN NEBRASKA* (1892)

To every nation there comes a time in its history when great and important issues must be met, that the peace and prosperity of said nation may continue.

That this may be accomplished, our wise Heavenly Father often calls out new and hitherto untried persons to carry out his plans and purposes.

In all ages since the creation, woman at critical times has come to the front and with her quick discernment and her great moral courage has so changed the onsweeping tide of sentiment for revenge and cruelty, that the Moral and the Spiritual have taken the throne and the nation has been saved.

This has never been more clearly demonstrated than during the past two decades. A great moral issue was to be brought before the people; one that would require the combined effort of all right-minded and thinking people, those who love God and their fellow-men; one that when the object was gained, would mean more to the homes of the Nation by the way of peace, happiness, and prosperity, than all other measures except the religion of the Lord Jesus Christ.

Then was it a strange thing that the women of the nation heard the call and obeyed the summons as coming from the Lord Jehovah? The hearts of the women were quick to respond because of the great burden which was upon them—they felt that relief must come or they die.

One after another of their precious loved ones was being taken from them and hurled into a drunkard's grave by the cruel liquor traffic, remorseless and as unfeeling as hell itself. The mothers, wives, and sisters could only turn their tear-filled eyes toward that God who has said, "ask and it shall be given," for there seemed to be no help in man. So when the fullness of time came, the fire was kindled which has sent a circle of light around the world.

In December, 1873, the gleam shot across the sky from Ohio. With eyes watching and waiting for the signal, with glad hearts we saw the gleam, and falling upon our knees, thanked our Heavenly Father that we could bring material to help continue the fire which had so recently been started.

Immediately, in many parts of the state prayer circles were formed, saloons were visited, public sentiment became aroused, and much good work done. In Ashland, the women were ill-treated by the saloon element and red paint was thrown upon them, spoiling their garments.

Not willing that this work should be lost as soon as active crusade work was over we began organizing societies but without name only as each one called their organization by such name as pleased them best.

As much of our early records were lost, I do not know which was the first organization, so in this history I cannot give the preference as I would like to do.

In the summer of 1875, after reading all that I could find concerning the work in other states, I grew very restless because we were not doing as other states were. I felt that we had no way of communicating with the societies which we already had in Nebraska, no concert of action, no systematic plan of work, and that under such circumstances, little would be accomplished.

I was sure then, as now, that God had called the women into this work, and that the command was to go forward. I would think upon it by day, and it was in my night visions, till I could see no rest. The words that . . . unceasingly rang in my ears were, "call the State together and organize it." I kept this matter buried in my own heart, feeling that I was not the one to make the call, until I could do so no longer and be at rest in my mind.

Early in August, I wrote Mrs. Slaughter to inform the Unions south of Lincoln, and I would those north and east of Lincoln, to meet in the Capital City to organize a State Woman's Christian Temperance Union.

The date was fixed for October 13–14, 1875. Miss Hattie R. Slaughter acting as secretary. We met in the Congregational Church at 2:30 P.M. There were but four regular delegates present. . . .

The address of welcome was given by Mrs. Angie F. Newman of Lincoln. Response by Mrs. Mary A. Hitchcock of Blair. The evening session consisted of singing by the Juvenile Templars, an essay by Mrs. Hitchcock, and short speeches. . . .

Thursday morning, the committee on permanent organization reported the . . . officers for the ensuing year.

The committee on resolutions offered the following, which were adopted:

Resolved, That the resolution of the National Temperance Union, expressive of the general spirit of our organization be adopted as the sense of this convention. Viz.:

Resolved, That recognizing the fact that our cause is, and will be combatted by mighty, determined and relentless forces, we will, trusting in Him who is the Prince of Peace, meet argument with argument, misjudgements with patience, denunciation with kindness, all difficulties and dangers with prayers.

Resolved, That we will pray and labor for the reform of the drunkard and tippler, yet we feel that our great work is with the youth to guard and prevent their falling into temptation.

To this end, we call upon every public teacher, and Sabbath school worker to assist us in our labor of love.

Resolved, That we look upon the beverage use of intoxicating liquors as a sin, and we call upon the clergy of the state to frequently preach against this most heinous practice.

Resolved, That in view of the fact that we look to God for guidance in this great work, we appoint a day of fasting and prayer once a quarter, to be observed by all the unions in the state.

Courtesy Nebraska State Historical Society, Lincoln, Nebraska.

TOPICS FOR WRITTEN OR ORAL EXPLORATION

1. Write an essay in which you explain why, in your opinion, Ántonia preferred men's work to women's work.

2. Pretend you are a pioneer on the plains during the nineteenth century. Create a mock journal in which you describe your daily life over a two-week span of time.

3. Write an essay describing the ways in which Marie Shabata *(O Pioneers!)* is a typical pioneer woman and the ways in which she is not.

4. Mrs. Bergson, Alexandra's mother, and Mrs. Shimerda, Ántonia's mother, are both similar to and different from each other. Discuss their similarities and differences in class.

5. Pretend you are a settler on the plains and write a mock letter to your relatives back home, updating them on your new life.

6. In *My Ántonia*, Lena Lingard describes marriage and motherhood in very negative terms. Write an essay that supports or refutes the following assertion: Lena Lingard becomes a successful businesswoman precisely because she rejects the traditional female roles of wife and mother.

7. Ántonia creates a scandal when she runs off with Larry Donovan and returns pregnant and unmarried. Would such a situation cause a scandal today? Express your opinions in a class discussion.

8. On the plains there was a clear division between "men's work" and "women's work." Although the distinction between them is not quite as clear today, many people still refuse to embrace the idea that any job is suitable for a woman who is willing and able to do it. Pick a job that you believe many people see as unsuitable for a woman and write a paper defending a woman's decision to pursue it.

9. In both *O Pioneers!* and *My Ántonia*, Cather sometimes describes the land in masculine terms and sometimes in feminine. Find examples of each and discuss the possible reasons for Cather's use of either masculine or feminine descriptions in each specific case.

10. Alexandra's brothers, Oscar and Lou, are often both embarrassed and perturbed by their sister. How much does their discomfort have to do with the fact that Alexandra is a woman? Would they be as upset with her if she were their brother instead of their sister? Defend your opinion in an essay.

SUGGESTIONS FOR FURTHER READING AND WORKS CITED

Armitage, Susan, and Elizabeth Jameson, eds. *The Women's West*. Norman: University of Oklahoma Press, 1987.

Brown, Dee. *The Gentle Tamers: Women of the Old Wild West*. New York: Bantam, 1958.

Cherny, Robert W. "Nebraska, 1883–1925: Cather's Version and History's." *Willa Cather: Family, Community, and History*. Ed. John J. Murphy. Provo: Brigham Young University Humanities Publications Center, 1990. 229–38.

Dick, Everett. *The Sod-House Frontier*. New York: D. Appleton-Century, 1937.

Farragher, John Mack. *Women and Men on the Overland Trail*. New Haven, Conn.: Yale University Press, 1979.

Foner, Eric, and John A. Garraty, eds. *The Reader's Companion to American History*. Boston: Houghton Mifflin, 1991.

Myres, Sandra L. *Westering Women and the Frontier Experience, 1800–1915*. Albuquerque: University of New Mexico Press, 1982.

Read, Georgia Willis. "Women and Children on the Oregon-California Trail in the Gold-Rush Years." *Missouri Historical Review* 39 (October 1944): 1023.

Riley, Glenda. *The Female Frontier*. Lawrence: University Press of Kansas, 1988.

———. *Frontierswomen: The Iowa Experience*. Ames: Iowa State University Press, 1981.

Royce, Sarah. *A Frontier Lady: Recollections of the Gold Rush and Early California*. Ed. Ralph Henry Gabriel. Lincoln: University of Nebraska Press, 1932.

Schlissel, Lillian. *Women's Diaries of the Westward Journey*. New York: Schocken Books, 1982.

Schlissel, Lillian, Byrd Gibbons, and Elizabeth Hampsten. *Far from Home: Families of the Westward Journey*. New York: Schocken Books, 1989.

Stewart, Elinore Pruitt. *Letters of a Woman Homesteader*. Boston: Houghton Mifflin, 1914.

Woodress, James. *Willa Cather: A Literary Life*. Lincoln: University of Nebraska Press, 1987.

Wyman, Walker D. *Frontier Woman: The Life of a Woman Homesteader on the Dakota Frontier*. River Falls: University of Wisconsin–River Falls Press, 1972.

Young, Carrie. *Nothing to Do but Stay: My Pioneer Mother*. New York: Delta, 1991.

6

The Disappearance of the Family Farm

For most of their history, Americans assumed that their civilization rested on a way of life that is now disappearing. That way of life was the family farm, which was at once an economic, social, and political ideal—an ideal the federal government once went out of its way to promote. Many American authors, like Hamlin Garland *(Main-Travelled Roads)*, John Steinbeck *(The Grapes of Wrath)*, Richard Wright *(Uncle Tom's Children)*, and Zora Neale Hurston *(Mules and Men)* also celebrate the family farm—or attack its alternatives. They describe those alternatives—tenant farming, migrant labor, and sharecropping—as forms of exploitation, the implication being that farming one's own land equals freedom. The view that the family farm is bound up with the American ideal of freedom, independence, and self-reliance is one that Willa Cather presents directly and positively in both *O Pioneers!* and *My Ántonia*. Perhaps the least-noticed major change in American society since her time is that the way of life that she, and many others, thought almost synonymous with that ideal has virtually disappeared and is now beyond the experience of the vast majority of Americans.

To understand why the ideal of the family farm was so important to Americans, it is essential to recognize how differently farming was organized in the "old country." Most Americans came from

European nations where the vast majority of farmers did not themselves own the land they worked. Rather, most had been tenants and had farmed land owned by the aristocratic class. That they were not "freeholders" meant that they were economically dependent on the nobility and the "landed gentry." It meant that they were politically dependent on them, as well. Where farmers could vote, during this time before the secret ballot, a vote against landlords could mean the loss of their farms. The ownership of one's own land, therefore, came to be seen as a good in itself, as inextricably bound up with freedom. As we are told by the narrator of *O Pioneers!*, "John Bergson had the Old-World belief that land, in itself, is desirable" (148). Having a lawful claim on a piece of land became one of the exemplars of American democracy, since without such a claim and the economic independence it brought with it, a man could not freely cast his vote according to his own conscience.

In American culture, the family farm has been associated with the most democratic parts of our political tradition. The whole idea of "Jeffersonian democracy" was based on the "yeoman farmer"—*yeoman* being the British term for a farmer who owned the land he worked, rather than working the land of another or living on rent paid by tenants, like a "gentleman." The less democratic forces, such as the Federalists in Jefferson's day, have been associated not with the family farm but with commerce, industry, or large-scale farming. The same belief that political franchise depended on land ownership underlay the call to provide all freed slaves after the Civil War with "forty acres and a mule," and many would say that the relegation of freedmen to the status of sharecroppers made it possible for southern states to deny black Americans their political rights until the 1960s.

With one major exception, the treatment of African Americans, and at least after democratic forces triumphed during the Jacksonian era, the government of the United States supported the notion that land ownership was the basis of democracy. That support for the yeoman farmer was made clearest by the Homestead Act of 1862. Rather than allowing the vast territories it was opening to white settlement to be purchased, the government gave them away freely, but only in lots of limited size (160 acres) and only to those who were willing to "improve" them—that is, to turn them into working farms. The act was evidence of the belief that to be a democracy, America had to be a nation of freeholders and not, like class-ridden Europe, a nation of landed gentry and tenant farmers. When Abraham Lincoln founded the U.S. Department of Agriculture in 1862, he declared its purpose to be the dissemination of useful agricultural information to all citizens. But to him the new agency was more than a useful bureaucracy. He referred to it as "the people's department," envisioning that widespread ownership of land and broadly based production of food would help ensure that "government of the people, by the people, and for the people" would remain strong in America.

Many would say, however, that the Department of Agriculture has been less than successful in the mission Lincoln envisioned for it. From his time to the present day, the USDA has produced one complicated farm policy after the other. The ostensible purpose of these policies has remained fairly constant: to support family-sized farms and to ensure farmers livable incomes by limiting the amounts of various crops produced on their lands (reducing the size of a crop tends to raise the price it brings) and by bolstering the markets for those crops. In practice, in contrast, from around 1930 on policies like farm subsidies and price supports mostly enriched large farmers at the expense of small ones. The government would set prices for the different crops raised by farmers and then pay farmers to leave a certain percentage of their land unplanted. When the crops were harvested on the remaining acres of planted land, the farmers would not receive less than the "support price" that had been set by the government. The reason that this kind of government intervention contributed to the death of the smaller family farm is explained by farm policy analyst Ingolf Vogeler:

> The larger producers are, the higher their total yields are and the more public assistance they have received. Thus, the net impact of public policy from the 1930s to the 1970s was to encourage farm size increase. Whereas farm subsidies have been defended to the nation as a means of preserving the political and social values of small-scale family farming, this kind of farming [consistently] declined. . . . In the 1930s there were hungry people and desperate farmers, but the U.S. government did not put the latter to work feeding the former. Instead, the United States adopted a policy of planned governmentally subsidized scarcity, which helped drive

family farmers and tenant farmers off the land, made people dependent on federal food handouts, and contributed mightily to the
growth of agribusiness. Over the years these farm programs have
continued the trend toward large-scale farming by disproportion-
ately benefiting these operators. (163)

While government policy ensured that farmers remained dependent on the government, which set their prices and determined
whether it would be more profitable to plant crops or leave the
land fallow, farmers became ever less able to influence the government. Farmers had once had great political influence, both through
the political parties and through organizations such as the Grange.
In addition, the sheer numbers of farmers gave them a good deal
of influence. Cather's two novels depict a world of virtually nothing but farmers, and except for those few who are described as
unable to make a go of it, like Carl Linstrum's family, they wielded
quite a large degree of power. But by the last quarter of the twentieth century much of that influence had evaporated, primarily because of the decreasing farm population. Put most simply, many
Americans were more interested in low food prices than in high
commodity prices. Even with the structural advantages (notably the
equal representation of all states, including the sparsely populated
agricultural ones, in the U.S. Senate) that gave farmers representation beyond their numbers in Congress, farmers' concerns carried less and less weight in the national debate.

Finally, the influence of money on American politics left the
small farmer at a profound disadvantage. The agribusiness lobbies
were in a much better position to contribute to political campaigns
than were the representatives of small-scale farmers, and therefore,
not surprisingly, the interests of these agribusiness lobbies were
more often reflected in legislation.

For all these reasons, the family farm became increasingly less
viable as an economic institution, even while it remained an important cultural icon. In the 1980s, when masses of Americans finally realized that farming as a way of life was disappearing even
as agriculture as an industry was growing, there was an astounding
outpouring of collective grief, even among people who had never
lived the farm life themselves. The news on television and in the
newspapers became increasingly grim as banks across the country
foreclosed on one farm after another. The number of suicides in

the farm belt rose markedly as desperate farmers succumbed to the stress and grief associated with losing what was to them a way of life, much more than merely a job. The murder rate in these areas increased as well. Some farmers focused all their anger on their local bankers, who refused to give them any more loans. One of the most widely reported stories was that of the murders of two bankers in Ruthton, Minnesota, on September 29, 1983, by two farmers, a father and a son, who supposedly had been driven to desperation by poverty and the prospect of losing their farm. A similar tragedy occurred in Johnson County, Iowa, on December 9, 1985, when an indebted farmer killed the local banker and then himself. Stories like these became common throughout the farm belt and were widely reported.

Many Americans reacted to the scenes they saw on television or read about in the newspaper either with numb disbelief or with horror and outrage. Admittedly, there were many Americans who were perfectly indifferent to the plight of the family farmer, but it is safe to say that the majority of people had some level of aware-ness that the demise of the family farm was deeply significant and disturbing, that it meant the end of the very way of life on which American democracy had been based.

Even the entertainment industry directed its attention to the farm crisis during the 1980s. Many artists used their considerable influence and visibility to try to save the family farm. In 1985, cer-tain popular singers and songwriters—Willie Nelson, Neil Young, Bob Dylan, and others—organized the first-ever "Farm Aid Con-cert." It took place in Champaign, Illinois, on September 22, draw-ing a crowd of eighty thousand people and raising over seven million dollars for assistance to family farmers *(Farm Aid)*. The concert is still held annually, and all evidence suggests that the tradition will continue.

Moviemakers, too, did their part to keep the spotlight on the farm crisis. In 1984 alone, Hollywood released three major movies about distressed farmers. Two of them—*Country*, starring Jessica Lange and Sam Shepard, and *The River*, starring Sissy Spacek and Mel Gibson—were set in the 1980s; the third, *Places in the Heart*, was set in the 1930s. All three showed the main characters strug-gling to hold on to their farms. Although these movies reflected the agony of the loss of the farm in sometimes sentimental and self-aggrandizing ways, they did achieve their goal of keeping the farm crisis fully in the public eye. Whatever one thinks of these efforts, either as works of charity or of art, the fact that people responded to them shows that many—including those who had never set foot on a working farm—saw the disappearance of the family farm as a real, almost personal, loss.

The outpouring of sorrow was only to be expected, for the power of the cultural ideal of the family farm has been, and continues to be, a strong one in America, even while real farms have been disappearing. Even though today very few Americans have any connection to farming in reality, the strength of the ideal is obvious. Evidence can be found in many works, both of literary and popular culture, in which the innocence and wholesomeness of the farm is contrasted with the corruption and evil of the city. To this day, most Americans can hum tunes from *Oklahoma!* and recall the books in the *Little House on the Prairie* series or episodes from the television version of those books; television advertisements for dairy products nearly always depict farm scenes, complete with red barns, silos, and grazing cows. Similar scenes are still often found on cardboard milk cartons. When Kellogg's or Post buys air time to sell Americans breakfast cereal, viewers often see as a backdrop fields of golden oats or wheat waving in the breeze under a blue American sky. Consider that one of our most beloved patriotic songs, "America the Beautiful," gives us phrases like "amber waves of grain" and "the fruited plain" as images of God's special blessings meant specifically for America. These phrases are unquestionably part of the national consciousness, and they are still associated in Americans' minds with the family, not the corporate, farm.

Of course, one of the things that made the end of the family farm so poignant was that at one time the ideal had, in fact, been a reality. America had been successful in creating the nation of yeoman farmers that Jefferson envisioned. In 1910, there were 6,366,000 farms for a population of 91,972,266, or about one farm for every fourteen Americans (USDA). In 1990, by contrast, there were 2,143,150 farms for a population of 246,081,000, or one farm for approximately every 115 Americans (USDA).

By the last decade of the century, then, America had all but abandoned its long-held ideal—and had undergone a good deal of trauma in the process. The idea of escaping the city for the life of the farm, once a real possibility, had become merely a pipe dream, possible only as a pastime for dilettantes. The "back to the land" movement, which started in the 1960s and was associated with the counterculture, was never very large and was never an important part of food production, whatever pleasure or enlightenment it may have brought to those who briefly played at working the soil.

That fewer people were living on the farm was by no means the only change. The lives of those few Americans who still made their livings from agriculture had changed dramatically. Fewer and fewer of them were the small freeholders who had been the mainstay of democracy in the view of Jefferson and his fellows. While the traditional plantation or the sharecropping system of the Old South had also been displaced by history, the ownership of agricultural land became more concentrated than it had ever been. Agribusinesses were created when certain corporations that dominated the processing of food moved from the control of milling, meat-packing, canning, and the cooking and packaging of "prepared foods" to the management and ownership of the farms themselves. Because of their size and vertical integration—that is, the fact that they controlled not just how the food was grown but also how it was processed, marketed, and sold—these corporations became competitors that small-scale farmers could never hope to defeat.

Corporations, of course, have "deep pockets" and can weather economic problems that would sink an individual farmer. Therefore, every disruption of the agricultural marketplace in the second half of the twentieth century led to a further consolidation of farming in the hands of corporate interests—or of the larger privately held operations. Such disruptions included the sorts of problems farmers have always faced: droughts or floods, plant and animal diseases, insect infestations, and ironically, the fall in the price of crops that results from bountiful harvests. Any of those misfortunes can lead to the sort of cash-flow problems that can only be solved by selling the one form of capital the family farmer has—the land itself.

Selling the land, in fact, actually became an increasingly attractive option, for during this period the price of most agricultural land rose—and that of land with any prospect of development for suburban housing soared. Besides tempting farmers to sell, rising land prices also meant the added burden of higher property taxes for those who remained in agriculture. Farmers who hoped to meet the competition of larger interests by increasing their own operations often faced a double bind. On one hand, they invested heavily in expanding their own land holdings and in updating their traditional farm implements with state-of-the-art machinery, found themselves heavily indebted as a result, and then were forced to sell everything when, because of one crisis or another, they were unable to make the payments on their loans. On the other hand, the produce of a small farm could no longer support a family—or even pay for the machinery then required—so that those who did not borrow to become larger operators would almost inevitably have to sell out.

The consolidation of farm holdings into the hands of fewer and fewer entities—many of them not individuals or families but corporations—was much more culturally traumatic than the same kind of consolidation in other areas of life. It is true that at the same time the family farm was disappearing, many other small-scale operations were vanishing from the American landscape as well. The "mom and pop" grocery store gave way to the chain supermarket, especially in suburban areas (although it did re-appear as the bodega or Korean market in many urban areas). Many intellectuals lamented the closing of independent booksellers, even as they bought their own books from Barnes & Noble, Borders, or Amazon.com. Even banks consolidated, until the local banker was no longer an independent local arbiter of credit but the agent of a corporation headquartered in a distant city. But none of these institutions, no matter what affection or respect people felt for them, had the cultural significance of the family farm, for the small farm means something that no other institution can. It unites several things that are deeply important to American notions of identity, things that may be found in other parts of the culture, but never in so pure a form. These are personal independence, family heritage, and connection with the one's country, both in the sense of one's nation and of one's land.

While in America the idea of the individual ownership of farmland reached its height in the era of Jeffersonian democracy, it had been there from the very beginnings of colonial America. Even though some colonies, including Pennsylvania and Maryland, began as private operations in the hands of single "proprietors," large-scale systems of tenant farming became established only rarely in colonial America. When they did, as in the "patroon" system of the Hudson Valley, it was considered a victory for American

democracy when they were dismantled. The continental government rewarded veterans of the War of Independence with land
grants, making clear the link between personal independence
through land ownership and national independence.

The link between the two ideals has an even deeper resonance.
Whatever later elements enriched it, American culture is at its roots
the culture of the Puritans. They came to America to create a society where they could worship God as they chose (albeit also,
admittedly, to prevent others from exercising the same option).
Their model of church government (congregationalism) and the
political ideal to which it gave rise (republicanism) were mirrored
in their arrangement of landholding—that is, one with many small
freeholders. The landlord-and-tenant system, with its echoes of the
feudal system, in which all land had been ultimately held in fief
from the king, was despised by the Puritans, because it echoed the
government of the established Church of England, whose ministers
were appointed by bishops, who were themselves appointed by
the king.

The Puritans saw themselves as the Children of Israel, leaving
the slavery of Egypt on an "errand into the wilderness," and their
methods of landholding echoed what the biblical Israelites created
in the Promised Land. In the Old Testament, the very image of
injustice is the consolidation of landholding. It is one of the great
evils the prophet Isaiah denounces: "Woe unto them that join
house to house, that lay field to field, till there be no place, that
they may be placed alone in the midst of the earth!" (Isaiah 5:8).
With the disappearance of the family farm, Americans lost the institution that had been since their earliest times and in their most
sacred documents the emblem of the freedom, independence, and
justice they cherished.

Second, it meant a loss of heritage. The family farm, more than
any other institution in the nation, linked one generation to its
predecessors and its successors. This intergenerational link is always true of landowners. In Europe, where land was held primarily
by aristocrats, it was the aristocrats who recalled their descent
through generations and planned for the future. They often took
their very names and titles from the land. Aristocratic names often
mark someone as being *of* a place, as in the French *de* and the
German *von*, rather than directly designating a family. The landless, who until recent centuries bore no family names, kept much

scantier records of their descent and had, in turn, little to pass on. In America, every landowning family, even if the holding was no more than a hardscrabble farm, had the same sort of heritage as that of the European aristocrat. Many farms were worked for five generations and more by the same family, and the tales of homesteading and the struggles of great-great-grandparents were carefully recorded. As families with that sort of heritage had to sell out, all of America felt an increase in the restlessness and *angst* that already marked so much of its culture. That is, as the family farm has disappeared, the sense of uprootedness, of being from no place in particular, has only increased, even for those to whom the family farm was a reality they contemplated only from a distance.

Finally, the link to the land as nation is weakened when the link with the *literal* land is no longer personal. A good example of that connection as it was understood in the past can be found in two of the great patriotic poems of American history, Ralph Waldo Emerson's "Concord Hymn," which he read at the dedication of the Concord Battle Monument in 1837, and Robert Frost's "The Gift Outright," which he read at the inauguration of President John F. Kennedy in 1961. Emerson emphasizes that the heroes of the American Revolution were not soldiers primarily but farmers: "Here once the embattled farmers stood / And fired the shot heard round the world." He also emphasizes the heritage that connects the generations, both past and future, a memory of which doubtless helped "those heroes dare / To die and leave their children free." In "The Gift Outright" Frost declares, "The land was ours before we were the land's," and he describes the way colonials made themselves Americans by giving themselves to the land. The implication is that Americans became citizens of their country through the effort they poured into its soil. That effort, of course, was made most directly by its farmers, and they alone kept the memory of that effort, acre by acre.

Considering all the changes that America has undergone in the last century, it is difficult to ascribe with certainty any particular social problem directly to the loss of the family farm. But that does not mean we would be wrong to wonder about the effects of that loss. Certainly the defenders of the family farm can correlate its disappearance with the rise of many social ills. Traditionally, social standards were maintained not primarily by law but by the knowledge that people's actions would be judged by their neighbors and remembered, for better or worse, into their children's time—and their grandchildren's. Once the tie to a single place—a single community—is cut, that natural mechanism of social control is lost. The very restlessness of Americans, expressed in their frequent moves from one community to another and even in their high divorce rate (things that can also be seen as the result of a loss of connection to land and place), clearly gives rise to a society where no one is directly responsible for anything and therefore no one need keep up a good name. Many would argue that the rise in crime and juvenile delinquency is a natural result.

These apologists for the family farm also point out that the consolidation of farm holdings leads to environmental destruction. While small farmers have not always been models of environmental purity, large-scale operators are even worse. A family farmer is almost forced to have at least some sense of stewardship; he must not spoil the land he will pass along to his children. A corporate farmer has no such commitment to the future. An eye to the next quarterly earnings report may lead such owners to farm in ways that will deplete the land in years to come—to say nothing of leaving it less beautiful, less habitable. That second sort of destruction is not at all uncommon. The consolidation of farmland, the impulse to turn larger and larger areas into a single field that can be worked with huge machines, leads to the destruction of the wetlands, areas of scrub, and woodlots that provide visual interest to the landscape, habitat for wild animals, and even living areas for bees and other pollinators on which agriculture itself relies. Some forms of large-scale farming also produce unmanageable amounts of waste. In several states, pig farms have reached sizes where their runoff can destroy all life in nearby streams and the stench of their sewage ponds blights the area for miles around.

Finally, we might wonder if, as the ideal of a nation of yeoman farmers disappears, the democracy that that social system was meant to underpin has itself been endangered. Some argue that it has. Here, perhaps, consolidation in areas other than farming is as important as that in agriculture, but it is most notable in farming. Where there were once many, many Americans who were "independent," in the sense that they worked for no one but themselves, there are now many fewer, proportionally. The farmer, who was independent even in growing his own food, was the purest example of that group, but the local banker, the owner of the small grocery or pharmacy, had some measure of independence too. Now, many of the economic decisions that affect Americans every day are made in distant cities. The man or woman who decides that a store or plant will close often lives a thousand miles away. Further, if in politics money is power, that money has been concentrated in fewer hands. Clearly American democracy goes on, but we should perhaps be at least uncomfortable that in our economic lives, fewer and fewer of us are yeomen and more and more of us are the retainers of the great magnates. These magnates are now corporations rather than individual aristocrats, but the fact remains that the control of our economic destiny is in the hands of others.

The farms in Cather's novels are idyllic, but they are not idealized. They feature much hard work, heartbreak, and failure. Disappointment drives one of her farmers, Mr. Shimerda, to suicide. But her fictional farms are depictions of what real farms once were to generations of Americans, and are no longer: real chances to be perfectly independent, to shape your own destiny, and to pass on as a legacy to your descendants the fruit of your labors, your place in the community, and perhaps most importantly, the land itself.

THE HISTORY OF AMERICAN AGRICULTURE: A TIMELINE

The following United States Department of Agriculture statistics show how the farm population has declined steadily since the late eighteenth century. Although the American public did not panic about these diminishing numbers until the mid-1980s, it is easy to see that the crisis was a long time in the making.

FROM U.S. DEPARTMENT OF AGRICULTURE, *HISTORY OF AMERICAN AGRICULTURE, 1776–1990: FARMERS AND THE LAND* (2001)

17th century

Small land grants commonly made to individual settlers; large tracts often granted to well-connected colonists.

18th century

English farmers settled in New England villages; Dutch, German, Swedish, Scotch-Irish, and English farmers settled on isolated Middle Colony farmsteads; English and some French farmers settled on plantations in tidewater and on isolated Southern Colony farmsteads in Piedmont; Spanish immigrants, mostly lower middle-class and indentured servants, settled the Southwest and California.

1776

Continental Congress offered land grants for service in the Continental Army.

1785, 1787

Ordinances of 1785 and 1787 provided for survey, sale, and government of northwestern lands.

1790

Total population: 3,929,214

Farmers made up about 90% of labor force.

The U.S. area settled extended westward an average of 255 miles; parts of the frontier crossed the Appalachians.

1790–1830

Sparse immigration into the United States, mostly from the British Isles.

1796

Public Land Act of 1796 authorized Federal land sales to the public in minimum 640-acre plots at $2 per acre of credit.

1800

Total population: 5,308,483

1803

Louisiana Purchase

1810

Total population: 7,239,881

1819

Florida and other land acquired through treaty with Spain

1820

Total population: 9,638,453

Land Law of 1820 allowed purchasers to buy as little as 80 acres of public land for a minimum price of $1.25 an acre; credit system abolished.

1830

Total population: 12,866,020

The Mississippi River formed the approximate frontier boundary.

1830–37

Land speculation boom

1839

Anti-rent war in New York, a protest against the continued collection of quitrents

1840

Total population: 17,069,453
Farm population: 9,012,000 (estimated)
Farmers made up 69% of labor force.

1841

Preemption Act gave squatters first rights to buy land.

1845–55

The potato famine in Ireland and the German Revolution of 1848 greatly increased immigration.

1845–53

Texas, Oregon, the Mexican cession, and the Gadsden Purchase were added to the Union.

1849

Gold Rush. [With it] the frontier bypassed the Great Plains and the Rockies and moved to the Pacific coast.

1850

Total population: 23,191,786
Farm population: 11,680,000 (estimated)
Farmers made up 64% of labor force
Number of farms: 1,449,000
Average acres: 203

1850's

Successful farming on the prairies began.

1850–62

Free land was a vital rural issue.

1854

Graduation Act reduced price of unsold public lands.

1859–75

The miners' frontier moved eastward from California toward the westward-moving farmers' and ranchers' frontier.

1860

Total population: 31,443,321

Farm population: 15,141,000 (estimated)

Farmers made up 58% of labor force

Number of farms: 2,044,000

Average acres: 199

1862

Homestead Act granted 160 acres to settlers who had worked the land 5 years.

1865–70

The sharecropping system in the South replaced the old slave plantation system.

1865–90

Influx of Scandinavian immigrants

1866–77

Cattle boom accelerated settlement of Great Plains; range wars developed between farmers and ranchers.

1870

Total population: 38,558,371

Farm population: 18,373,000 (estimated)

Farmers made up 53% of labor force

Number of farms: 2,660,000

Average acres: 153

1880

Total population: 50,155,783

Farm population: 22,981,000 (estimated)

Farmers made up 49% of labor force.

Number of farms: 4,009,000

Average acres: 134

1880's

Heavy agricultural settlement on the Great Plains began.

1880

Most humid land already settled

1880–1914

Most immigrants were from southeastern Europe.

1887–97

Drought reduced settlement on the Great Plains.

1890

Total population: 62,941,714
Farm population: 29,414,000 (estimated)
Farmers made up 43% of labor force.
Number of farms: 4,565,000
Average acres: 136

1890's

Increases in land under cultivation and number of immigrants becoming farmers caused great rise in agricultural output.

1890

Census showed that the frontier settlement era was over.

1900

Total population: 75,994,266
Farm population: 29,414,000 (estimated)
Farmers made up 38% of labor force.
Number of farms: 5,740,000
Average acres: 147

1900–20

Continued agricultural settlement on the Great Plains

1902

Reclamation Act

1905–07

Policy of reserving timberlands inaugurated on a large scale

1910

Total population: 91,972,266

Farm population: 32,077,00 (estimated)

Farmers made up 31% of labor force

Number of farms: 6,366,000

Average acres: 138

1909–20

Dryland farming boom on the Great Plains

1911–17

Immigration of agricultural workers from Mexico

1916

Stock Raising Homestead Act

1920

Total population: 105,710,620

Farm population: 31,614,269 (estimated)

Farmers made up 27% of labor force.

Number of farms: 6,454,000

Average acres: 148

1924

Immigration Act greatly reduced number of new immigrants.

1930

Total population: 122,775,046

Farm population: 30,455,350 (estimated)

Farmers made up 21% of labor force.

Number of farms: 6,295,000

Average acres: 157

Irrigated acres: 14,633,252

1932–36

Drought and dust-bowl conditions developed.

1934

Executive orders withdrew public lands from settlement, location, sale, or entry.

Taylor Grazing Act

1940

Total population: 131,820,000

Farm population: 30,840,000 (estimated)

Farmers made up 18% of labor force.

Number of farms: 6,102,000

Average acres: 175

Irrigated acres: 17,942,968

1940's

Many former southern sharecroppers migrated to war-related jobs in cities.

1950

Total population: 151,132,000

Farm population: 25,058,000 (estimated)

Farmers made up 12.2% of labor force.

Number of farms: 5,388,000

Average acres: 216

Irrigated acres: 25,634,869

1956

Legislation passed providing for Great Plains Conservation Program

1960

Total population: 180,007,000

Farm population: 15,635,000 (estimated)

Farmers made up 8.3% of labor force.

Number of farms: 3,711,000

Average acres: 303

Irrigated acres: 33,829,000

1960's

State legislation increased to keep land in farming.

1964

Wilderness Act

1965

Farmers made up 6.4% of labor force.

1970

Total population: 204,335,000

Farm population: 9,712,000 (estimated)

Farmers made up 4.6% of labor force.

Number of farms: 2,780,000

Average acres: 390

1980

Total population: 227,020,000

Farm population: 6,051,00

Farmers made up 3.4% of labor force.

Number of farms: 2,439,510

Average acres: 426

Irrigated acres: 50,350,000 (1978)

1980's

For the first time since the 19th century, foreigners (Europeans and Japanese primarily) began to purchase significant acreages of farm-land and ranchland.

1986

The Southeast's worst summer drought on record took a severe toll on many farmers.

1987

Farmland values bottomed out after a 6-year decline, signalling both a turnaround in the farm economy and increased competition with other countries' exports.

1988

Scientists warned that the possibility of global warming might affect the future viability of American farming.

1988

One of the worst droughts in the Nation's history hit Midwestern farmers.

1990

Total population: 246,081,000

Farm population: 4,591,000

Farmers made up 2.6% of labor force.

Number of farms: 2,143,150

Average acres: 461

Irrigated acres: 46,386,000 (1987)

USDA Web site: www.usda.gov/history2/text3.htm.

DEBUNKING THE ROMANTIC MYTH OF THE FAMILY FARM

It must be admitted that not everyone who lived and worked on a family farm mourned its passing. Some, in fact, believe that the tendency of many Americans to romanticize farm life has prevented them from seeing its harsh realities and from even considering the possibility that being driven off the farm might be the best thing that could happen to many families. In the following article, published at the height of the farm crisis in the mid-1980s, Jeffrey L. Pasley makes precisely such a point and attempts to replace Americans' romantic image of farm life with what he views as a more realistic one.

FROM JEFFREY L. PASLEY, "THE IDIOCY OF RURAL LIFE" (1986)

> The bourgeoisie has subjected the country to the rule of the towns. It has created enormous cities, has greatly increased the urban population as compared with the rural, and has thus rescued a considerable part of the population from the idiocy of rural life.
>
> —Marx and Engels, *The Manifesto of the Communist Party*

> If we let Republican farm policies drive our family farmers off the land, then your food won't be grown by farmers whose names are Jones or Smith or Anderson. No, your food will be raised by Tenneco corporation, or Chevron, or ITT.
>
> Senator Tom Harkin, Democrat of Iowa

The idea that people still farm for a living in 1986 is an alien and yet somehow romantic one, redolent of grandparents and "Little House on the Prairie." A 1986 *New York Times* poll reported that 58 percent of Americans believe that "farm life is more honest and moral than elsewhere," and 67 percent think that "farmers have closer ties to their families than elsewhere." Images of rural life dominate the "Americana" that passes for tradition in the United States. At a holiday like Thanksgiving, when we are supposed to give thanks to our Pilgrim ancestors and the "bounty" before us, we pay homage to the values embodied in the idea of the "family farm."

At one time, this reverence for farm life made sense. The United States began as an agricultural nation. In 1790, 93 percent of the American population worked on farms. Agricultural products made up 80 percent of exports. The Founders, knowing which side their breadbasket was buttered on, heaped extravagant praise on the nation's farmers. "Cultivators of the earth are the most valuable citizens," wrote Thomas Jefferson. "They are the most vigorous, the most independent, the most virtuous, & they are tied to the country & wedded to its liberty and interests by the most lasting bonds."

The "family farm" remained a powerful myth long after it ceased to be a political fact. "The great cities rest upon our broad and fertile prairies. Burn down your cities and leave our farms, and your cities will spring up again as if by magic; but destroy our farms and the grass will grow in the streets of every city in the country," thundered Populist leader William Jennings Bryan. Yet as the myth gained strength, Americans were actually leaving the farm by the millions. Though the number of farmers continued to grow until 1920, the cities grew much faster, and the percentage of the American population working in agriculture declined with every census after 1790. . . . As the country grew, it exposed its citizens to creature comforts and other opportunities to prosper more easily, which made it hard to keep the farmers down on the farm. As farmers sold out or quit, those who remained bought up their land. Average farm size increased from 152 acres in 1930 to 441 acres in 1985.

I grew up outside Topeka, Kansas, attended a rural high school that had an Ag-Science building but no auditorium, and graduated from a college in the Minnesota farm country. In my experience, the standard image of the farmer has more to do with urban romanticism than with reality. Yet when the most recent farm crisis hit the nation's front pages and movie screens in 1985, the "family farm" captured the national imagination. Journalists suddenly found the stuff of Greek tragedy in Ames, Iowa. "Beauty is a cruel mask," wrote Paul Hendrickson of the *Washington Post*, "when the earth rolls right up to the edge of the interstate, freshly turned. When the rosebud trees are bleeding into pinks and magentas. When the evening rain is soft as lanolin." And so on.

With the papers full of stories about farmers going out of business, committing suicide, or shooting their bankers, farm-state politicians and activists began to campaign for a program specifically to help "family" farms, a proposal that evolved into the "Save the Family Farm Act." Introduced in October by Harkin and Representative Richard Gephardt of Missouri, the bill would impose mandatory controls on the amount farmers could produce and the extent of land they could farm, and would force larger farmers to set aside a larger percentage of their acreage. The bill would roughly double commodity prices (followed by additional yearly increases), sharply increasing the cost of raw food products. A small price to pay, its proponents say, so that family farmers can afford to maintain their traditional way of life. For supporters of the bill, the question is not primarily economic. On humanitarian grounds, they want to preserve the family farm as a way of life. On social grounds, they want a Jeffersonian countryside of small, independent landowners. Yet when I asked Charles O. Frazier of the National Farmers Organization, which supports the Harkin bill, whether the measure might hurt farmers in the long run, he replied, "To hell with the long run, we're talking about running a business."

Farmers are just like everyone else. They want to make money and live better than their parents did—and better than their neighbors, if possible. Urbanites often confuse the folksy ways of some farmers with an indifference to material wealth and the refinements that it brings. The difference between farmers and city-dwellers lies not in a different attitude toward money, but in different choices about what to spend it on. Washington lawyers want to make money to buy a BMW and a vacation in Paris. The average farmer may prefer a big pick-up truck with floodlights on top and a motor home he can take to Florida for the winter. Indeed, the young farmers who are in the most trouble today got that way by expanding their operations too quickly in the 1970s. Farmers aren't uniquely greedy, just ambitious like any other businesspeople. . . .

The USDA divides farms into five classes: rural residences ("hobby farmers"), small family, family, large family, and very large farms. The farm crisis has left the large and very large family farms relatively untouched. Because of their economies of scale, even when prices drop they can still make a profit. . . .

What the Pa Ingalls fans have in mind are rural residences and small family farms, which usually occupy 300 acres or less. Although these small farmers make up two-thirds of the total, however, they do not depend on agriculture for their living. According to the USDA, their "off-farm income" has exceeded their "on-farm income" ever since 1967. The yeomen of 1986 till the soil only as a sideline, and make 90 percent to 100 percent of their income from jobs or businesses off the farm. So the "farm crisis" isn't impoverishing them. . . .

In fact, just about the only ones really endangered by the current crisis are medium-sized family farmers. . . . Unlike small farmers, who have other sources of income, or large farmers, who have diversified multimillion-dollar operations, the family farmer gets paid only when he sells his crops. In between harvests, he must borrow money if he is to stay in business and feed his family. In no other industry does a worker need to take out loans in order to keep his job.

These family farmers occupy a precarious center between the larger and smaller operations. Their farms are big enough to require full-time work but not big enough to lower costs or allow them to take full advantage of new technology. . . . His high costs relative to his size make his profit margin razor-thin when it exists at all.

Thus medium-sized family farmers rely heavily on the increasing value of their land to help them pay their debts and get new loans. While inflation plagued the rest of the country in the 1970s, family farmers experienced a boom, as food prices and especially land values climbed to unprecedented heights. When inflation slowed down in the 1980s, so did the farm economy, sending land values through the floor. The farmers who invested heavily in new land on the wave of rising values found themselves hopelessly trapped when the values fell. The moral of this tale cannot be missed: those family farmers' fortunes depended not on their farming abilities, but on land values, a factor out of their control. Their ownership of land made them only more dependant. According to the USDA, farmers that leased more land weathered the crisis better, since they had fewer debts to pay at inflated interest rates. The family farmer has always walked this economic treadmill. . . .

How, then, did American family farmers become, in Harkin's words, "the most efficient and productive in the world"? Family farmers can keep labor costs very low because the family provides the bulk of the labor. . . . "[C]hild labor laws do not apply to family farms because family farms must have child labor to survive," wrote Minnesota politician and family farm alumnus Darrell McKigney. . . . From a very early age, family farm children participate in every phase of the operation, from work with dangerous heavy equipment to close contact with carcinogenic chemicals and disease-carrying animals. . . . Practices that would be outrageous at a textile mill suddenly become all warm and cuddly when they appear on the family farm.

Family farmers also achieve efficiency through a draconian work schedule that no self-respecting union would allow. "[T]he farm family does physically demanding and highly stressful work at least 14 hours a day, . . . seven days a week, 365 days a year without a scheduled vacation or weekends off," wrote McKigney. "The farmer must endure all of this without the benefit of a health plan, safety regulations, a retirement plan, workmen's compensation, or any other of the benefits that most U.S. labor unions demand." Peter Keller, past president of the Association for Rural Mental Health, pointed out that many farmers are permanently tied to their farms. A dairy farmer, for instance, cannot just take off for a two-week vacation and not milk his cows. "Farmers lose perspective on the other things in life," said Keller. "The farm literally consumes them."

And the family farm physically consumes those who work on it, too. According to the National Safety Council, farming is the nation's most dangerous job—more dangerous even than working in a mine. . . . Farmers working with powerful farm machinery face death or maiming by crushing, chopping, asphyxiation, or electrocution. . . . They may be poisoned by the nitrogen dioxide gas that accumulates in grain silos, or have their lungs permanently damaged from breathing the air in enclosed hog pens. They may be crippled by "farmer's lung disease," caused by moldy grain dust. They may develop leukemia from contact with herbicides used on corn. (Iowa farmers contract leukemia 24 percent more frequently than the average American.) . . .

But what about the benefits of good-old-fashioned-lemonade values and the supportive friendliness of a rural community? Though hard data is difficult to come by, many small towns appear to suffer from teenage pregnancy, alcoholism, and other social maladies at rates that are higher than average. One New England study showed relatively high suicide rates among farmers during a period antedating the farm crisis. And rural communities haven't always stood by their financially troubled members. . . . At a "town meeting" with Representative Tim Penny, Democrat of Minnesota, in New Market, Minnesota, I heard farmers ridicule the idea of slightly higher property taxes to improve the area's meager school system practically in the same breath that they demanded higher subsidies for themselves. These things never happened on "The Waltons."

The usual lesson gleaned from the facts of farm life is that there is nothing wrong with the family farm that higher commodity prices won't solve. Yet farm programs have come and farm programs have gone, and still farmers (and especially farmers' children) have left, for the simple reason that life is usually better off the farm. "It is a way of life, but so was the village blacksmith," says economist William H. Peterson. The urban "wage-slave" worker, for all his lack of "independence" and supposed alienation from his work, has some decided advantages over the rural yeoman. He has the security of a regular income, and definite hours set aside for his leisure. More often than not, the law guarantees the non-farmer a safe place to work, and protects him from the whims of his employer. The urban wage-earner has daily contact with a wide variety of other people, and access to cultural events and decent public services.

Proponents of Harkin-Gephardt and similar measures worry about where farmers will go once they leave the land. Yet former farmers do not just fade away. They have skills and work habits that many employers find attractive. . . .

I saw the movie *Country* on a rainy Monday night in Topeka. Two farmers and their wives and a group of teenage girls were the only other people in the theater. The farmers complained loudly throughout the first hour of the film, and then left, shaking their heads in disgust. The girls sat through the final credits, sniffling at the plight of Sam Shepard and

Jessica Lange. At a farm protest rally in Minnesota, I heard a song that went like this:

Now some folks say
There ain't no hell
But they don't farm
So they can't tell.

We should take the singer at his word. Tyrants from Stalin to Mao to Pol Pot have subjugated their populations by forcing them to "stay on the land." Given the conditions of life on the family farm, if ITT or Chevron or Tenneco really does try to force some family farmers off their land, they might well be doing them a favor.

The New Republic, December 8, 24–27.

GOVERNMENT HEARINGS ON THE FUTURE OF FAMILY FARMING

On September 6, 1985, a subcommittee of the House of Representatives Committee on Small Business convened to take testimony about the future of the family farm in the United States. Convening in Albany and Perry, Georgia, the subcommittee heard from many different kinds of experts on the farm crisis, including university professors, economists, representatives of agribusinesses, directors of agricultural investment corporations, and, perhaps most importantly, Georgia farmers themselves. The purpose of these hearings was to try to ascertain whether or not America was actually in danger of losing the family farm, and if so, to try to determine what would happen to those farmers who did lose them.

The first statement is by Charles Hatcher, the subcommittee's chairman; the first witness was Garland Thompson, the president of the Georgia Agribusiness Council of Atlanta, Georgia; Donnie Doles was a farmer from Fort Valley, Georgia; and Neal Talton farmed in Bonaire, Georgia. These transcripts are drawn from U.S. House of Representatives, *Hearings before the Subcommittee on Antitrust and Restraint of Trade Activities Affecting Small Business of the Committee on Small Business*, 99th Congress, 1st session, 1985.

FROM CHARLES HATCHER, "THE FUTURE OF FAMILY FARMING"
(1985)

Clearly, there are many problems facing our farmers in south Georgia and throughout the country today. A severe trade imbalance in agriculture, as well as in many other sectors of our economy, highlights the problem our own farmers are having in competing in the world market with an overvalued dollar and oversubsidized foreign commodities. The financial crisis that gripped us in the South some 4 or 5 years ago, has now gripped the Midwest even more severely than it is affecting us right now, perhaps. . . .

We in Congress, I think, should be very careful about making changes that could potentially hurt our farmers. A good example of such a change that I see . . . is President Reagan's proposal to repeal capital gains taxation on timber. This proposal would require timber management expenses to be capitalized rather than deducted as permitted by current law, and it would repeal the special reforestation incentive for small timber owners. Now, I certainly believe that there is room for tax reform in this country, and I hope we will be able to achieve something that will be fairer and simpler this year. However, this particular timber proposal would have a devastating effect on Georgia's economy because its impact would really fall on the small timberland owner. . . .

We have long passed the time, I think, when ignoring the farm problem or applying quick fixes will suffice. Again, that is why we are here today. What are your thoughts and your ideas about the future of family farming in south Georgia, and in the country? Today we will be hearing testimony from a number of different people representing both agricultural and small business interests. I think and hope this will be a very informative meeting not only for those of us here, but for everybody back in Washington, because that is where we expect to take this testimony.

Congressional Hearings. Washington, D.C.: Government Printing Office, 2–3.

FROM GARLAND THOMPSON, "THE FUTURE OF FAMILY FARMING" (1985)

I am employed by the Trust Company Bank of Coffee County in Douglas, which is in a very heavily oriented agrieconomy. I am also serving as president of the Georgia Agribusiness Council, which has over 300 members of the agribusiness firms throughout Georgia. . . .

The noted American poet, Carl Sandburg, once said when a nation or a people perish, one thing can always be found: They forgot where they came from. Many people today are saying that American agriculture is about to perish. So I think maybe we ought to remember where we came from, that is a nation of farmers, and a look back reveals the transition of average farm size that has moved from mostly small to medium-sized farms of the fifties.

There are three types of farm operators in the 1980's. These include, nationally, about 175,000 large commercial farms, 650,000 medium-sized family farms, and 1,450,000 small farms where anywhere from 50 to 85 percent of the income is from off-farm employment and I stress that.

The situation in Georgia is similar to the national picture and the total number of farms here has shrunk to less than 50,000. The average debt load of Georgia farmers increased by 390 percent over the 1970 levels. Georgia farm income as a net percent of gross receipts has fallen from

26 or 27 percent in the mid-seventies to the 13-percent range in the 1980's.

Bankruptcy was a term almost never associated with farming until 3 to 5 years ago, but increased capital needs, loss of foreign markets, high interest rates, adverse weather conditions, along with other problems have changed that and according to information from Iowa State University, approximately 40 percent of American farmers today face problems with debt to asset ratios that range up to 100 percent for at least 10 percent of them. . . .

[I]n the seventies, our nation's exports reached $44 billion. Two of every five acres was being exported. This caused marginal land to be brought into production. In turn, this caused high rents, overbuying of land, equipment and machines. Then came high interest, a strong dollar, cargo preference laws, changes in lending policies, droughts, and a downturn in global economic conditions. All of this caused a reduction in our commodity exports. Hopefully, our markets will be increased by improving as many of these factors as we can.

On credit, one-fourth of Georgia farmers have a Farmers Home loan which amounts to a $1.2 billion in principal alone. Some 5,500 of these over 9,000 loans are delinquent in their payments and it amounts to $700 million and more than 2,000 of these borrowers are not expected to ever meet their obligation. . . .

In the 1950's, commercial banks nationwide made over 50 percent of agriculture loans and this has now decreased to slightly over 20 percent, with many not making any due to the track record of the past few years. Unfortunately, many small banks are located in areas that are totally agriculture oriented which means that it is the only business they have. These are the ones that make up the majority of the 69 that have failed so far this year. Others are expected to close their doors making this a record year for such failures.

In summary, . . . agriculture . . . is too important to be left just to farmers. We do have to have Government involved and at all levels we must have Government making sure that our roads, our railroads, airports, and our ports are in place. Now this can be accomplished by direct Government investment and monetary inducements to the private sector. Transportation is the key to survival in many rural communities.

Tax-exempt loans have been mentioned, and they are being used by many states for loans to farmers as well as agribusiness that add value to our farm products and priority could be given to these . . . businesses and some limitations now could be made for those in existence that could be removed.

Federal crop insurance has saved many farmers from failure and I think it is [something] that can be strengthened and improved and used to protect the majority of our farmers. The availability of these off-farm jobs is the most pressing economic need for some of our small farmers. Again, tax-exempt IRB's [Industrial Revenue Bonds] have brought many jobs to these rural communities which have saved some from being lost. . . .

[Recent] record corn and soybean crops are causing markets that bring farmers less than their cost of production. I think with some Government encouragement there is still a place for gasohol plants. They can use the surplus corn and we can have a renewal fuel that would reduce our output for foreign oil.

Tax writeoffs . . . should not favor the nonfarmer or the hobby farmer at the expense of the full-time farmer. Some farms will again fail to find operating loans for the next crop year. I believe that some help could be given if Farmers Home loans could be made through or in connection with commercial banks, letting the bankers do the paperwork with some type of guarantee by Farmers Home.

At this time, the future for the small family farm looks bleak. It is doubtful that survival will be easy with the outlook being what it is for credit in farm programs in general.

Congressional Hearings. Washington, D.C.: Government Printing Office, 47–49.

FROM DONNIE DOLES, "THE FUTURE OF FAMILY FARMING" (1985)

The question was asked about the future of the family farm. From my perspective, it is pretty dim, awfully dim. And the reason I say that . . . is profit is not in it today, profit is not there. I have done a better job of farming in the past several years. I have upped my production, I have used as good techniques as I know how. I have cut . . . corner[s,] . . . and what have I done? I have contributed to the surplus that . . . others have spoken about. So, surplus and overproduction is one of our main problems and we have got to find some way to control that. . . .

I was averaging about 30 bushels of wheat back in 1975, and now I am averaging 50 bushels of wheat. And . . . I have not benefited from it. Who has benefited? The consumer has benefited from my efforts. The information that I was getting from the people that I borrow money from, magazines, agricultural experts, and all, was that in 1975 we had to feed the world, and we set out to do it, and we are about to break ourselves doing it.

Land values have plummeted. And how that affects me is that it affects my equity in my farm. The last several years, I have probably backed up a little bit. I have not met production costs; therefore I am eating into the equity of my farm, the only thing that I have to retire. I am now 57 years old and I am entitled to a retirement as well as anybody else. . . . But I will not have it if things continue as they are going. It will be eroded away to zero, and a lifetime of work will be for nothing. . . .

I have got three sons. Two of them are interested in farming, and have been. We tried it together. Two of them are now doing something else. The one that was not interested never did try farming. . . . There is no way that I could sell my farm, even give it to them, and they could continue on and make a go of it. That is pretty discouraging.

There is a lot of blame to go around. I blame myself for part of it. I went through some years when I probably should have put some money aside. But we have had lending agencies and others that have encouraged farmers to grow more, to produce more. On the one hand, we have one service or Government agency say you have got to produce more to make a go of it. They have encouraged irrigation in some places, hog houses in other places, renting of land, purchase of equipment. Every single one of these things made the debt load go up and we have not been able to pay off that debt load.

. . . [T]he American . . . farmer has probably done more [to make] this country strong [than anyone else]. We are the breeding places of some of the best folks in the world. . . . I think [the family farm] is worth saving, myself.

Congressional Hearings. Washington, D.C.: Government Printing Office, 107–109.

FROM NEAL TALTON, "THE FUTURE OF FAMILY FARMING" (1985)

I would like to thank you for inviting me to discuss the problems faced by today's family dairyman. My father was in the dairy business for over 25 years. As I was growing up on our dairy farm, I saw my father making a comfortable living for a family of six. I always enjoyed living and working on the farm and hoped one day I could dairy and raise a family of my own on this same farm. In 1980, my father sold his dairy herd so I could enter the dairy business alone. At the age of 21, I got my loan while the dairy farmer was still making a good living. Everything seemed to be looking bright for me, but 5 years later the dairy industry has hit an all-time low.

In these 5 years, I have gotten married and have one son. I would like very much to raise my children on a dairy, but with the current dairy situation, I do not feel I could support a family on my income. Officials have been telling dairymen to hang on for 2 years, and now after 2 years they say hang on for a few more. With the current dairy situation and the near future not pointing in a positive direction, I am fearful of having to leave my dairy and the family farm to look for a new way of life.

[Because I am] a relatively new dairyman, my debt load is higher than a lot older dairymen. As of right now, I am paying all my bills and loans on time. However, if the dairy situation gets any worse, I would be in a real tight bind. Last year, when feed prices climbed so high and my cow numbers were down and cash-flow was low, I got behind on my feed bill and some others were not getting paid on time. Not only was this putting a strain on me, but on my family as well. However, I kept working and my cow numbers got back up, as did my cash-flow, and I caught up on my bills.

With the cash-flow up, the price of milk up somewhat, and feed prices way down, I began to see some daylight. As I see it now, though, milk prices have dropped and will continue to drop because of the big surplus. I also do not feel feed prices can stay this low for an extended period of time. With my present debt load, there is not much difference in what it costs me to produce milk and what I receive for my milk. So, if there is a rise in feed cost or lower milk prices, you can see where that leaves me. . . . I really enjoy what I do for a living but it takes all the enjoyment out when I cannot make a decent living now and the near future looks even worse. Life is too short for all the worry and stress that today's dairyman has to put up with. . . . As to what to do with the large surplus of milk in the dairy industry, I do not have the answer. I do have a couple of opinions or ideas. One is to put a quota on milk. Maybe take a producer's previous 2 or 3 years' milk production and pay top price for base milk and pay a lower price for any milk over his base. The second would be to divide the country into zones or sections.

I do not feel that loaning more money is the answer. By doing this, you are keeping more people in the dairy business and in turn keeping more milk on the market. If I [were] in the situation of needing more money, which I may be in the near future, and I could not pay my existing loans, I would not want more [borrowed] money. The most important reason is I would run the risk of losing the farm that has been in my family over 100 years. The second reason is I do not feel you can borrow yourself out of debt. I also do not think low interest loans for new farmers [are] the answer. Even if a new farmer borrowed money with no interest, it would be almost impossible to pay back with the current dairy situation. We have tried these types of loans before and the only thing I see that it has done was put more milk on the market that would not have been there before. That is one thing we do not need—more milk.

I would also like to say the average age of a dairyman is a lot higher than in the past. We need young dairymen like myself or the family farm will no longer exist. But I can see why a young man would be skeptical [about] enter[ing] the dairy business today. Everything you read and hear about the dairy business is negative. I know if a young man came to me and asked my opinion, I would tell him to find a job in another field. Even if my son were old enough to dairy, I would definitely persuade him against making a career in this business. I know these are sad things to say, but this is how I feel. If I [had known] in 1980 what I know now, I would not even have thought about entering the dairy business or any other field of agriculture. Without new, young farmers, I feel the family farm will eventually be a thing of the past.

This is why I feel corporate farms will slowly take over. I do not feel a corporate farm that relies solely on agriculture as its source of income will fare any [better] than the family farmer. I do feel the corporate farms, with the backing from groups of lawyers, doctors, and foreign investors will survive. But I feel this will be worse for the consumer in the long run because these types of farmers will be less efficient than a farm owned by an individual. [Because they will be] less efficient, these farms will demand a higher price for their products and the consumer will end up footing the bill.

Congressional Hearings. Washington, D.C.: Government Printing Office, 113–117.

THE END OF THE LINE: THIRD AND FOURTH-GENERATION FARMERS TELL THEIR REAL STORIES OF LOSS IN PERSONAL INTERVIEWS

The following two interviews were conducted by the author on December 13 and 14, 2000. Mr. Louis Forbes and his son Steven, third and fourth-generation farmers near Grand Rapids, Michigan, agreed to recount their stories of losing the family farm in the mid-1980s, a period in which thousands of other farmers across the country were forced to put their land, buildings, equipment, and in fact their very ways of life on the auction block.

FROM LOUIS FORBES: A PERSONAL INTERVIEW (2000)

SLM: Tell me a little about your personal history and the history of your farm.

LF: I am a member of the third generation born on the farm that belonged to my grandfather. His first name was Louis, and I'm named after him. He cleared that forty-acre farm with an ax and a team of oxen. My own father, of course, was also raised on that same farm. During World War I, he left the farm to join the army and was stationed in Oklahoma. While there, he met and married my mother and brought her back to the farm after he was discharged. I was born on August 28, 1920, and am the oldest of their four children. We were all raised on that same farm. We walked together to a one-room country schoolhouse together. We had a good life back in those days. There was no electricity or any conveniences like that, but we all thought life was pretty good. Even during the Depression when it was more of a struggle, things were not as desperate for us as they were for many other people.

SLM: So you were able to keep the farm during the Depression?

LF: Well, times were tough—very tough—but, yes, we did survive and keep the farm, and we never went hungry. My dad bought a few more cows, and we never knew what it was like to be without meat, potatoes, milk, and butter on the table.

SLM: Did you ever think of doing something else besides farming?

LF: No, not really. All I ever did after I graduated from eighth grade was help my dad on the farm, and my sisters and brother and I never fully realized how bad the times really were. I loved farming and stayed right with it. We gradually got more cattle, enough so that my dad could go to FHA and borrow a little money, and he and I continued to farm. We never made much money, but we lived good.

SLM: So you simply assumed that you would stay on that farm and raise your own family there?

LF: That's right. And that's exactly what I did. I met my future wife at one of the local camp meetings that were occasionally held in the area. We went together for about a year, married in 1941, and moved to the farm with my dad and mother. My wife was a city girl. She knew nothing about life on a farm, but she took to it right away. She loved the farm. She really did. [During] World War II . . . , we had two small children, and it looked as if I'd have to go into the army. By then, though, we were farming enough that I could get a deferment and stay home. Around that time, threshing machines were being replaced by combines. One of the neighboring farmers had bought one and needed help running it, so I hired myself out to him for one dollar a day to supplement our income.

SLM: Did you continue to farm uninterruptedly from that time until you retired?

LF: That is almost true, but not quite. There was a bit of an interruption during the Korean War. I had a brother twelve years my junior, who by that time was farming with me and my dad. While the three of us farmed together, things were all right, but my dad was getting older and slowing down, and he decided it was time for him to retire. So when my younger brother went into the army, I had little choice but to get out of the farm business. We sold off the cattle and most of the machinery, but my wife and I and our children (by then we had four) stayed in the same house. We never sold that. I got a job at a dairy company in town, and when my brother returned from Korea, he took a job at the same place. He and I would often talk about how working in a dairy company was just not the life for us. When we couldn't take it anymore, we quit, borrowed money, bought a herd of cows, and started milking again.

SLM: Were there no more interruptions after that?

LF: No, there weren't. When my brother and I went back into farming after our short-lived attempt to do something else, we continued to expand our operation until we had about 250 cows, including milk cows, dry cows, and young cattle. We spent the better part of the 1960s and 70s expanding the farm because it had to support two families. By then my brother and his wife had four children of their own, and my wife and I had had a fifth child. My other four children were growing into adulthood, and everyone helped work the farm in one way or another. It was during those decades, too, that my mother and father died, and after that it was just the third and fourth generations farming the place.

SLM: All of this farm expansion was accomplished on borrowed money, I assume.

LF: That's right. We built a brand new milking parlor, new barns, bought more machinery—everything. And to do all that you have to borrow money. We did make more money, but we were also deeper in debt, so the profit margin wasn't that much greater than it ever had been. In fact, milk prices for farmers weren't much higher than they had been 50 years before.

SLM: Were you able to make the payments on your loans?

LF: We did all right, but in the early '80s we could see the handwriting on the wall. It looked as if we wouldn't be able to make enough profit to support two families and still make the payments on the loans forever. The banks were foreclosing on one small farmer after the other.

SLM: Were you and your brother still running the farm together, or had your son officially come into the operation by then?

LF: My second son, Steve, became a partner with us in the early 80s. My oldest son was never interested in farming for a living, so my plan was to have both Steve and his younger brother come in as fourth-generation partners, and then I would gradually retire. But it didn't work out that way, and to this day it makes me sad to think about it.

SLM: Can you explain why it makes you sad?

LF: I believe that farming as a way of life usually makes for a much closer family than other ways of life. It's hard to explain. Kids learn more about life from farming than they could possibly learn from any other way of life. Also, farming is a dawn to dark enterprise—sometimes even dawn to dawn. And the whole family is involved in it. Farm kids don't have time for much tomfoolery. I will go to my grave believing that children raised on a farm generally have better values and know more about the importance of family and about life in general than those not raised on a farm. I could probably never prove that to people who have no farm experience, but I believe it's true, nevertheless. It simply is. Also, we were four generations in one place—*our* place on the earth—and we lost it. It's still hard to believe. But I'll let my son tell you the story of losing it.

FROM STEVEN FORBES: A PERSONAL INTERVIEW (2000)

SLM: You are a member of the fourth generation to be born and raised on the farm your father has just described. Is that right?

SF: Yes, it is. I was born in the spring of 1953 on that same farm. I grew up there with my two brothers and two sisters.

SLM: I'm sure you have very strong memories of those growing-up years. Are they are mostly positive ones?

SF: They are mostly positive, yes. I guess what I liked most is that the family was always together—parents, siblings, grandparents. We ate 3 meals a day together, we worked together, we played together. That was extremely valuable to me. And I liked the whole lifestyle.

SLM: Your father says that it was dawn to dark work everyday, for the most part. What about that aspect of farm life?

SF: Well, there was actually some flexibility built into the routine, but he's right in that you had to be totally committed to whatever had to be done on any given day. What I mean by flexibility is that there were different *types* of work to be done. It was never repetitive work like some factory jobs, for example. But we never had the kind of flexibility that would allow us simply to take time off if we didn't feel like working.

SLM: Are there any negative sides to the farming life?

SF: Sure there are. As we've already said, the hours are long, and you never get a day off. Also, farm life is dangerous. You work with animals and huge machines day in and day out. Just to give you one instance, when I was 12 or 13 years old, it was my job to feed the cows. At that time we had an auger type feeder that ran out a long way into the barnyard. I would turn the silo motor on and wait for the hopper to fill with feed. Then the auger would distribute it down the length of the feeder. It was like a huge spiral meat grinder that kept turning and pushing the silage along. One very rainy night in the early fall, I walked down through the milking parlor to get to the barnyard. My dad was in the milking parlor, and as I passed him, he said, "Now whatever you do don't get up on that thing and rake that silage down." He knew it would probably not slide down on its own because it would be damp. Well, his warning went right in one ear and out the other. As it turned out, the silage was packed just as he'd thought, and it wouldn't slide down the chute into the hopper. There was no stick or anything around there that I could use to dislodge it, so I jumped onto one of the wooden sides that held the auger so that I could reach up and rake the silage down with my hands. Of course the wood was wet and slippery, and I fell into the auger. Everyone talks about those instances when people's lives flash before their eyes, and that really happened to me in just an instant. I knew that I couldn't get out and that the auger would probably grind me up and spit me out the other end. I was screaming and flailing, knowing all the time that it was to no avail. Then suddenly, the auger stopped, and my dad was right next to me. He had seen me fall in because he suspected that I wouldn't listen to what he had said, and he had come out to check on me. He had to turn the auger backwards so that I could get out, since the thing had already drawn one of my legs into it. We went directly to the hospital. My leg was pretty chewed up from the knee to the ankle, and there was some concern that it wouldn't heal properly because the wound was so full of silage. It did, though, but it was a very long process. Even so, I was extremely lucky. I was just seconds away from being totally chewed up. That happened about 35 years ago, and my leg still hurts a bit sometimes, and the scar is still very large and very visible.

SLM: Considering the danger and the relentless work, would you have traded the farm for another way of life?

SF: Absolutely not. And my friends and relatives who lived in town seemed to have the same feelings about the farm as I did. They always wanted to come to visit me on the farm. It was the farm that was the attraction. My cousins regularly came from Grand Rapids and Detroit to spend time with us, and to this day they talk about the time they spent on the farm with me and my family as some of the best days of their lives.

SLM: Would you have chosen to stay on the farm and raise your own family there if you could have?

SF: Without a doubt. My younger brother and I both wanted that, but by the time it was our turn to take over, farming was not a profitable enough enterprise to sustain a family.

SLM: Why not?

SF: I think it was largely because we didn't have enough land to make it profitable. Ours was a dairy farm, and we were trying to sustain 300 cows on the 60 acres of land we owned. We had to rent a lot more land to farm. That all costs money, as does buying more land. On top of that, the rented land became increasingly scarce, either because the landlord would rent it to someone who was willing to pay more than we were or because he had decided to sell the land to developers. So we had to go further and further away from our own farm to find land to rent.

SLM: As your father has said, the more you tried to expand, the more money you had to borrow. Do you agree that that was a major problem?

SF: Yes. The scarcity of available and affordable land, the high cost of machinery—and of overhead in general—and the high interest rates in the 1980s all played a part. It got to the point where the revenue from milk sales alone could not pay the bills. No way. We and all the rest of the family farmers in America at the time were faced with the same choice—go heavily into debt in order to expand or get out of farming.

SLM: How hard did you resist selling out even after you realized that there was very little likelihood that you could remain in farming?

SF: We fought very hard against what we knew deep down was inevitable. We tried a lot of things: we rented another farm and milked twice as many cows for a while to try to catch up on our loan payments. That didn't work. We tried farming more acres to sell more crops, thinking that cash crops would subsidize the milk industry. That didn't work, either. Nothing worked.

SLM: How long did that struggle go on?

SF: About three years. For three consecutive years, starting in the spring of 1983, we borrowed $100,000 for operating expenses. All we could ever do was pay interest on those loans. Crop prices were down; fertilizer prices were up; milk prices were lousy. Farmers are always dependant on the weather, too, of course, and it very seldom cooperates perfectly.

SLM: Didn't the bank eventually become reluctant to lend you money?

SF: Our bankers were pretty good to us, but, yes, they did start balking. In the spring of 1986 when we went ask for our third $100,000 loan, they told us point blank that while they would agree to loan us the money this time, they were not going to do it another year. They recommended that we take the loan, raise the crops, fill everything up, and sell out in the fall because they were simply not going to loan us any more money. They said they knew we couldn't pay it back.

SLM: But you were still paying the interest on the loans?

SF: Yes, we were, but our overall debt load had increased tremendously, and the bankers could see that we didn't have enough collateral to be a good risk. After all, we only actually owned 60 acres, some equipment, and a herd of cows.

SLM: If they didn't feel you had enough collateral to borrow against, what made them think selling the farm would net you enough money to pay back your loans?

SF: They didn't think that. They said if we sold the farm in the fall, they'd be willing to take their lumps and losses, and we'd part as friends. They even agreed to loan us $5,000 to make a new start in something. Our attorney advised us to accept the bank's proposal. He also suggested that we go to all our other creditors—the neighbors we rented land from, equipment dealers, the mill, and whoever else we owed money to—and ask them to accept 50 cents on the dollar for what we owed them. If they refused, they'd very likely get nothing at all. All but one of our creditors agreed to those terms. They did it as a favor to us. They were not just businessmen; they were our friends. The one creditor who did not agree thought he could get more out of us than half what we owed him. He ended up with nothing at all.

SLM: At that point, then, did you finally face the truth that you were losing the farm forever?

SF: We had no choice. It was a harder truth to face than people who have never experienced it can imagine. I mean, my father was born on that farm, and his father before him. It was my great-grandfather's farm originally. I have a picture hanging above my fireplace today of the cabin in the woods on the edge of the original cleared 40 acres. Now, I was being forced to accept the fact that my own children would be the first generation not to be born and raised there. Still, it had to be faced. I told my brother he had to find another job because he wouldn't be able to draw a paycheck from the farm much longer. He nearly refused to do it. I had to push him hard, but he finally did it.

SLM: What was it like farming full-time for what you knew would be your last season?

SF: It was not pleasant, to say the least. We knew that we were planting the crops, milking the cows, and doing all the other things that had to be done, not for ourselves, but for the bank. Again, though, we had no choice.

SLM: In several of the 1980s Hollywood movies about the loss of the family farm, the bankers are generally portrayed as pure villains. Do you think of your banker as a villain?

SF: No. In the end, the bank, like all our other creditors, agreed to take 50 cents on the dollar. In other words, the proceeds from the sale of our farm could only pay for about half what we owed. And they were glad to get that much. But there certainly were some villainous bankers out there. We were just lucky not to have had one. I know how some of the other aggressive types of bankers operated. A farmer would go to one of them and want a loan to buy, say, a new corn picker. He would trust the banker the same way he trusted the man he'd dealt with years before at the same bank—a man who was completely honest and above board with him. But this new banker says he wants to take a lien on the farm. Many farmers agreed to that, which meant that with any little bump in the road, the bank had a legal right to take away from them something they'd had for generations. And the banks often got it, too. These types of bankers don't care at all whether or not the farmer survives. They're only looking at bank assets.

SLM: How did you handle the actual sale itself—watching your whole way of life being auctioned off?

SF: It was not good. Not good at all. We spent the last month before the sale cleaning things up and getting everything ready for the auction. It was a two day sale. We sold the cattle the first day and the machinery and all the rest the next. I think it was even harder on my dad than it was on me, if that's possible. It had been his whole life. Mine, too, of course, but his life was simply longer. As I watched it go, bit by bit, I didn't know what was in store for me, either. It was the first time in my life I'd ever had to look for a job. I can only keep saying that it was not a good day.

SLM: What do you do for a living now?

SF: I'm a field supervisor for a construction company. The farm prepared me well for this job. On the farm we could build nearly anything and fix nearly anything ourselves—and we did. The farm is a good training ground for a lot of things.

SLM: Would you still like to go back to farming if that were feasible?

SF: I do still think about it. In fact, my wife and I even talk about it occasionally. Could we milk 40 or so cows and survive? But no matter how we look at it, we know we just couldn't make it.

Here's what it comes down to: It used to be that if you loved the land and were willing to work, you could go into farming and rely on the feed man to sell you feed at a fair price. And you could get a reasonably fair price for what you were selling, milk or crops. You could also more often than not rely on the local banker to deal honestly with you. In the early days it seemed that everyone was fairly honest with each other. Most deals were made with a handshake. Now you need something like an MBA to make any money farming. I know a guy who recently came from California to establish a farm here in Michigan. But he didn't come with just his hands in his pockets; he came with a whole lot of money. He hardly knows which end of the cow to milk, but he's a very shrewd businessman. He'll hire people to feed and milk his 3,000 cows. He plans to buy all his feed and grow nothing himself. So what you have is the owner of a farm who is not himself a farmer and who lives 2,000 miles away from his operation. That means that the direct connection between the owner of the farm and the farm itself is gone. And it's gone forever. It's the end of the line.

TOPICS FOR WRITTEN OR ORAL EXPLORATION

1. For Cather's characters, America was the place where everyone could own his own farm and thus be his own master. Americans still prize personal independence highly. Discuss how they achieve that ideal today.

2. Cather's immigrants also thought of America as a place where they could own their own farms. What, in your opinion, draws immigrants to America today, now that the nineteenth-century vision is just a historical memory?

3. In the course of the twentieth century, succeeding generations saw the disappearance of institutions that had been profoundly important to them in their formative years: the family farm, the "mom and pop" grocery store, the locally run diner, etc. What familiar institutions do you anticipate losing as the twenty-first century progresses? Discuss your ideas in class.

4. Pretend you are a fourth-generation farmer who has come to realize that the farm that had belonged to your family for well over a hundred years will have to go on the auction block. Write a mock journal in which you describe the days leading up to the sale. Talk about the preparations, both emotional and physical, that must be made before the actual event occurs.

5. Write an essay on how the disappearance of the family farm has changed the way Americans think about the treatment of domesticated (food source) animals.

6. Write an essay on how corporate farms have changed many of the agricultural products we consume.

7. In class, discuss how the disappearance of the family farm has changed the way Americans think about environmental issues.

8. Farmers in Cather's novels have found a profession that will last a lifetime. Many Americans now must change professions two or three times before retiring. Does this life pattern change the way we think of ourselves, our work, and our society? Write an essay in which you defend your answer to this question.

9. Watch one or all of the 1980s movies about the loss of the family farm (*Country*, *The River*, and *Places in the Heart*). What groups or institutions do these films blame for the farm crisis? Do they make any effort to present the complexities of the issue, or do they provide only stock villains and simple explanations for what is in fact a very complicated situation? Present your answers in an essay or as part of a class discussion.

SUGGESTIONS FOR FURTHER READING AND WORKS CITED

"Amber Waves of Debt." *Time*, March 3, 1986: 67

Bauer, Douglas. "Broken Heartland." *Esquire*, January 1987: 68–77.

Berry, Wendell. *The Unsettling of America: Culture & Agriculture*. San Francisco: Sierra Club, 1977.

Bosc, Michael. "Learning to Survive on the Land." *U.S. News & World Report*, February 2, 1987: 30.

Farm Aid Official Web site: http://www.farmaid.org/org/historical/1985/, February 10, 2001.

Houston, Patrick. "Hard Times Will Get Harder Down on the Farm." *Business Week*, January 13, 1986: 76–77.

Marton, Larry B., ed. *United States Agriculture in a Global Economy: Agriculture Yearbook, 1985*. Washington, D.C.: Government Printing Office, 1985.

Mueller, William. "How We're Gonna Keep 'Em Off of the Farm." *American Scholar* 56 (Winter 1987): 57–67.

Shilling, A. Gary. "Should Uncle Sam Save the American Farmer?" *Los Angeles Times*, February 24, 1985, sec. 6: 3.

"Singing for AID." *Nation*, October 5, 1985: 300.

U.S. Department of Agriculture. *A History of American Agriculture 1776–1990: Farmers and the Land*. http://www.usda.gov/history2/text3.htm, February 26, 2001.

Vogeler, Ingolf. *The Myth of the Family Farm: Agribusiness Dominance of U.S. Agriculture*. Boulder, Colo.: Westview Press, 1981.

Williams, Simon, and Ruth Karen. *Agribusiness and the Small-Scale Farmer*. Boulder, Colo.: Westview Press, 1985.

Index

About the Author

SHERYL L. MEYERING is Professor of English at Southern Illinois University, Edwardsville, and associate editor of the literary journal *Papers on Language and Literature*. She is the editor of *Charlotte Perkins Gilman: The Woman and Her Work* (1989), *Sylvia Plath: A Reference Guide* (1990), and *A Reader's Guide to the Short Stories of Willa Cather* (1994). She has also written extensively on Nathaniel Hawthorne as well as on several nineteenth-century women writers.